A SAMURAI DREAM OF AZAD HIND

RASH BEHARI BOSE

Prasun Roy

Vitasta
LET KNOWLEDGE SPREAD

A middle-aged Rash Behari Bose in Japan
Creative Commons

In our struggle for the independence of our country, we will have to fight; some with the rifle, some with their brains and others with their wealth...

We will have to go through a Modern War, which is really a war, more of brains than of brawn...

We Indians should intensely LOVE OUR MOTHERLAND — INDIA and be proud of being Indians!

—*Rash Behari Bose*

Published by
Renu Kaul Verma
Vitasta Publishing Pvt Ltd
2/15, Ansari Road, Daryaganj
New Delhi-110 002
info@vitastapublishing.com

ISBN 978-93-90961-84-9

First Edition 2022
Second Reprint 2022

MRP ₹ 595

Edited by Papri Sen Sri Raman
Cover by The Book Bakers
Typesetting by Somesh Kumar Mishra
Printed by Chaman Enterprises, New Delhi

Devoted to all the unsung children
of Mother India
for whose heroic sacrifices we now
live freely in Azad Hind

For my beautiful children
Ekalavya and Ekantika
You are my biggest gifts from God

Rabindranath Tagore with Aizō and Kokkō Sōma, and the family children when he visited Japan. Rash Behari is seen seated on the extreme left
Creative Commons

CONTENTS

The Nakamuraya* Curry dinner set in which the curry Rash Behari invented in 1927 is traditionally served in the still popular Tokyo restaurant.
Creative Commons

---

* After his wife Toshiko died, a grief-stricken Bose threw himself into work.
Two years later, he decided to partner with his father-in-law to set up a small restaurant on top of the Nakamurya bakery that would sell Indian-style curry and rice.
The selection of ingredients and preparation of the dish – named Indo Karii – was personally supervised by Bose who wanted Asians to experience India's food and culture without the exchange being mediated by Westerners.
Nakamuraya's curry clicked instantly with the locals, quickly becoming more popular than the bakery's signature item, custard buns.
Thanks to newspapers that zealously wrote about his struggles against imperialism and his romance with Toshiko, 'Bose of Nakamuraya' became a household name in Tokyo and his 'Indo-Karii' was famously christened the 'taste of love and revolution'.
The curious citizens of Tokyo began flocking to the restaurant to taste authentic Indian food and soon the restaurant grew into such a big venture that it became one of the first food companies to go public. on the Japanese stock exchange.

Publisher's Note

While everyone today knows Netaji Subhas Chandra Bose and his Indian National Army, very few know of THE OTHER BOSE, a man who dreamt of revolution long before Subhas came into the picture. He was a young ten-year old affectionately called Rasu whose dream for a free India began in the 1890s. Throughout the heyday of colonial rule in India, he became a bane for the British Raj, an icon for proponents of armed revolution in the subcontinent and abroad to free India in the first two decades of the twentieth century and who later came to be known as 'The Bose of Nakamuraya' in far-off Japan.

Japan embraced several hundred Indian revolutionaries from 1900 to 1945, just like it had done Buddhism some 2,500 years ago, providing shelter and material support to Anushilan Party and Ghadar Party activists who had death penalties hanging over their heads in British India. Among them was Rash Behari Bose; the little Rasu who had turned into a firebrand inspiration for armed revolution for an Azad Hind. As early as in 1925, he had set up the Indian Independence League, an international advocacy platform, and the Indian National League and Asia Lodge in Japan and other south

Asian countries, all solidarity forums for India's cause. In 1942, Rash Behari rescued thousands of captured Indian soldiers by his intervention with Japan and set up the Indian National Army. In his time Netaji Subhas had an oak to shade him.

Through the last decade, Vitasta has had the privilege to bring to our readers meticulously researched stories of Subhas Bose. We now bring you another stellar tale of our freedom struggle, one man's *Samurai Dream of Azad Hind.*

Due to lack of credibly sourced details on Rash Behari's early life, this biography adopts a narrative style, adding flesh to the academic information made available by scholars in Bengali, English and Japanese. The fictional interventions are an attempt to bring this roller-coaster of a life story alive and more accessible to the modern young reader just like a high-octane adventure story, through cautious use of the creative license.

Revolution is not necessarily armed struggle. It can be a strategy, a plan and in the 1940s Rash Behari acknowledged Gandhi's non-violent struggle as a part of his global overview. So, this book is also the story of how in the 20th century, the world became a continuum in war and peace, in victory and defeat and colonialism became an obsolete and unsustainable political venture.

FOREWORD

From Tokyo, Rash Behari Bose wrote to Subhas Chandra Bose on 25 January 1938, 'What is now wanted for the Congress to lead the country correctly is to have a revolutionary mentality. It is now an evolutionary body. It must be made a pure revolutionary body.... The fetish of non-violence should be discarded, and the creed should be changed. Let us attain our goal through all possible means: violence or non-violence.'

The letter, as you can guess, was intercepted by the British intelligence.

Subhas Chandra would have indeed written similar lines himself, for he too believed the time was right to move away from parliamentary concessions doled out by the British and fight for Indian rights. The two Boses possessed one soul, as Tōyama Mitsuru had said when he met them later.

Unlike Subhas, Rash Behari, however, had taken the fiery revolutionary road early in life. His acts of personal daring and courage, too, were unlike those of many other leaders of the time. He had been the mastermind behind the bomb thrown at Lord Hardinge, Viceroy of India, in 1912. He had not only manufactured the bomb, which severely wounded the Viceroy, but was also present when it was hurled by an 18-year-old companion dressed as a girl. Three of Rash Behari's accomplices had been arrested and executed for this.

Rash Behari and Subhas shared the same passion for liberation of their motherland. Both advocated the use of force, if necessary, to achieve their purpose. In a letter, published in *Young India* on 23 November 1922, Rash Behari had said:

No people on earth can consent to be governed by another people... there can either be freedom or the opposite of it... slavery. There is no mid-way. For India to desire to remain within the Empire is to acknowledge herself as a slave. Freedom and slavery cannot go together....'

Rash Behari was prescient. In Subhas Chandra Bose's context, he said, 'Gandhi is a person whom I respect but he is an Indian saint and a person of yesterday whereas Subhas Chandra Bose is the person of today.'

Introducing Subhas Chandra Bose to his compatriots in Japan in 1942, Rash Behari said, 'I have brought you one of the most outstanding personalities of our motherland...I resign from my office as president of the Indian Independence League in East Asia. From now on, Subhas Bose is your Leader in the fight for independence.'

As the two Boses stood together next to a bay window, Rash Behari's life-long friend and mentor in Japan, Tōyama Mitsuru, commented, 'You both have the same surname. But I think that you both have by now one soul. Hence, you both should fight for the freedom of India.'

More than 12,000 men and officers had answered his call, when an ailing Rash Behari had travelled to Bangkok in June 1942 where, in a first of its kind effort, he had motivated Indian prisoners of war, held by the Japanese during World War II, to take up arms for their country's liberation from the British rule. The Indian National Army was founded on 1 September 1942.

Ten months later, Rash Behari Bose handed the Azad Hind Fauj to Subhas Bose – the 'person of today', and walked into the sunset. The man who had played the pivotal role in creating India's first army, had not hankered after any credit though.

Rash Behari Bose's act of stepping down from the presidentship of the Independence League was, in fact, the most selfless act of heroic nationalism in the annals of India's freedom struggle. It paved the way for the most abiding memory of Subhas Bose and the Azad Hind Fauj.

Rash Behari may not have taken any credit; those times were uncertain and circumstances compelling. It does not mean today's India, with one of the finest standing armed forces in the world, forgets to honour him.

Prasun Roy's book captures the bold acts of defiance and derring-do against the British by Rash Behari in lucid details. He was a hero like no other – a man of valiant spirit desperate to free India from British rule. Prasun traces the revolutionary's historic journey with eminent freedom fighters like Jatindra Nath Mukherjee, Shrish Chandra Ghosh, Aurobindo Ghosh, Moti Lal Roy, Amarendra Nath Chatterjee, Sachindra Nath Sanyal and others with great fidelity.

Of particular interest to the reader would be how the Ghadar uprising among Indian soldiers of the British Army was planned by him, and how it failed due to traitors and spies. The action stretches from cantonments of Bengal to Punjab. It is testament of Rash Behari's organisational skill and daring against all odds.

Though Rash Behari Bose was the most wanted man on the Indian sub-continent, the British could never lay their hands on him. Such was his audacious courage that he once travelled on a train with a British Superintendent of Police tasked to secure his arrest. He sat in front of him throughout the journey and even made small talk, but the policeman could not recognise him from his disguise.

Rash Behari Bose escaped to Japan, dressed as an elite member of the Tagore clan
Creative Commons

Rash Behari arrived in Japan in 1915 – a penniless fugitive and with the knowledge of just four Japanese words. But when he died on 21 January 1945, the imperial carriage of the Japanese Emperor was sent to receive his body.

He was recipient of the highest civilian Japanese award Order of the Rising Sun. He had, in his own way, also given back to Japan's cultural and political life. Rash Behari's culinary creation, The Nakamuraya Curry sells 2 billion servings even to this day.

The revolutionary's life story reads like a super thriller – full of mystery and intrigue, adventure and daring, commitment and selfless service. He was a multi-faceted personality, who not only charmed everyone he met with his sincerity of purpose, but also inspired them to action. Love for his motherland was the bedrock on which he built his name and fame.

Prasun Roy's book takes in the entire sweep of Rash Behari's life in all its splendour. It is an honest attempt to capture the events and essence of Rash Behari's momentous life through painstaking research, and some deft writing. I am sure readers will be inspired by the national hero's zeal and indomitable spirit to secure a better life for his countrymen.

Ashwini Bhatnagar

April 2022

Ashwini Bhatnagar is a veteran journalist who has served as Professor and Dean at the Faculty of Mass Communication and Media Technology, SGT University, Gurugram. He has worked with leading Indian newspapers such as *The Pioneer, Times of India, Sunday Mail* and *The Tribune* in editorial leadership positions. He has published eight books so far, both fiction and non-fiction. He is also a well-known documentary filmmaker, columnist, travel writer, satirist and contemporary-history enthusiast.

Picture from *Rash Behari Basu: His Struggle for India's Independence*

PREFACE

In our beloved country, India, where the names of many great freedom fighters float in the lore of recent history, *A Samurai Dream Of Azad Hind – Rash Behari Bose* is an endeavour to revisit the life and works of the one man who had silently striven for nearly half a century to liberate his motherland from Britain's colonial rule.

I must acknowledge that this book's attempt is to give my readers a glimpse of the life and times of one of the greatest revolutionary leaders of India, Rash Behari Bose, whose gypsy life lived in a whirlwind of sacrifices as he worked towards his free India rattled the mighty British Raj to the core. With a single-minded focus throughout his life, he had dedicated his entire existence to achieve this much-sought-after freedom for his beloved countrymen.

Adopting a semi-fictional style, with words from fellow revolutionaries and official documents of that time, the dramatic accounts of the first thirty years of Rash Behari's life read like a typhoon on the move. Many years later, Rash Behari's sister, Sushila Devi claimed that she and her older brother Rash Behari were both born in their maternal uncle's house at Parala-Bighati, in the Hooghly district of Bengal. The fact that is of much more importance than the ambiguity of his birthplace is that the boy with the Lion's Heart was born in Bengal and wrote his own fate with the ink of supreme sacrifice and valour. That story is yet to be told.

This chronicle just skims the surface of a deep, dark and dedicated personality and brings to an average reader the story of a lifespan filled with intrigue; being a master of disguise, he was perhaps the one man who the frustrated colonial government failed to capture, despite all efforts. Rash Behari provoked the rulers by simply eluding their hawk-eye while many others chose martyrdom in that phase of our freedom struggle. Rash Behari Bose emerged as *the* mighty opponent who simply couldn't be found and remained undefeated. He took to heart the very English phrase, 'you live to fight another day'.

Through all his travails, Bose never lost his mettle. Thus, when British Intelligence Services closed their fist around him, he chose the life of a fugitive, far away in Japan, to continue his struggle for armed intervention, which he and many others considered and still consider righteous. In a way that makes him a pioneer in the modern history of militancy in the subcontinent.

In the distant land of Japan, Rash Behari Bose found refuge, a home and hearth, parents, mentors, scholarship, a political foothold, love and a family. The life of Rash Behari Bose in the Land of the Rising Sun is a perfect example of the thousands of years of cultural bonding between the two nations, India and Japan. This book touches briefly upon that wonderful element of harmony between the sentiments of the two countries and empathy that has been long-standing. Rash Behari not only established himself as a respectable citizen of Japan, but also created a volcanic uproar within entire Asia that led to a massive anti-colonial movement and the world-wide call for a Free India. Japan bestowed its highest honour, the Order of the Rising Sun, on Rash Behari while he was still alive.

With the fire of Swaraj (self rule) burning deep within him, Rash Behari managed to finally bring all the disparate elements of armed revolution's proponents in South Asia together to established the Indian Independence League and the Azad Hind Fauj. This Azad Hind Fauj actually served as a strong lifeline for thousands of Indians forming the British Indian contingents in WWII, taken prisoner by Japan.

Being the internationalist that he was, Rash Behari saw a future of a comity of friendly and peaceful free nations and envisioned a free India as a part of this South Asian alliance. In 1945, this free-standing army called the INA, fully trained and armed, frightened a fatigued and economically devastated Britain more than any politicking and pleading could. Though outside India, the possibility of INA-inspired armed rebellions across the length and breadth of their Jewell in the Crown was not something the Raj found palatable; it was not 1857 and it was not something they could quell. Giving India its freedom was the only way. Most of India does not know that it was Rash Behari Bose's persistent lobbying for end to colonial rule that brought freedom closer to India.

Rash Behari's life, activities and achievements carry a message for everyone. He depicts that true spirit that strives against all odds to attain the success of a supreme dream. The story of this valiant man deserves to reach every reader and this book is a modest effort towards that goal.

In India, amidst our myriad tales of sacrifices by thousands of freedom-fighters, Rash Behari is one man who chose to remain in oblivion, so that his motherland could become free. Like the swansong of a Hero, in his last years, he handed over the reins of his best projects, the Indian Independence League and the Azad Hind Fauj, to Subhas Chandra Bose, so that his dream becomes the first ray of light in the new dawn of independent India. People know of Subhas and his association with the INA but little about Rash Behari. This book also attempts to bring out the intelligence, strategic thinking and selflessness of these two monumental Indian leaders. It was a seamless union of two heroes who admired and respected each other, where the former was a master strategist while the latter was a valiant man of action.

This book is also an attempt to portray, in the history of our freedom movement, the role of India's revolutionaries who offered the British armed resistance to colonialism. These unsung heroes had worked silently and often sacrificed their lives on British gallows, striving to shake off the shackles of bondage. Rash Behari Bose had remained resolute in his mission while he collaborated with other eminent freedom fighters like Jatindra Nath Mukherjee, Shrish Chandra Ghosh, Aurobindo Ghosh, Moti Lal Roy, Amarendra Nath Chatterjee, Sachindra Nath Sanyal and many other brave men and women of that era.

Rash Behari was the leader who was able to bridge the struggles for freedom between united Bengal, and the united Northern Provinces and Punjab. Inspiring the trust of the Sikhs, he actively participated in the Ghadar Movement and motivated trained cantonments to rebel, striking at the morale of the colonial Raj lethal blows. Prominent members of the

Ghadar Party like Lala Har Dayal Singh, Sohan Singh Bhakna, Kartar Singh, Vishnu Ganesh Pingle, Mula Singh and Nidhon Singh worked tirelessly with Rash Behari to chalk one of the greatest armed uprisings in India. The sacrifices of these men are not remembered any longer with the passage of time. This book is a tribute to all such brave souls whose valour deserves greater celebration in India today.

Lines soaked in high voltage adrenaline swept through the alert mind of the feeble man reclining on the hospital bed. It was an electric flashback of his own voice thundering before a multitude of awestruck spectators. Two drops of precious tears trickled down his cheeks. Then he closed his eyes softly and after a while, a delicate smile spread across his countenance.

The year was 1945 and the month was that of January. At a wintry junction of war-torn Tokyo city, inside the closed chamber of an old hospital building, a doctor stood beside the bedstead of this ailing patient. The Indian-origin frail gentleman, lying on the bed, looked pale and weak.

Before entering the room, the doctor had studied the progress report of the patient and had consulted the nurses.

He had sadly remarked, 'The condition of our patient is not showing very positive signs of improvement. But, he is a fighter. His inner strength emanates from a deep desire to witness something that he has strived for throughout his life! I wish his dream comes true and he is able to witness it with pride.'

He paused a while and sighed, 'Alas, our famous patient, the man behind the innovative brilliance of the Nakamuraya Bakery, will perhaps never be completely healed.'

The doctor checked his vitals and asked, 'Sir, how is your appetite? The nurses are telling me that you don't feel like eating. Sir, is there anything that appeals to your palate?'

The man looked at the doctor, smirked a little and replied, 'Yes… the Indian Curry of Nakamuraya!'

With collapsed lungs and heavily impaired respiratory function, the fragile old man stared at the closed window wanting a glimpse of the crimson rays of the rising sun and his mind floated into a déjà vu.

In that brief moment of silence, his own words again reverberated in his mind, '*Best results are only produced when valour and intelligence are combined....'*

And then, the vision of two little children cuddled up against an innocent Japanese woman draped in an Indian saree flashed past his eyes.

The cold morning breeze knocked upon the tightly shut glass window, as if trying to share the harsh reality playing out inside. The Cherry Blossoms will again bloom four months later, but one pair of eyes will perhaps not witness them ever again.

The doctor continued with a smile, 'Of course! The Bose of Nakamuraya no doubt loves his favourite creation. Alas sir, you know that we cannot get that for you. Yet, why do you still ask for it?'

The latter responded with a mild grin, 'I have always been a disobedient boy. '

Thus, the déjà vu continued….

SUMMER OF 1886

ACROSS THE SOUTH China Sea, in the Bay of Bengal, in a small house deep inside the mud-soaked village of Subaldah, in the Burdwan district of Bengal, a child was born on a humid morning of the summer of 1886. The infant arrived riding a thunderstorm that brought the village a soothing relief from the scorching heat. Incessant showers welcomed the arrival of the baby boy on 25 May.[1]

Only destiny knew that just like the accompanying storm, the boy himself was destined to be a typhoon that would touch the hearts of millions in two subcontinents.

Binod Behari Bose looked at his son and clasped his hands in prayer. Embracing the baby nestled at her breast, Bhubaneswari Devi kissed his forehead tenderly. The family lovingly named him Rash Behari.

---

1 *Rash Behari Bose: The Father of The Indian National Army* Vol-1 by Elizabeth Eston & Lexi Kawabe, page numbers 52-62.
The information has also been sourced from two Japanese books:
Dokuritsu no Tōsō by Rash Behari Bose.
Seinen Ajia no Shōri by Rash Behari Bose (published in 1937).

As the tides of time passed, the infant began to grow up. The initial years were cradled in the loving warmth of Bhubaneswari Devi and she fondly nicknamed her son, Rasu. The rural atmosphere of Subaldah was serene and passive and the little child remained nestled within the undisturbed tranquility of his immediate family.

Three years later, Binod Behari and Bhubaneswari were blessed with a girl-child, Sushila. However, the happiness of the family was fated to be transient. In an abrupt assault of destiny, Bhubaneswari Devi passed away in the year 1889. Little Rasu was three years old and Sushila was just a newborn. The death of their mother left the two children in an unfathomable void that could never be filled up.

The vast abyss created by the death of his wife left Binod Behari without many options about the upbringing of his children. However, destiny always has a plan. Those are plans that have inherent and far-reaching plots which nobody can comprehend. Such a divine plan unfolded before Binod Behari when Kalicharan Bose, his father, suggested, 'Let the children remain under my tutelage. In Subaldah, they will grow up within the familial canopy until they are ready to face the harsh world.'

Binod Behari was, however, not destined to live the life of a villager. Employed as a government servant, he had to relocate to French Chandannagore. Kalicharan's offer was a blessing for the devastated young father. He felt content that the children would not be left at the mercy of an unsympathetic upbringing.

Satisfied with the proposal, Binod Behari was ready to travel to Chandannagore. Social norms in those days obliged him to marry again and Tinkori became Rash Behari and Sushila's stepmother. However, she had to accompany her husband to the French colony of Chandannagore, where Binod Behari had purchased a house and established his residence. The first word that comes to mind when one thinks of France is Revolution and Rash Behari's connect to revolution actually began under his parental umbrella, in his grandfather and father's homes.

A GRAND MENTOR

SEVERAL YEARS PASSED and Rash Behari grew into an astounding young boy, a rebel who was not born to be tamed. Under the auspices of his grandfather, Kalicharan Bose, the child listened to fantastic tales of the country's revolutionary movement. The impact of this early influence of radical philosophy transformed him from within into a person who always chose to swim against the tide.

On a humid, yet, starlit night, sitting upon the wooden bedstead inside his little room, Kalicharan narrated to his grandson India's stories of valiance. 'Our country, our great mother, India, has always borne fearless children who have never hesitated to sacrifice their lives for the sake of honour and national integrity. The greatness of our country is unmatched by that of any other in this entire world', he said. On hindsight, a biographer can safely say, this is what finally shaped Rash Behari's life.

Sitting beside him inside the dark room, little Rasu's eyes lit up like glowing fireflies and glittered like gems in the feeble light of the flickering earthen lamp. 'Please tell me more stories. I want to listen to all of them', the child pleaded.

Kalicharan replied, 'Our country is bountiful in all her natural resources. Mother Nature's treasures are immeasurable. We have the lofty Himalayas that reach up to the heavens. We have numerous rivers and tributaries. We have vast stretches of fields that are fertile enough to produce grains and vegetable to feed the entire country. From time immemorial, our Motherland has been blessed with so much.'

Looking into the passionate glow in the eyes of the little boy, he continued, 'Alas, the filthy chains of servitude under the British Raj has left us caged and helpless. I have lived my life, but you, and thousands like you, my child, are born in this caged existence. This pains me. I hope the fire of being free burns in your heart and moulds your soul to strive to break down these chains, so that, in a distant future, perhaps our countrymen will be able to breathe the fresh air of independence.'[1] It was the 1890s, Queen Victoria had taken over the reins of India and the British were India's master since the 1870s.

Rasu was too little to fully understand the import of his grandfather's words. However, the intensity of the sentiment was too strong, and it pierced through his delicate heart and left a lasting impact. Thus, he kept listening to these tales of bravery as he sat huddled close to his grandfather.

On another instance, Kalicharan narrated to him the story of the great upheaval of 1857. In a passionate voice, Kalicharan

---

1 The stories of childhood in this section of the narrative are all sourced from historical facts referenced from: *Two Great Indian Revolutionaries-Rash Behari Bose & Jyotindra Nath Mukherjee* by Uma Mukherjee, page numbers 40-120.
Uma Mukherjee used references from Prof Bejon Behari Bose's (Rash Behari's younger brother) Bengali work, *Karmabir Rash Behari*, published in 1956.

said, 'They call it the Sepoy Mutiny. Dear Rasu, my child, it was not just a mere mutiny. It was an unprecedented upheaval by our countrymen in an attempt to overthrow the foreign rulers. Those were the first rays of a great revolution. It showed our countrymen that, together, we can rise against oppression. However, a few cowards betrayed the brave revolutionaries and the fantastic attempt failed. What a misfortune. Thus, we remain in chains....'

Little Rasu's eyes became moist as he heard this account while he shuddered with fear and crouched up against his grandfather. Kalicharan cuddled him and continued, 'This was not the first time my child. Our brave countrymen have always fought for the freedom of our country. A century before the Sepoy Mutiny, the Battle of Plassey was valiantly fought between the Nawab of Bengal Siraj ud-daulah and the treacherous British East India Company. Alas, a traitor betrayed Siraj and our motherland was left at the mercy of foreigners.'

At that tender age, the stories of the struggles for independence left a deep imprint on Rash Behari. Unknowingly, the fight for India's freedom from the British became permanently etched in the character and personality of the young Rash Behari. While the flickering light from the lamp danced upon his countenance, Kalicharan said in his most dramatic voice, 'It was not just a mere revolt of a few rebels. The audacious act of defiance in 1857 was the foundation stone of India's Freedom Movement. The blaze of that volcano is still alive.'

The animated recounting by the old soul was soaked in patriotism, but for the child, it was the allure of the unknown. He understood some of it and remained perplexed about the remaining bits. Yet, his heart was filled with a nameless desire.

Geographically, Subaldah was far away from the raging revolutionary hotspots of the country at the time. However, the sentiments of breaking free from the oppression of the colonial Raj was predominant even among these villagers in a far corner of Bengal. The revolutionary novel *Ananda Math* had been published in 1882; though not targeted at the British, it had created a stir. The 1857 Sepoy Mutiny was still fresh in people's minds.

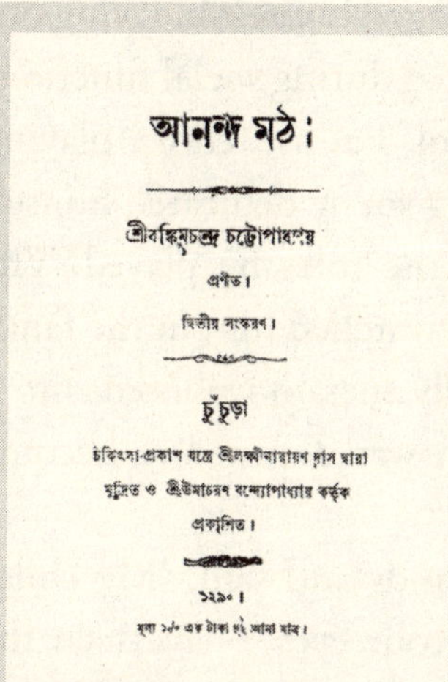
আনন্দ মঠ।

শ্রীবঙ্কিমচন্দ্র চট্টোপাধ্যায়

প্রণীত।

দ্বিতীয় সংস্করণ।

চুঁচুড়া

চিকিৎসা-প্রকাশ যন্ত্রে শ্রীলক্ষ্মীনারায়ণ দাস দ্বারা
মুদ্রিত ও শ্রীউমাচরণ বন্দ্যোপাধ্যায় কর্ত্তৃক
প্রকাশিত।

১২৯০।

মূল্য ১৵০ এক টাকা দুই আনা মাত্র।

Ananda Math book cover

A few more years passed and Rash Behari matured into a bright young lad whose existence in the mortal world was about to set foot into a realm of rebellion.

Rash Behari, or Rasu, studied at the village pathshala. Along with the other kids, he sat under the shade of a big banyan tree, beside a dilapidated structure that acted as the lone shelter for the rural school. As the teacher taught the routine chapters of the textbooks, Rash Behari felt a steep disconnect between what was being taught and what he wanted to know. His eyelids shut in that heady concoction of boredom and imposed education.

Bookish knowledge failed to attract his interest and the young boy focused on sharpening his physical strength and analytical skills. Thus, during leisure hours, he was an active participant in games of fist-fighting, aiming with catapults and even climbing trees. Sitting with his peers, he would say, 'The

Shlokas, the Epics, the Poems are all full of stories and morals. However, I don't feel any connection between them and the life that we are leading.'

Speaking to his gathering of schoolmates, he often said, 'Oppression is an offence. However, to remain oppressed is also an offence. To protest oppression, we must fight. We must be strong to break any blow that falls on us.' It was wisdom pouring out of the mouth of a baby.

From an early age, little Rasu engaged himself in trying out various radical ideas. In skits performed during social functions within the village locales or in school, he insisted on playing the wildest of characters. While doing so, he dedicated himself to trying different camouflages for the roles he played. The spectators felt entertained while they watched him in the fancy costumes. However, thus he gradually metamorphosed into a master of disguise. It was a skill that was destined to become one of his most powerful weapons.

One day, Kalicharan held his hands and said, 'My child, I want you to learn something. In your eyes I have seen the fireball of a revolution. However, a rebel is nothing if he cannot protect himself and his fellow people. So, today, I want to take you somewhere....'

Kalicharan took Rash Behari along with him and headed towards the outskirts of the village. At a distance from the edge of the village, where the rice fields met the earthen roads coming out of the human settlements and where the stretches of plush green stretched towards the horizon, the grandfather and grandson came and stood near a flat square space of bare land.

With eyes filled with awe Rash Behari saw a group of young men who were diligently practicing a fantastic from of martial art. It was the bizarre style of fighting that made him dumbstruck. The beauty and passion with which the players practiced was indeed worth a show. It was the game of war!

Kalicharan held Rasu's hands and said softly, 'The precision of their strokes is worth noticing. Rasu, look closely. It is not only assault, but also defense that is very important. Remember this my child. Your defense must be as strong as your assault. Else, your fight will always be incomplete.' It was a lesson that sustained Rash Behari throughout his heady and exotic life.

'Why have we come here to see this?' asked an amazed little Rasu.

'From today, I want you to learn this very special form of martial art that is indigenous to our motherland. It is called *Lathi Khela*. The knowledge of this art form will make you an expert in attack and self-defense and also give you physical strength to enable you to endure all hardships in life', replied Kalicharan.

An aged man, with gray-hair, but a strong body, came forward and knelt down in front of Rash Behari. Then, he said, 'My pupils call me Guruji. I am the teacher of all these boys and men here. Are you scared? Or would you like to try it? What is your name?'

Rash Behari looked into the man's eyes and then clasped the thin bamboo stick that Guruji was holding. Even though he was a young boy, his posture and the expression in his eyes showed a strong resolve. Then, he replied, 'My name is Rash Behari Bose. My grandfather and all the other villagers call me Rasu. Guruji, I am not scared. Take me as your disciple and teach me the skills. I am ready to fight....'

Seeing his conviction, Guruji smiled a bit, held his hand and took him inside the fighting arena. Kalicharan stood outside the boundary and watched with pride. Guruji took Rash Behari to the center of the arena and announced, 'Dear pupils, let me introduce to you our youngest member of this forum. This is Rash Behari Bose, or our young Rasu. From today, he is one of us. I shall myself train him. Let us all welcome him.'

The group of young men huddled together around Rash Behari and patted him. One of the men brought forward a firm stick and handed it over to him. Guruji looked into his eyes and said, 'May the art of Lathi Khela be your weapon to build your strength and fortitude. I pray to god that with confidence and poise, you will be like a tiger leaping ahead to squash every oppression and injustice.'

From that day onwards, for several years to come, Rash Behari Bose became an ardent student of India's traditional martial art. His exceptional skill in Lathi Khela or stick-

Lathi Khela Arena
Creative Commons

fighting, displayed his passion for the art. Indeed, it not only helped him build his physical strength and stamina, but also boosted his self-confidence and firmness of character.

The books on freedom-struggles, in the collection of Kalicharan, were like the first rays of light that opened Rash Behari's eyes towards a disruptive world view. Listening to militant poems and speeches by patriotic leaders became a constant in the life of the little boy.

One more year passed, and the season of autumn festivals arrived. For traditional Bengali families, Durga Puja is the biggest carnival of the year and it is celebrated as a community event since the 1780s. The small village of Subaldah dressed up like a newlywed bride while the residents of the village immersed themselves in the worship of the goddess.

Guruji, whose name was Sangram, proposed a unique performance on the eve of Maha Ashthami, the most significant day of Durga Puja. A makeshift stage had been set up beside the Pathshala for the nine days of various cultural activities by the village. Guruji announced, 'We will perform on the open ground, in front of the stage. It will be a very special show....'

As the evening sky became dotted with numerous twinkling stars and a cool breeze started to blow, the villagers gathered in the open ground adjacent to the makeshift stage. The local priest completed the evening worship amid the customary sounds of the drums and conch. The atmosphere was highly charged, and everyone waited for the special performance to begin. Kalicharan sat down under the banyan tree, along with the other elderly men.

Like a gust of wind, the performers arrived at the specified area before the stage and began their performance. Dressed in exquisite costumes, Guruji's students enacted a fantastic sequence of war, while one of them narrated the storyline: *This is a nameless tale of an act of bravery that lit up the vast rural landscape of Mother India. When the oppressions of the colonial rulers became unbearable, a band of lionhearted youth decided to revolt. With their age-old skills, Lathi Khela, they inflicted a jolt upon the oppressors.* It was wishful thinking at its best.

As the discourse continued, another group of students entered the arena, along with Guruji, and a wonderful performance began. Divided in two groups, the students started a magnificent display of Lathi Khela. One group was dressed as colonial soldiers, while the other was dressed as native revolutionaries. The villagers stood in complete silence while they witnessed the performers maneuver their bamboo sticks and flaming torches with utmost dexterity.

Performance of Lathi Khela in rural Bengal
Creative Commons

Then, to everyone's surprise, young Rasu arrived on the scene. The other performers encircled him while Guruji came forward and the two charged ahead at each other with their respective weapons for another breathtaking bout of Lathi Khela. As the performance ended, the crowd exploded in cheers while the troupe took a bow in front of everyone. Through the performance, the troupe had successfully upheld the sentiment of uprising against the oppressive British Raj and created a patriotic atmosphere among the spectators.

Without doubt, Rash Behari was the star of the show and he stood with a confident look in his eyes and determination in his composure. As everyone praised him for his skills, Rasu felt content and smiled at Kalicharan. His content grandfather smiled back.

A young boy from the neighborhood came up to Rash Behari and said, 'Rasu, the performance was excellent. I really loved it. However, there is something that I don't understand.'

Rash Behari asked in response, 'What is it that you don't understand?'

The boy questioned back, 'Do you really think we can drive away the oppressive British Raj by the simple art form of Lathi Khela? Do you think we stand any chance to win against them? Can we really fight against all their weapons and their huge army?'

The words were simple, but they left a lasting mark on Rash Behari's mind. That night, his inner voice asked him a question that kept on haunting him for the years to come. It told him, 'Indeed… a simple combat is not what we need to learn.' It asked, 'How can we grow up to fight against the army of the mighty British Raj?' Even though he was too young to ask such a question of himself, Rash Behari's subconscious self was already beginning to get radicalised.

Tinkori Devi, Rash Behari's foster mother, came to visit Subaldah a few days after Durga Puja. Even though he was not her son by birth, the gracious lady had a soft corner for him. Sitting beside Rash Behari, in the open courtyard of their house, she took out a piece of sweetmeat and lovingly gave it to him. As Rash Behari savoured the delicacy, an emotional Tinkori Devi embraced him close to her heart, and whispered, 'Rasu, my son, God has not given me the good fortune to bear you as my own, yet, my almighty knows, how dear you are to me. It is fate that has destined me to stay away from you. However, every day that I pass in Chandannagore, my heart cries out for you, my child. I hope, I can be a good mother to you and my love is able to touch your innocent and beautiful heart.'

Young Rash Behari hugged her back. Deep within, he was still a child who craved for a touch of motherly warmth. As tears appeared on the brim of his eyes, Rash Behari replied, 'Maa... I don't know why I am feeling like crying, but I promise you, for me you will always be my beloved Maa.'

This untarnished love between the two fostered as the sun went down the horizon and ushered in twilight. Tinkori Devi's visit to Subaldah soon came to an end and it was time for her to travel back to Chandannagore. Rash Behari felt sad and sat gloomily in a corner of the courtyard. His inner turmoil was multifaceted. His head was deliberating the question that the little boy had asked him during Durga Puja, while his heart wept at the departure of Tinkori Devi.

Looking at the upset countenance of his sister, Sushila, Rash Behari wiped away his own melancholy and said mischievously,

'Sushila, when Maa leaves for Chandannagore, will you mind if I chop off your long hair?' and thus the siblings engaged in a playful war, dispelling their sorrow.

At the railway station, Tinkori Devi boarded the train and bid her children farewell through the open window of the compartment. Rash Behari stood near that window and said his goodbye. Then, he came closer, and said in a firm voice, 'Maa… I want to join the Army. I will become a soldier in the British India Army. Isn't that wonderful?'

The train had already started to leave the platform, and an astonished Tinkori Devi sat with eyes wide open. Extending her hand through the open window, she exclaimed at Rash Behari, 'Rasu, my boy, don't do anything in haste. I will be worried about your safety. Discuss your plans with your father, write him a letter. Be safe my child… be safe!'

Despite the warning, a cyclone had already started to form within him. Rash Behari told himself, 'The questions that boy asked are very pertinent. Grandfather tells me the tales of revolutions and how the spirit of freedom must bloom within our hearts. However, it is not an easy task. We can never defeat the British with our inexperience and insufficient knowledge of warfare.' His head told him, 'we need experience.'

Sitting inside his little bedroom, he clasped his hands and made up his mind. 'To defeat the enemy, we must learn the skills of the enemy. I must join the British Army to be trained in their techniques and become an able commander… only then can I lead the others towards a successful retaliation.'

Sensing a presence within the room, Rash Behari turned back and saw that Kalicharan was standing behind him. Kalicharan sat down beside Rash Behari and said softly, 'If you have made up your mind, then prepare for the next step. Write your future to secure what you want.'

In the coming month, Rash Behari sent out an application to the British Army, for joining the forces as a native soldier. His heart brimmed with hope as he saw the culmination of his journey into becoming a well-groomed soldier. With great enthusiasm, he posted the letter and waited eagerly for the response to arrive. At times, the long wait seemed unbearable, but Rash Behari held his resolve. It was 1898.[2]

Then, one morning, a reply reached the post office in Subaldah and with extreme eagerness, Rash Behari brought it home and opened it in front of Kalicharan. As his eyes scanned through the typewritten response, the radiant glow in his face slowly turned into dejection. Rash Behari thumped the letter down on the table and said sadly, 'It's a rejection. They said that I am too young.' Rash Behari was just twelve years old.

Before the conversation between Kalicharan and Rash Behari could progress further, a bullock-cart came to a stop before the house and two people entered the courtyard. Sushila rushed into Rash Behari's room and announced, 'It's Baba and Maa!'

Indeed, Binod Behari Bose and Tinkori Devi had arrived suddenly, without notice. However, it was a sweet surprise, and the household was happy. Rash Behari was happy too, but he hid the rejection letter so that his father didn't get to see it.

That day, after a sumptuous lunch, Binod Behari sat in

---

2 *Rash Behari Bose: The Father of The Indian National Army* Vol-1 by Elizabeth Eston & Lexi Kawabe, page number 66.
Referenced from Japanese books: *Dokuritsu no Tōsō* by Rash Behari Bose.
Seinen Ajia no Shōri by Rash Behari Bose (published in 1937).

the open courtyard along with Kalicharan. Tinkori Devi sat at a corner with Rash Behari and Sushila. Binod Behari looked at Rash Behari and then at Kalicharan and then said, 'Baba, I have arrived at a decision. I am taking Rasu and Sushila along with me to Chandannagore. We will travel after two days. Rasu is almost thirteen years old. In Subaldah, his education cannot continue further. I have decided to enroll him at the Dupleix College in Chandannagore. He will get a good education there.'

Rash Behari was not expecting this news. He looked perplexed and questioned, 'But… how can I leave?'

Kalicharan raised his hand and stopped Rash Behari midway. Then he replied with a smile, 'Rasu, don't worry about me. I will be fine. All the villagers are here to take care of me. Go to Chandannagore. Remember… the light of education and knowledge is very important. It is the most powerful weapon. In that new place, you will meet new people with a bouquet of world views. You will become stronger, my son….'

Rash Behari wanted to protest but refrained from doing so. Tears welled up in his eyes as he struggled to come to terms with the sudden change in life his father had decreed. Tinkori Devi hugged him. Deep within, she knew about the inner turmoil within Rasu and she wanted to keep him safe.

Mysteriously, the cards of fortune always played a magical game in his life and drew Rash Behari towards a journey that was to remain etched in the altar of history.

The next day passed in packing. Rash Behari took all his stuff but left his Lathi in Kalicharan's room. Looking at his old and frail mentor (his beloved grandpa), Rash Behari said, 'This will remind you about me and everything that you taught me….'

That evening, Rash Behari went to meet Guruji to bid him

farewell. He touched the feet of his guru and said, 'Bless me Guruji, so that I can become what my heart truly aspires to be. Tomorrow morning, I will leave for Chandannagore.... Goodbye Guruji.' Guruji touched his head in blessing and then hugged him. Then, he held Rash Behari's shoulders firmly and said, 'Never say goodbye. We shall meet again. Remember, your strength is your biggest weapon. Don't let it fade. And... keep practicing your skills.'

MEETING REVOLUTION IN CHANDANNAGORE

Chandannagore Railway Station

THE MORNING TRAIN from Subaldah took the family of Binod Behari Bose and headed out for Chandannagore. The quaint little town was a slice of France and for young Rash Behari, it was a big transformation, both in terms of geography as well as cultural settings. As they alighted on the platform of Chandannagore railway station, Rash Behari was overwhelmed by the French architectural grandeur all around.

As the family of Binod Behari Bose entered their house in a residential locality, it was already late in the afternoon. The beautiful buildings all along the way had left a lasting impression on Rash Behari. The longing for Subaldah and the face of his beloved grandfather was still very fresh in his mind. He sat by an open window and looked outside, while many fond memories created a mêlée of emotions within him.

As the evening approached, Binod Behari understood the turmoil in his son and said, 'Rasu, come with me. Let us go around the town. I am sure you will like the place.'

The father and son went for a stroll, as the cool evening breeze from the Hooghly River lent a soothing touch. They went past the Strand, the Sacred Heart Church, the French Cemetery and then arrived at the crescent shaped Ghat of the Hooghly River.

The Strand, Chandannagore

Standing in front of the glittering water under the silvery moonlight, Binod Behari looked at Rash Behari and said, 'Son, here in Chandannagore, if you delve deep, you will be able to get a taste of the French culture. In contrast with whatever you have learned so far, I am sure that your education will flourish. Next week, I will take you to the Dupleix College and get you enrolled there.'

Then he added, 'There is a library in the lane adjacent to our house. You can enroll your name there. I have been told that the library has a rich collection of books.'

As his hair fluttered in the breeze, Rash Behari looked blankly at the river and replied, 'Yes Baba.' He was just too overwhelmed by all that he had seen of the town.

Binod Behari patted his son on the shoulder and said with a smile, 'Rasu, you must learn to tame the turmoil within your heart and mind. That will enrich you and make you a stronger person.'

The next morning, Rash Behari found the library nearby. As he stepped inside the old building, the gloom within his heart lifted a little. The sight of shelves and shelves of books was overwhelming and Rash Behari stood astounded by the large collection.[1]

The old librarian, Das Babu, smiled at him and asked, 'So, Mr Bose, is there any specific book that you are looking for?'

---

1 The mention of the books he read and loved dearly has clear references in:
A Life Story Of Rash Behari Basu by Kshitish Chandra Das, pages 10-25.
Rash Behari Bose: The Father of The Indian National Army Vol-1 by Elizabeth Eston & Lexi Kawabe.
The narrative style has been adopted to fill in the gaps in the story.

Rash Behari nodded, indicating that he was still unsure about what he wanted. Das Babu added, 'You are new to this place. I guess, the French culture needs to settle down in your system before you can appreciate the beauty of this place and understand the people here. Can I make a suggestion?'

'I think the culture of my motherland is vast and I don't need to imbibe a foreign culture. Moreover, I believe that the native people who live here are more Bengali than French. Does one need to know them afresh', asked Rash Behari.

Das Babu laughed dryly and responded, 'I see the flame of nationalism burning bright in your young heart. If you listen to this old man, you must read about the French Revolution.' Das Babu handed over three books to Rash Behari and said, 'Come and meet me once you have read them. Trust me... you won't be disappointed.'

Then he turned back and took out another book and gave it to Rash Behari. Rasu looked at the title. It read, *Ananda Math* in Bengali. Das Babu said softly, 'Your tumultuous heart will find solace in this book and your analytical mind will discover a rhythm in it that will echo in the other books I gave you.'

Rash Behari smiled back and replied, 'Thank you!' Young Rasu's quest for knowledge had at last really begun.

Over the next couple of days, Rash Behari immersed himself in the books that he had received. Sitting within the serene settings of the French Cemetery or upon the paved stairs of the crescent Ghat of the Hooghly, Rash Behari drank the potion of knowledge hidden in their pages. The fiery sentiment of *Ananda Math* and the account of the Sannyasi Rebellion in Bengal in the 18th century mingled with the blatant struggles of the French Revolution of 1789 and created a chiaroscuro of

A front view of the famous Dupleix College

turbulence in his mind. The stories of a nationwide uproar to overthrow monarchy and establish a republic, via a catalysed violent political upheaval, created a deep impact. The militant ideology hidden in the pages of *Ananda Math* blended with the actual rebellion in France and germinated in Rash Behari's young mind a hope of freeing India through armed struggle. The imagery of the times was very strong. India, the land was portrayed as a woman, everyone's mother who was in shackles and had to be freed. The association of ideas touched every heart, old and young.

Rash Behari reiterated his own words, 'To defeat the enemy, we must learn the skills of the enemy. I must join the British Army to be trained in their techniques and become an able commander… only then can I lead the others towards a successful retaliation.'

With a spark in his eyes, Rash Behari said to himself, 'Indeed, the cultural and historic knowledge of the French is worth knowing. Even though Chandannagore is a colony under their rule, the rich fragrance of revolution in their blood is worth knowing. Only by knowing about such brave endeavours, can we garner the courage to rise against the mighty British Raj.' Clearly, relocation to Chandannagore was beginning to have a wonderful effect on the life of Rash Behari Bose, broadening his vision of revolution and giving him a global perspective. With a mind that was like an empty canvas, Rash Behari absorbed the overdose of this diversity that he observed in Chandannagore's busy streets, the lively shops, the people and their urbane behaviour.

The concoction of Indian and French cultures opened up a new vista in his world view. Rash Behari's first direct interaction with a foreign culture, that too one replete with a revolutionary zeal, began a philosophical transformation which included the young boy's own vision of a grand finale that would bring freedom to his own country.

One week flew by and Binod Behari felt happy to see that Rash Behari was slowly beginning to like the new place. Thus, on a bright Monday morning, he told his son, 'Rasu, get ready. We are going to the Dupleix College today.'

Under the long pillars of the huge complex of Dupleix College, designed in typical French style, the passageway to the building had a quiet ambience. Even though the atmosphere was different, Rash Behari entered the institution with an open mind. It was his first experience of an urban educational institution, very different from his village pathshala, and he wondered what spectacles awaited him. Getting him enrolled

Dupleix College Entrance

was not a problem for Binod Behari, as he was a government employee. As the formalities got completed, Rash Behari received a fresh set of books and was all set to begin his classes.

The next morning, dressed in clean clothes, Rash Behari entered his new classroom. The students were mostly Indian and Rash Behari chose an empty seat in the middle of the classroom. A few boys came up and an informal introduction started before the routine classes commenced. Being a keen observer, Rash Behari focused his energies on the subjects that were being taught.

During the afternoon break, Rash Behari chose to sit at his desk and go through the notes, while the other boys went out for refreshments. As he was immersed in the pages of his handwritten notes, a boy came and stood in front of him. Rash Behari lifted his head and looked at him. With typically

Bengali features and large intelligent eyes, the boy was dark complexioned, and had a thin but strong built.

The boy pulled up a chair, sat in front of Rash Behari and said in a mocking tone, 'So, you are the newcomer. I believe you are here to gain the pearls of wisdom so that one day you can become a loyal civil servant to the Imperial government. Isn't that your dream? To be a Royal Servant.'

Rash Behari replied sternly, 'I don't reveal my intentions to strangers. What I desire is far from the ken of blubberers.'

The boy came closer to Rash Behari and said in an angry voice, 'Either answer my question or fight.' The boy folded his sleeves and placed his arm on the wooden bench, challenging Rash Behari to a fist fight. By this time, a band of boys had gathered around them to see the little drama unfolding. Rash Behari looked around and then, accepting the challenge, folded his own sleeves and placed forth his right arm.

Thus began a teenage show of strength as the two boys, their faces puckered, tussled to down each other's arms. While the enthralled audience watched silently, the minutes seemed to move at the speed of a snail. Then, with a thud on the wooden desk, Rash Behari thumped down the hand of his opponent and commanded a mini roar of appreciation from his spectators.

Looking into the eyes of his opponent, Rash Behari said, 'The power of a rebel is not just in his words. It resides within his mind. You cannot extract from me by force what I want to become in life.' As he got up from the chair, the other boy stood up and extended his hand towards Rash Behari for a handshake.

Unable to refuse the magnetic attraction of his rebellious arrogance, Rash Behari held out his hand in response. The boy smiled and said, 'My name is Shrish Chandra Ghosh. In those fiery eyes of yours, I have got my answer. I am glad to meet you. Your strength and your wit, both speak the truth. Can we be friends?'

Rash Behari smiled back in response and replied, 'I am Rash Behari Bose. My family and friends call me Rasu. Yes, we can be friends.... And you guessed it right, I am not planning to be anybody's servant.'

The band of boys surrounding the two of them burst into cheers as the two aggressors hugged each other. Only destiny knew that it was the commencement of a lifelong friendship that was ordained to go beyond the boundaries of time.

Shrish asked enthusiastically, 'You seem to be new in Chandannagore. Where are you from?'

'Yes. I am new here', replied Rash Behari. 'I have come from Subaldah, my ancestral village. My sister and I used to live with our grandfather. My father is employed here, and I have come here a few days ago to live with him.'

Shrish's eyes lit up and he said, 'This cannot be just a coincidence. Even I belong to Subaldah. I was born there in my maternal uncle's house and had lived there while I was a toddler. Then, my parents brought me here so that I get a proper education.'

'The soil of Subaldah perseveres', smiled Rash Behari. 'Perhaps, that is what attracted us, I am glad that I met you.'

Friendship with Shrish was like a gust of fresh air for Rash Behari. Their dreams were yet to crystalise, but in Shrish, Rash Behari found the same ardent desire to know, the zeal to learn and that mysterious something, undefined yet, which drew them to each other.

Sitting in the classroom of Dupleix College, the two friends dreamt of a free India, Relaxing under the shade of the old banyan in the French Cemetery, or in the open field beside the banks of Hooghly, Rash Behari could speak his heart out to his new-found companion. Their free and untamed minds needed the tether of a tutor and destiny seemed to have just the right man for the job.

Two months later, a visiting faculty arrived at the Dupleix College. Edward Gomes was a teacher of the English language and had come to Chandannagore from Kolkata for taking special classes. As the class started, Edward Gomes began with the statement, 'Inherently, the people of Bengal have very little courage.'

On hearing his opening line, several students clenched their fists, among then Shrish. Rash Behari held his hands and quietened him. The insult was great, but the time to respond impulsively was not appropriate.

Gomes continued, 'It's a pity that you all were born in this race. Birth does not come by choice. However, with proper education, I am sure you will be able to refine your cultural disadvantage and become respectable civil servants of this colonial society. Hence, to gauge your abilities, I have decided to conduct a creative writing contest for you. So, tomorrow, you must submit your individual entries and I will personally read them and evaluate each one of you. Remember, your submissions will tell how efficient you will be, to become successful in your careers.'

For the rest of the class, both Shrish and Rash Behari remained infuriated but refrained from doing anything drastic. As the class ended, the two looked at the insulted yet timid faces of the other students and walked out. 'I just cannot swallow the insult', Shrish shook in anger. 'We must give an appropriate reply.'

'Shrish, have you read *Ananda Math*? Isn't it wonderful?' said Rash Behari in the evening, as the two buddies sat near the Strand and sipped coconut water, to cool off the heated encounter that they had experienced in the classroom.

Shrish replied, 'Yes. The sentiment is excellent. I see so much potential in it. Being a resident of Chandannagore and having heard about the French Revolution, when I look at that book, I firmly believe that even I can protest. However, we are just gobbling up the insults and not doing anything.'

Rash Behari looked at his friend and replied, 'You know, I always believed that a formal military training would enable us to become real fighters, rather than mere rebels. We must erase the blame that we carry upon us. We are not cowards. And I shall prove that tomorrow.'

'So will I. But how?', replied Shrish with an equally determined countenance.

Rash Behari looked into his eyes and said, 'Tomorrow we will submit our written articles for the creative writing competition. In that endeavour, my subject will be REVOLUTION. As Edward Gomes will surely read the articles, it will be my apt response to the insult we have faced today.' Shrish Ghosh's eyes glittered like gems, and he smirked at his friend's cleverness.

The next morning, Rash Behari and Shrish Ghosh entered the classroom at the stipulated time. As Gomes sat down at his desk, one by one, the students went up and submitted their entries. Gomes kept the papers inside a folder and went on with the class.

At last, before culminating the session, he said, 'I will

read them tonight. Tomorrow morning, I shall declare the best entries in the presence of the School Principal, Mr Charu Chandra Roy.'

As Gomes walked out, Rash Behari looked at Shrish and said with a smirk, 'Wait for the upcoming fireworks tomorrow.'

The following morning, the class for the special session began in an electrifying atmosphere. The students, dressed in neat uniforms, sat in their respective places and awaited the arrival of Edward Gomes along with the principal.

Shrish looked at Rash Behari and said, 'Do you know anything about Professor Charu Chandra Roy? I have heard that he is a man who strongly opposes the colonial rule and is vocal about the rising concerns of the common people.'

Rash Behari nodded his head, indicating that he had not heard anything about the man.

Soon, Gomes entered the classroom along with another man. The latter, dressed in a crisp white Indian attire, had a charismatic personality. His tall stature, his intelligent eyes and his serene countenance reflected a brilliance that filled the room with a strange positivity.

The man stood in front of the class, beamed at the students and said in a heavy baritone, 'Good morning everyone. I am Charu Chandra Roy, the Principal of Dupleix College. Due to my work engagements, I didn't have an opportunity of meeting every one of you. However, today is a wonderful occasion, when in the presence of Mr Gomes, I will be able to interact with all of you.'

After the initial greetings, Edward Gomes began speaking. He picked up a few pages and appreciated the efforts of the boys and then held out two pieces of paper and spoke in an arrogant voice, 'Behold. These two entries are from Mr Rash Behari Bose and Mr Shrish Chandra Ghosh. May I request these two gentlemen to stand up in front of the classroom.'

With an air of confidence, both Rash Behari and Shrish stood up and looked ahead. The two knew that the subjects of their bombastic essays were sure to raise the teachers' eyebrows. They quickly glanced at each other and then stood straight.

Edward Gomes continued in his haughty tone, 'These two gentlemen have written about the seeds of revolution in Bengal. The two essays have described in detail how the people of Bengal had fought in the Battle of Plassey and stood up against the British. They have had the audacity to criticise the imperial rule and tell us how the sons of Bengal have done whatever they did.'

Gomes then looked sternly at Charu Chandra and said loudly, 'I take this as a personal insult on behalf of the British. Let me tell you folks that none of the efforts that you have written about, ever succeeded. Moreover, you live in a fool's paradise, if you think that India will ever be able to fight the British.'

Finally, Gomes threw down the two essays and said in a loud voice, 'Mr Roy, I wanted to bring this act of audacity to your notice. I refuse to take further classes here and am leaving for Kolkata immediately. I will lodge my complaints to higher authorities if you don't take strict actions against these two rebels. Goodbye.' Nobody noticed, but Charu Chandra's eyes sparkled momentarily. Then, maintaining his composure, he said, 'Alright Mr Gomes. You can go back to Kolkata. Leave this matter in my hands and I will do whatever rightly needs to be done.'

As silent spectators, Rash Behari and Shrish watched, while Edward Gomes walked out from the room. Charu Chandra picked up the two essays, and before leaving, said in a grim voice, 'After the school gets over today, the two of you come and meet me at my office.'

The tense mood of the class prevailed the entire day and when the school got over, all the boys rushed out. Rash Behari and Shrish Ghosh went up to the principal's chamber and knocked at the door. A voice asked the two to enter the room and close the door.

As Rash Behari and Shrish Ghosh stood in front of the large desk, Charu Chandra observed them silently for a few moments. Rash Behari noticed that their essays were kept on the table meticulously, under a paperweight.

Then, Charu Chandra spoke. 'What do you think? Are the few brave sons of Bengal sufficient to overthrow the British Raj? Will writing a fiery essay and submitting it to a British-origin teacher be a powerful blow to them? Can the entire country get rid of the imperial rule by simply doing these stupid things? What qualities do you have to become revolutionaries?'

Shrish Ghosh was speechless. The questions were indeed pertinent, and he didn't know what to say. However, a few moments later, Rash Behari held his hand firmly, looked into Charu Chandra's eyes and said in a confident voice, 'We don't know the answers to the questions you ask.'

A surprised Charu Chandra stared back at him and said, 'So...?'

Replied Rash Behari, 'Sir... teach us how to answer them.'

An instant of deadening pause intervened and then Charu Chandra sighed, with the words, 'Come back and see the school's notice board tomorrow morning. You will get my reply.'

The next morning was unlike any other, ever since Rash

Behari had arrived in Chandannagore. As Shrish Ghosh and Rash Behari reached close to the school's notice board, a mini crowd had gathered around it with a murmur reverberating in the air. The two peeped in through a gap and saw that the school's principal had put up their essays on the notice board as 'Recommended Reads' for the week. The crowd noticed their presence and a sound of applause filled the air. It was a victory that the two had never experienced before. It filled their hearts with an ecstasy that was novel and pure.

As they were still basking in their glory, Charu Chandra came and stood behind them. When the two children turned around and saw him, he said softly with a smile, 'Yes, I will teach you. Meet me at my residence on Sunday.'[2]

Forging Iron Men

The following Sunday brought with it the dawn of discipline in the lives of the two boys. Early in the morning, the two of them arrived at the gate of the little bungalow where Roy lived. Through the wrought iron gate, they could see the beautiful garden surrounding the tranquil white house. They walked past the gate and up the gravel pathway to stand at the entrance of the house. The sound of their stride announced their arrival. Charu Chandra Roy opened the wooden door and came out to welcome them. Dressed in a crisp white kurta, he looked as serene as a sage.[3]

---

2 The historical facts have been referenced from: *Two Great Indian Revolutionaries-Rash Behari Bose & Jyotindra Nath Mukherjee* by Uma Mukherjee, page numbers 40-120. *A Life Story Of Rash Behari Basu* by Kshitish Chandra Das. *Rash Behari Bose* by Satyavrata Ghosh & Luis Fernandes.

3 Saree, Kurta are Indian clothing.

'Come boys', said Charu Chandra in a commanding voice, sprinkled with enthusiasm. Rash Behari and Shrish Ghosh followed him and went inside.

There were tasty refreshments waiting for the boys and after they had had their fill, Charu Chandra said, 'Revolution is not defined by just opposing something with sheer repulsion. It is not about stubbornly resisting. Neither is it about doing outrageous acts without a proper focus. The life of a revolutionary is extraordinary, and it needs astonishing skills of decision-making.'

Rash Behari looked at Charu Chandra with utmost attentiveness while the guru spoke, 'A revolutionary must take tremendous strides, but must protect himself from being crumbled by the opponent. He must be a master of disguise, a commander of mass conviction and a person who will be able to accomplish a mammoth rebellion. Yes, he must do that. However, the rebellion must rise like a wildfire and consume the entire woodland. Even though a wildfire often mellows and is contained by mankind, but the human mind grapples with the impact it leaves behind. The aftermath of a revolution must be like that of a wildfire. Even though the revolution might not be able to accomplish its target, its jolt must unnerve the opponent with its sheer strength.'

Charu Chandra's words were like arrows that pierced through the hearts of the two young boys. The rush of adrenaline brought with it visions of great adventure and excitement.

Charu Chandra paused a little and then said, 'Let us go outside. With the sunshine bathing us, we must sit close to the soil and feel the touch of Mother Earth and our country. In that natural motherly affection of our nation, I shall hold your hands and help you take your first steps into the new world. The old banyan in my garden is like a family member for me. Let us go and sit under her tranquil shade.'

Thus, inside the serene quarters of the little bungalow, under the shade of the banyan, for the first time, the two young boys listened to Charu Chandra Roy and his radical world views. With wide open eyes, they heard his words and gulped down the doses of an alternate concept of nationalism that steered them towards revolutionary politics as grownups.

The months moved ahead and metamorphosed into years and as Rash Behari Bose grew to a strapping teenager he started to get moulded into a person whose only focus in life was to bring about a colossal revolution that would free his beloved motherland from the shackles of colonialism.

Years ago, by a stroke of luck at the library near his house, Rash Behari had gained access to the book, *Ananda Math,* written by noted Bengali novelist Bankim Chandra Chatterjee. It was a revolutionary novel, whose vast content was too big for his young mind at the time. However, as the years went by and Rash Behari grew up, he became more and more aware of the implication of a revolution and this book ignited the flames of a subconscious dream of a militant bid for freedom within his heart.

Soon, he became consciously involved in making his dream a reality. Rash Behari was now no longer a dreamer. The book was not only an eye-opener but also a source of knowledge that made Rash Behari think about a modus operandi for a organised protest and uprising. He gathered more and more books on revolutionary thinking and immersed himself in the ocean of knowledge that the authors had portrayed within the pages of such books. And French Chandannaagore became the perfect foil for his kind of revolution.

Secretly, he discussed his ideas with his friend Shrish Ghosh and their resolve to free their country grew. The fiery speeches of Surendranath Banerjee and Swami Vivekananda acted as further catalysts to their way of thinking.

Often, during the humid summer afternoons, Rash Behari and Shrish Ghosh sat in front of their mentor and debated the daring ideas that came to their minds.

'The country needs the sacrifices of young men and women', Charu Chandra said in a restless tone. He was getting on in years and desperately wanted to see India free. 'Only by the combined efforts of an entire generation will our forsaken motherland become free from the shackles of bondage to a foreign power. Alas, that dream is yet to be dreamt by the multitude and we are unable to foresee the day when the unborn children of our country will open their eyes in a free land.'

Rash Behari argued, 'Sir, the responsibility rests on our shoulders. We, the educated youth, need to do something to awaken that spirit within the ones whose eyes still remain closed.'

As the discussion continued, Rash Behari added, 'Sir, I strongly believe that we, the eager and revolutionary youth of this country, lack proper training to carry out a war against the military prowess of the British Army. We must learn the skills of the opponent from them and use that same skill to fight them.'

'My dear, your words are both right and wrong', replied Charu Chandra. 'On one side, you are correct about the lack of skill, but I doubt how much our youth will be able to learn from the enemy, because they are very shrewd. On the other side, I believe that the journey of revolution must be traversed over generations, because a mammoth task like this cannot be completed by a single generation. The mistakes of one generation teach the next and that will pave the path for the final victory. My conviction says, we don't need to learn from the enemy. Our sacrifices will teach our children to carry out the final assault.'

Rash Behari was young and adamant, and he felt that his own thinking was right. When alone with Shrish Ghosh, he told his trusted buddy, 'Nobody will know, but I will try my luck with the British Indian Army. Let me see if I can achieve what I am hoping to do.'

With waves of aspiration soaring high within his heart, Rash Behari enthusiastically wrote an application letter to the British Army officials of Fort William in Kolkata. He was applying to entre the Army for the second time in his young life. However, his castle of dreams crashed after a month, when he received yet another letter of rejection.

'The letter states my physical unfitness as the reason of this rejection', Rash Behari fumed as he tore the reply to bits. 'It says that the British Army will not recruit a Bengali since they are physically unfit. How can they judge a person without even testing him?'

Shrish Ghosh sat beside him and replied, 'Don't you think that the revolutionary background of Bengal is the prime cause of this rejection?' Ever since the 1856-57 mutiny and its leadership by soldiers like Mangal Pandey of the 34th Bengal Native Infantry (BNI) regiment of the British East India Company, the British had distrusted the Bengalis, the Bengal regiments and Bengal.

'Yes. You are correct Shrish', replied Rash Behari, 'However, I will keep on trying until I can make a breakthrough. Now I understand the value of patience and perseverance. Being

An old photograph of Fort William

impulsive is detrimental to the philosophy of success.'

That evening, in Charu Chandra's garden, under the shade of the banyan, Rash Behari told his mentor, 'Sir, you were correct. I was wrong. I promise you, I will never let emotions drift me away into the darkness of failure.'

The aging Charu Chandra Roy embraced his protégé lovingly.[4]

---

4 The storyline so far is based on historical facts that have been referenced from: *Two Great Indian Revolutionaries-Rash Behari Bose & Jyotindra Nath Mukherjee* by Uma Mukherjee, page numbers 125-140. Many references in the book by Uma Mukherjee come from Prof Bejon Behari Bose's (Rash Behari's younger brother) Bengali work, *Karmabir RashBehari*, published in 1956.

Anushilan Samiti

Anushilan Samiti, the parent organisation of Jugantar

The next two years passed like the turning pages of an epic and Rash Behari grew up into a very intelligent teenager. The canopy of knowledge provided by his teacher Charu Chandra and the shield of friendship bestowed upon him by Shrish Ghosh polished him into a man of steel.

Holding the hands of his two disciples, Charu Chandra Roy introduced them to the revolutionary wing of the Anushilan Samiti, of which Jugantar was the wing that was active in Kolkata. Thus, while living in Chandannagore, Rash Behari became associated with the local wing of the Anushilan Samiti, a Bengal-based organisation that supported radical violence as the means for ending British rule in India. Prominent members of the organisation included nationalists Aurobindo Ghosh and his brother Barindra Ghosh. Despite the fact that he was not a member of the organisation, even at a young age, Rash Behari's mind and soul were one with the ideologies of these revolutionary leaders and their fundamental viewpoints. Even though Rash Behari and Shrish were not yet active members, they ardently followed the preaching of revolutionary politics propagated by this group and its affiliates.

OUTLAW IN SCHOOL

AT THE DUPLEIX College, Rash Behari remained a student with a radical mindset. Even after Charu Chandra Roy had retired as principal of the college, Rash Behari continued to stand up for his own stubborn beliefs. Thus, as a student of the Second Class (Class 9) at the Dupleix College, Rash Behari had yet another blunt confrontation with his teachers that steered the course of his life away from school altogether. The year was 1902, he had been away from Subaldah now for nearly four years.

'I feel humiliated by the amount of hatred displayed by the British teachers. We, the native students of this country, are forced to study under the tutelage of these foreign teachers who have no respect for our country', said Rash Behari one day as the last class for the day ended.

Shrish Ghosh replied, 'I know. Alas, we have to remain calm and composed and tolerate their contempt. I don't know how long generations of Indians will have to face this ordeal.'

School hours were over. Students from all the classrooms were preparing to leave as they were hurrying down the staircase. A group of three Englishmen were standing near the corridor and they overheard the conversation of the boys. They

Corridor of Dupleix College

were three British teachers who were employed at the Dupleix College at that time. Among them, Howard Rothman was the most notorious.

Rothman intercepted Rash Behari and Shrish and said sternly, 'I believe that you two gentlemen have a serious grudge against the British teachers. Alright, then speak up.'

Rash Behari came forward and said calmly, 'Sir, we don't have a grudge against the British. We simply don't support your colonial rule that is forcibly imposed on this country and on her people. Moreover, this is my personal conviction. None of my companions have any opinion on this.'

While the other students gathered around them, Rothman came closer to Rash Behari and then shouted, 'This country was always destined to be ruled and will remain so in future as well. That is why Bakhtiyar Khilji was able to conquer Bengal with just seventeen cavalrymen. You must feel blessed that the British have chosen to rule you. That is the reason why you fools are getting good education.'

Rash Behari could not control himself further. He shouted back, 'That is a wrong statement, Mr Rothman, the vile Bakhtiyar Khilji had many more men behind him... your knowledge of history is incomplete. Mother India and her children are not cowards. One day, we will prove that to the entire world and overthrow the colonial rule.' Rash Behari then stormed out of the premises of the school,

The next day began within the closed chamber of the Principal of Dupleix College. In front of a small assemblage of teachers, Rothman pointed at Rash Behari and screamed, 'This boy has the audacity of confronting the teachers with contempt. He dared to insult me in front of the entire school. His mindset dwells upon radical nationalism. He does not have the right to study in Dupleix College. He must be expelled from here before he corrupts the minds of other students.'

The teachers gathered in that room nodded in agreement. None of them dared to oppose Rothman's opinion. He was British and speaking against him was considered a taboo. Thus, silence prevailed. Even the Principal of Dupleix College was like a puppet who dared not say a word against Rothman, though this was French Chandannagore.

Rash Behari replied in a furious tone, 'I reject the allegations. It is Mr Rothman who inflicts heinous abuse upon Indians. I had simply put forth my objection. Yes, I did, because I am proud of my birth and ethnicity, as a son of Mother India. Moreover, I won't allow you an opportunity of expelling me. Before that, I myself am leaving…' and the angry young man strode out.[1]

As the door of the Principal's room was flung open, Rash Behari walked out with a conqueror's stride. Students of the entire Dupleix College witnessed the final departure of this brave son of mother India. Standing by the corridor, Shrish Ghosh silently wiped away his own tears and whispered to himself, 'One day, his strides will jolt the entire colonial Raj.' That was the last day for Rash Behari at the Dupleix College. The school etiquette had been breached and Rash Behari's name was permanently removed from the school's rolls.

At home, Binod Behari Bose was furious. The news struck him like a thunderbolt, and he sat speechless for some time. Then, he said in a grim voice, 'Rasu, my boy, your desperate views and your growing inclination towards revolutionary activities is making me feel scared and worried. I was never so afraid in my entire life. I feel apprehensive about your future.'

Rash Behari sat down beside his father. There were tears in

---

1 *A Life Story Of Rash Behari Basu* by Kshitish Chandra Das.
Rash Behari Bose by Satyavrata Ghosh & Luis Fernandes.

both their eyes. He understood that his rebellious behaviour was causing pain to his father. He touched his hands lightly and said softly, 'Baba, I cannot restrain myself when someone abuses my motherland. The behaviour of these British teachers at the Dupleix College had crossed the threshold of my tolerance. Please forgive me for whatever happened. It was beyond my patience. However, I promise you that I will obey whatever you tell me to do.'

Binod Behari hugged his son lovingly and said, 'Rasu, on Saturday, I will take you to Kolkata. From now onwards you shall stay in Kolkata, at my cousin's house. I will use my influences and get you enrolled in the Morton School. You must complete your studies from there.'

The decision was a painful one for Rash Behari. The life of a revolutionary is never painted in the hues of stability. A revolutionary is like a vagabond who roams around the world to create his vision of freedom and himself remains a nomad. Rash Behari did not know that his life of a nomad had already been written in his stars.

In the next few days, Rash Behari said his goodbyes to everyone. Going away from Shrish Ghosh and Charu Chandra Roy was not so easy. It was a huge emotional burden on the young Rash Behari, but he gathered all his courage and resolved to remain strong.

Charu Chandra blessed his loving disciple and said, 'Life will not be kind or compassionate to you. Junctions in your journey will bring immense difficulties. However, you have chosen a path where you must walk upon fire. Keep the flame burning within you. We might be apart physically, but our souls remain united.'

Shrish Ghosh hugged his buddy and said, 'Our friendship is beyond the barriers of distance. Our sole resolution remains strong, and our friendship will remain etched on the embers of time.'

Lady luck relocated Rash Behari to another unknown city at the impressionable age of sixteen. Once again, he settled himself in a completely different environment and pretended to adjust to the world that surrounded him.

Binod Behari got him enrolled at the Morton School and Rasu restarted his routine student's life in a high school. However, Kolkata being a big city and a hub for various revolutionary activities, Rash Behari soon found himself engrossed in the work of the Anushilan Samiti and its fledgling wing, Jugantar. He was still not an active member, but his heart and soul were fully dedicated to all that the organisations were doing. In good faith, it was his father who had brought him to Kolkata, not knowing that this was revolution's opportunity to grab Rash Behari into its fold.

Rash Behari tried to focus on the school curriculum but at every step, he strongly felt that whatever was being fed to him as a student was unnecessary to learn. His young mind was agile and bubbling with zeal. Despite being forced to live in Kolkata, Rash Behari kept shuttling between Chandannagore and Kolkata. This kept the flame of revolution ignited within him. The visits to meet Charu Chandra and Shrish Ghosh were his lifeline.

Meanwhile, undeterred, Rash Behari sent out numerous letters to the British Indian Army and visited several military cantonments seeking an opportunity to get recruited in the army. However, every time, his high hopes crumbled under the weight of rejection. At the end of two more years, Rash Behari finally fled from the Kolkata guardian's house to seek employment within the British armed forces, but success continued to refuse to embrace his endeavours.[2]

A worried Tinkori Devi and Binod Behari brought their son gone astray back home and sat him down for a serious discussion. Binod Behari spoke in an anxious tone, 'Why are you doing this? Rasu, we are so worried about you. First you left the house in Kolkata without informing us and I had to go through a great ordeal to find you. Next, I stumbled upon this letter from the British Army. Why are you applying to seek employment there?'

Rash Behari tried his best to pacify the apprehension of his parents, but his father said in a concerned tone, 'Rasu, my son, please don't do anything drastic. I request you from deep within my heart. Please refrain from doing anything radical. Listen to me. Complete your education and then do what you aspire to do....'

'Rasu, my dear, I always believe that you are my own child. I don't want to lose you. Please listen to your father', cried Tinkori Devi.

Rash Behari understood that his impulsive behaviour had only caused despair in his parents. He apologised and calmed their concerns. Yet, this was just an eyewash. Despite all his promises, Rash Behari couldn't resist what his heart truly desired. Rash Behari's rebellious character made him even more

---

2 Year is around 1902-1903.
This has been referenced from: *A Life Story of Rash Behari Basu* By Kshitish Chandra Das.

restless. Disinterested in formal education, he finally left school and went back to Chandannagore.

Binod Behari Bose understood the turmoil within his son. He comprehended the desire within his firstborn to be a part of India's freedom struggle. However, the father within him dreaded such a young man's fate and worried about the safety of his son. Sitting in the living-room of their house, Binod Behari told his son, 'Rasu, I understand the unrest within your heart. However, I fear for your security. What will you be able to achieve against the mighty imperial rule? You cannot do anything alone. The entire revolutionary fraternity is struggling to carry on their fight. How will you be able to bring about a transformation?'

Rash Behari replied grimly, 'Baba, I do not have any answers to your intriguing questions. I only know what my heart wants. I don't know whether I will be able to succeed. Yet, not doing anything is equal to accepting defeat. I must do something. I cannot remain silent when I see the injustice of the British Raj.'

Binod Behari raised his voice to calm his 18-year old son's outrage and said, 'Rasu, I will not tell you to continue your education. However, you must promise to listen to me. I will consult my cousin and try to find you a job. You have to promise me that you will listen to me and take it. This is my final decision.'

Rash Behari couldn't refuse his father. Even though reluctantly, he replied, 'Yes Baba.'

Soon, an elite recommendation fetched Rash Behari Bose a job at Fort William, in Kolkata. For long, his dream had been to get into Fort William, the English army's headquarters. It was the job of a clerk and Rash Behari went back to Kolkata and joined work. 'It is true that the job of a clerk is poles apart from the job of a soldier. However, being employed here will help me learn more about the British Army', he told himself. At least, now he would be an insider, he thought.

Alas, despite all his efforts, Rash Behari's quest for more information on the British Army was never destined to be a smooth one. Within a few weeks, an unpleasant encounter sealed the fate of his job at Fort William. At that time Kolkata was the capital of the country.

On a fateful day, the Commanding Officer spotted Rash Behari and summoned him to his office. As Rash Behari entered, the Commanding Officer asked him, 'What is your full name? I see that you have been working here for the past few weeks. Answer me....'

Fort William

Rash Behari felt insulted at the scornful tone of the man. He replied, 'My name is Rash Behari….'

The Commanding Officer interrupted him midway and raised his own voice, 'Isn't your full name Rash Behari Bose? You are a damned Bengali. Don't you know that the volatile nature of the Bengali youth is the prime reason why the British Raj abhors you folks? Still, shamelessly, you have come here for a job. The Bengali youth are visionless and are aggressive towards us.'

The allegation was too much for Rash Behari to bear. He thumped the table and replied, 'Bengal and Bengalis are not against the British, but against their colonial rule. However, because of heartless men like you, the friction will never end. I am quitting this job right now.' Saying this, Rash Behari walked out of the office while the Commanding Officer screamed and hurled abuses at him. Rash Behari was hurt and insulted. The words of the Commanding Officer no longer mattered. He felt happy that he had walked out of the job. Yet, he was apprehensive about the agony this would cause his father.

IN THE LAP OF THE HIMALAYAS

VOLATILE EPISODES IN Rash Behari's life were like a persistent fountain and Binod Behari Bose was worried about the future of his son, given the history of angry encounters with the British Rasu had had from a young age.

The incident at Fort William left the father at his wits end. Rash Behari's parents were greatly upset that their attempts to tame the young rebel faced roadblock after roadblock. Binod Behari was now stationed in Shimla and was even more anxious about his son. In her motherly concern, Tinkori Devi then told her husband, 'Please send him away from Bengal. Bring him to Shimla, far from all the turmoil. Let him settle down in a professional environment where his mind will be at ease.'

'Yes, I believe you are right. Let me see what I can do', Binod Behari told his wife thoughtfully. In a few months, Binod Behari used his professional contacts and succeeded in finding a new job for his rebellious son. According to his father's wish, Rash Behari joined the Government Press in Shimla. At the press, he got appointed as a copyholder.

The serene beauty of Shimla somewhat helped to ease the storm that brewed in the young man's heart ever since Rash Behari had left Dupleix College. In the beautiful mountains and the Himalayan climate, he tasted another kind of freedom in the vastness of mother Nature. As a boon, this job earned him proficiency in the English language and the skill of typewriting.

Even though Rash Behari was unhappy with the political turmoil in the country and his multiple job changes, as he traveled far away from Bengal, he became acquainted with the subcontinent's varied people and their cultures across the country. Through his interaction with the locals, he learnt their languages and their notions. He got to know his country and its people and their dreams and aspirations. He understood their pains and their sublime desire to be part of a nation that would be free from colonial domination. He felt united with the dreams of India's people – at last he felt one with the common man's aspirations and goals – a free India.

Sitting inside the quarters of his new residence, he once told Brijraj, his manservant, 'Birju, within such a small span of time, I have traversed from Bengal to the Northern Provinces. I have tried my luck at several jobs, met numerous people and witnessed the convictions of so many of our countrymen. Yet, I never found solace anywhere. However, here in Shimla, when I talk to the locals, the poor, I feel a connect with them, just like I used to find in Bengal.'

Brijraj sat and listened to the young man. Even though Rash Behari was a man from a different province, he liked him. He taught him the local language and made him taste the flavours of local cuisine. Across the barriers of ethnicity and birthplace, he felt Rash Behari was not someone alien. He was like a man in whom Brijraj could confide.

Rash Behari continued, 'I have befriended so many people over here, within such a short time. I can understand their pains. I can feel their anxiety and their desire for freedom.' The young Rash Behari had started to command the love and faith of the people around him. He was becoming a man whose words had the power to convince the multitudes. He had started to acquire the flair of a true leader.[1]

At the Government Press, the prejudices of the staff were split between two different kinds of politics, so their beliefs divided them into two distinct groups. One group comprised men who strongly supported the policies of the British Raj, while the other, a relatively smaller group, comprised men who proactively raised their voices against the atrocities of the Raj rule. Rash Behari became a proactive member of the second group. Being an impulsive nationalist, he became vocal against anything that he felt was a wrongdoing against Indians.

'I cannot resist myself from opposing what is wrong', Rash Behari said at a meeting of the nationalist group, after office-hours. 'I will continue to be vocal against it, even if it costs me my job. The local people are like my family now. I will not let any injustice happen against them.'

Soon, however, the news about Rash Behari's growing prowess as a vocal rebel within the Government Press reached Binod Behari Bose. He again became anxious about his son. The aging father again tried to do something that would ensure the security of his child. Before anything drastic happened, with great concern, he devised a new plan and wrote a formal letter to Rash Behari, so that his verdict would remain as proof, in

1 *Two Great Indian Revolutionaries-Rash Behari Bose & Jyotindra Nath Mukherjee* by Uma Mukherjee, page numbers 90-120. The year was 1905.

case any controversy arose with the British. He hoped it would save his son from the angry retributions of the colonial rulers.

> *My dear Rasu.*
> *I am deeply concerned about the ongoing agitations against the British Raj, while you are an employee at the Government Press. I don't want my son to be entangled in any controversy. I, as your father, command you to resign from this job and head to Kasauli.*
> *I have made arrangements for your employment at the Pasteur Institute in Kasauli.*
> *My dear son, before anything disastrous happens, please listen to me and do as I instruct. As your father, I urge you to give me your promise again. I will look forward to your reply.*
>
> *Your Loving Father*
> *Binod Behari Bose.*[2]

Thus, yet again, this job too was short-lived and Rash Behari resigned from the Government Press, bid farewell to his parents and joined the Pasteur Institute in Kasauli. Even though he was like an untamed horse, he loved his father immensely. He could never refuse him.

Despite all setbacks, something phenomenal was taking place in his life. As his vagabond life kept him on the move, Rash Behari Bose became an independent thinker and a self-governing disciplinarian who mastered the ability to survive

---

2 *Two Great Indian Revolutionaries-Rash Behari Bose & Jyotindra Nath Mukherjee* by Uma Mukherjee, page numbers 90-120.

Pasteur Institute, Kasauli

in all kinds of adversities and in unfamiliar social settings. It was a blessing in disguise that was to become his big shield all through his life.

Life at the Pasteur Institute was normal and politically nonproductive. Cradled in the lap of the Himalayas, Kasauli was a tranquil hill-station that witnessed a glimpse of the lofty snowcapped peaks every day. However, the days were uneventful, and the place was secluded away from the rest of the country. At first, Rash Behari felt good in the beautiful scenic beauty of the place. However, the boredom and lack of activity soon made him restless.

Then came the blatantly communal partition of the State of Bengal in 1905 by the British Viceroy in India, Lord Curzon, despite strong opposition from Indian nationalists. This was not 'just an administrative divide' as the British proclaimed, but constituted the creation of a State in united India, based on the religion of the population in the region. It was an abysmal political move to create a crack among the people of Bengal and undermine their spirit. Rash Behari was upset that the British did what they pleased with his beloved Bengal while he was not able to see his vision of free India make any progress. Stuck as he was in monotonous Kasauli, Rash Behari ultimately left his job again and returned to Chandannagore.

Charu Chandra was no longer a school principal and Rash Behari did not live in Chandannagore any more. Yet they met every time Rash Behari was in Chandanagore, visiting his parents. 'The Englishmen, and their Indian servants who drew the borders to divided Bengal, do not even have the slightest knowledge of the demography or geography. They are completely unaware of the emotional and social attachments of the people of Bengal, irrespective of religion. How can they just split up everything?' wept Rash Behari.

Neither he, nor his parents understood what the future really held for Rash Behari. Binod Behari, who was also in Chandannagore at that time, was devastated by the events that had conspired against his son's luck. Binod Behari held his son close to himself and pleaded, 'Rasu, please calm your desperate instincts. Become docile. Become submissive. I don't want to lose you....' The soft touch of his father again melted Rash Behari's resolve. For the young Rash Behari, his life was like that of a moth in a wildfire. The more he tried to escape the flames, the more the snaring blazes burnt him deeply.

At last, upon the advice of a close acquaintance, the twenty-year-old Rash Behari Bose went to Dehradun in 1906 and began work as a guardian tutor in the house of Prafulla Nath

Tagore.[3] At the same time, he got employed as a clerk, under Sirdar Puran Singh, who was the in-charge of the Chemistry Department at the Forest Research Institute.

Forest Research Institute, Dehradun

3 Historical fact from: *Two Great Indian Revolutionaries-Rash Behari Bose & Jyotindra Nath Mukherjee* by Uma Mukherjee.
Mukherjee quotes from an article by SN Ganguli in the Bengali weekly *Basumati*, 12 August 1965.
In this article Ganguly says, Prafulla Nath Tagore was the grandson of Kali Krishna Tagore. Prasanta Nath Tagore, the third son of Prafulla Nath, told author SN Ganguli that their villa in Dehradun consisted of 100 bighas (an Indian measure) of land and was looked after by a caretaker whose house was situated at a remote corner of the estate. It was this outhouse where Rash Behari lived since 1906, planned and plotted, and made the bombs for the Hardinge attack.
Raja Prafulla Nath Tagore belonged to the Pathuriaghata branch of the Tagore family and was married to Rabindranath's sister Saudamini who was the mother of the artist Abanindrananth Tagore.
In retrospect, it appears, the owners may have known about caretaker Atul Ghosh's connections with various pro-freedom anti British activists and did not mind offering them occasional refuge.

Tagore Villa, Dehradun. Now it is a commercial complex
Photo credits: Aerial shots of the Tagore Villa Park and buildings, roughly locating where Rash Behari Bose lived in Dehradun and manufactured his bombs are by Maanas Lal, (Author, Columnist and acclaimed Painter).

No one guessed it, but this destination had something different to offer Rash Behari that no other previous place had. Atul Chandra Ghosh, the care-taker of the Tagore Villa, welcomed Rash Behari with a wide grin and said, 'In your young eyes, I see the fire of the Bengal Tigers. Even though I am old, I have not become a cripple yet. My cognition never fails me. I know what I am seeing, and I am happy that you have come.' Rash Behari didn't reply. He smiled in response and went with Atul, who showed him his room. In his heart he felt an unknown positivity that he was yet to discover fully. Intuition told him that his life would be redefined in Dehradun. Yet, the cover of unfamiliarity veiled everything.

For the first time in his life, the twenty-year old Rash Behari restrained himself from being impulsive. The experiences at Fort

Prafulla Nath Tagore

William, Shimla and Kasauli had taught him many lessons. He sat alone and told himself, 'In all these years, through all the turmoil, I have learnt a big lesson. Being a revolutionary nationalist is not an easy task. An impulsive mindset with a verbose mouth can spoil every opportunity. Being resolute, shrewd and thoughtful are the true colours one must adopt. From today onwards, I shall carve out my own niche and become a responsible person. The phoenix within me will rise from my ashes, here in Dehradun, and show me my path ahead.'

A keen observer always, Rash Behari soon mastered the careful art of mixing chemicals, under Sirdar Puran Singh, in the chemistry lab of the research institute.

A week after Rash Behari arrived in Dehradun, Atul Chandra told him, 'Rash Behari, today is Sunday. If you agree, I would like to take you somewhere. I want you to meet somebody.' In the absence of any other engagement, Rash Behari agreed to the proposition. That evening, Atul Chandra took Rash Behari to a small congregation of Bengalis who were living in Dehradun at that time. In the social gathering, Rash Behari felt good. Atul Chandra introduced him to the people and a jovial discussion on various topics ranging from cultural to political was soon underway.

Presently, a man came forward and sat beside Rash Behari. Away from the eyes of the crowd, this man had been observing Rash Behari and had been keenly following his opinions while he spoke with a few others. The man looked at Rash Behari and introduced himself, 'My name is Amarendra Nath Chatterjee. I was listening to your views about the political atmosphere in the country and felt interested.'

Amarendra Nath Chatterjee

Amarendra had a magnetic personality and great charm that attracted Rash Behari. Thus began the bonds of patriotism and friendship that tied the two men together for life. At first, Amarendra was a bit skeptical of Rash Behari's views. However, as their friendship deepened, their discussions became more focused on subjects that formed the basis of Amarendra's own existence.

Away from the glare of publicity, Amarendra's life had a reality of its own. He was in-charge of raising funds for the Jugantar movement. His activities largely covered revolutionary centers in Bihar, Odisha and the United Provinces. Away from Bengal, he covertly carried out his own mission of amassing support for armed revolt from Bengalis and others living and working outside Bengal. Jugantar was the young wing of the Anushilan Samiti. Led by Jatin Mukherjee (also known as Bagha Jatin in Bengal), the organisation with which Rash Behari identified with a hypnotic attraction, nurtured the revolutionary vision.

One evening, sitting inside the outhouse of Tagore Villa, Amarendra said in an excited voice, 'Last week, I had the great fortune to meet Sri Aurobindo Ghosh. His versatile and attractive personality mesmerised me completely. He knew everything about me and he was so happy with whatever I have done so far.'

Atul Chandra sat with the two of them and listened silently. Despite being non-active in any nationalist activities, he wholeheartedly supported the cause of India's freedom struggle. Rash Behari felt excited on hearing what Amarendra said. He said, 'This is brilliant. Tell us more about the meeting....'

Aurobindo Ghosh and Barindra Kumar Ghosh

Amarendra continued animatedly, 'He told me... *Surrender yourself to God and in the name of the Divine Mother, get along with the service of India. That is my message to you. If we want to secure the freedom of our country, we have to sacrifice everything. We should be ready to give up even our life for it. If we want to free the country, we shall have to conquer the fear of death!*[4]

Rash Behari felt elated. The words of Aurobindo Ghosh reverberated his own sentiments. He asked, 'What is your plan now?'

Amarendra zealously replied, 'He encouraged me to the highest degree. As per his instructions, I will collect funds for our future movements. I shall meet Jatin Mukherjee to discuss the future plans. He is the face of the new era of revolution, not only in Bengal but also across the country. I know that our association will yield fantastic results.'

Rash Behari felt happy about the encounter his friend had had with Rishi Arubindo. He said enthusiastically, 'My heart has always desired to dedicate myself completely in the struggle for freedom of Mother India. Do hold my hands and take me along in this journey. I will feel blessed to be associated with you and with Jatin Mukherjee.'

That day marked a big step in Rash Behari Bose's life. At last, his revolution appeared to be real. This was the moment when Rash Behari entered nationalist politics as a real freedom fighter. This was the moment his grandfather Kalicharan and his teacher Charu Chandra had guided him to. Amarendra

---

4 *Terrorism in Bengal* by AK Samanta (editor), Vol V, p 63.

Chatterjee hugged him while Atul Ghosh stood beside them and clapped his hands, as tears rolled down his eyes. For Rash Behari, his never-ending dream actually began to see the first rays of light. His training as a professional revolutionary began in Dehradun and indeed, his stint at Dehradun was unlike all his escapades across the country till date.

Surendranath Bannerjee

NO LONGER JUST A WISHLIST

WITHIN A FEW months of Rash Behari's arrival in Dehradun, at the wedding of the eldest son of Purna Chandra Banerjee, a local acquaintance, Rash Behari had met a man from Saharanpur. With a nondescript look but a magnetic personality, this man drew Rash Behari's attention, they were both invitees at the ceremony.[1]

'I am Jitendra Mohan Chatterjee', the visitor from Saharanpur introduced himself. He had a commanding voice that had an overdose of a sentiment that Rash Behari was very familiar with.

'I am Rash Behari Bose', replied Rash Behari while he looked into Jitendra Mohan's eyes. Here again, a magnetic attraction pulled them together. As the two discussed a gamut of subjects, they took each other's measure and what attracted them became clear to each. It was revolution. Understanding the unrest within Rash Behari, Jitendra Mohan tried to gauge how ardent Rash Behari was about freedom from the British.

---

1 *Two Great Indian Revolutionaries-Rash Behari Bose & Jyotindra Nath Mukherjee* by Uma Mukherjee, page numbers 90-120.

That evening, before saying goodbye, Jitendra Mohan looked at Rash Behari and said, 'Farewell my friend, but not for long. My instinct tells me that we will meet again and on many more occasions. Within those fiery eyes of yours, I can see the volcano that is about to erupt. In them I can see the smouldering fire of our struggle for Swaraj.'

Har Dayal Singh

Over the next few months, in numerous communications and in numerous meetings, Rash Behari became an ardent follower of Jitendra Mohan. Jitendra Mohan had gained prominence as a leader of the radical movement under the tutelage of Sardar Har Dayal Singh,[2] who had left the local baton of the revolution in the hands of Jitendra Mohan when he was forced to leave India for his radical views. As Jitendra Mohan traversed the country to build the plinth of their mission,

2 Lala Har Dayal was an Oxford educated Sikh who, on his return to India, wrote extensively and explored anarchist and revolutionary ideas. His radical writings drew the attention of the British India government. So, on the advice of Lala Lajpat Rai, Har Dayal went to France.

In Paris, he edited a magazine called *Vande Mataram*. He moved from Paris to Algeria and from there to Martinique where he led a life of asceticism.

He then moved to the USA and lived all his life there, supporting the Ghadar movement in the second decade of the twentieth century. He wrote on Karl Marx extensively and was involved in creating industry unions in the USA.

Rash Behari told him, 'At Chandannagore, meet Shrish Ghosh, the most desperate and dangerous figure among the revolutionaries there. Tell him my name. Even though miles apart, we still remain the best buddies… a bond that has remained forged in gold ever since our childhood.'

Amarendra was aware of Rash Behari's potential and how Jitendra Mohan had influenced him with his own charismatic persona. Amarendra felt happy that Rash Behari was finally actually becoming leadership material for the proponents of armed struggle.

Soon, a year had gone by, and it was 1907. Rash Behari sat with his guru Charu Chandra Roy, inside the secret den that they had created in a covert location in Chandannagore. Away from the prying eyes of everyone, this was a deadly asylum where Rash Behari had started to groom his own self. He was now convinced that it was time for him to take his own political decisions. With utmost dexterity, he immersed himself in the lethal art of making explosives. Grasping the dangerous ingredients and mixing them in the right quantities, Rash Behari became an expert in the art of making country bombs, an important part of a militant freedom fighter's arsenal.

Then came the day when he held out an earthen shell towards Charu Chandra and said with a smile, 'The fireworks are ready. Sir, the bombs made with our deadly ingredients are no match to the explosives broiling in the young blood of our motherland. Still, let me give you a demonstration.' The two men were standing near an abandoned Ghat of the Hooghly River. The entire town was immersed in the celebrations of the final day of Jagadhatri Puja, the most popular celebration in Chandannagore of that time.

Hooghly Ghat, Chandannagore
Creative Commons

Rash Behari flexed his wrist and threw the shell far away at a distance. The shell took a big trajectory and landed on an empty piece of land. Then, with a flash of blinding light, a huge explosion rocked the neighbourhood.

Charu Chandra looked around cautiously, after balancing himself carefully, shaken by the impact of the explosion. Far away, the people of Chandannagore were unaware of what had just conspired. Charu Chandra patted his disciple and said, 'Rash Behari, my lionhearted child, may you achieve the trophy of Independence for your motherland. My blessings are with you. And yes… the fireworks have just begun. The ideologies of my dear "Suhrid Sammelani" will remain burning within you, even if the enemy eradicates our existence.' Suhrid Sammelani was Charu Chandra Roy's brainchild, an organisation that was created to further revolutionary activities and Rash Behari was its brilliant product.

However, Roy's disciple, Rash Behari was destined to march ahead into far more ruthless terrains. In the folds of the dark alleys of time, a daring plan was already in place and soon Rash Behari Bose was to be pulled into its vortex.

Then Came April 1908...

In April 1908, a desperate attempt to kill Presidency Magistrate Douglas Kingsford in Muzaffarpur was undertaken by Bengali nationalists, Khudiram Bose and Prafulla Chaki. This attack was taken extremely seriously by the colonial rulers and was marked as an act of 'Waging war against the Government' of the British Raj. As an aftermath of this dare-devil attempt, a series of notorious trials of Indian nationalists began. Collectively, they became known as the infamous 'Alipore Bomb Case' as the cases were heard at the Alipore sessions court in Calcutta.

Many prominent members of the Anushilan Samiti came under the British intelligence radar. Both Aurobindo Ghosh and Barindra Ghosh were accused along with thirty-seven

Khudiram Bose

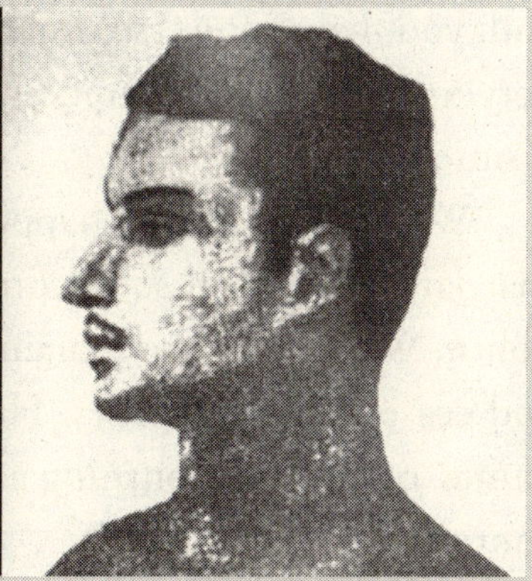

Prafulla Chaki

other members. Following their arrests, Bengal witnessed a succession of violent unrest across the land. An invisible sword hung above the heads of everyone associated with the Anushilan Samiti as the government tried to break up the organisation and shut down its networks.

Rash Behari knew that the government's gaze would not overlook him, although he was in no way involved with Khudiram's assassination attempt, nor was he directly involved with the Anushilan Samiti. The execution of many young men, including Khudiram Bose and Prafulla Chaki, made Rash Behari angry as he could do nothing to prevent them. Rash Behari quickly left Chandannagore and went back to work in Dehradun.

Both Amarendra Chatterjee and Rash Behari Bose were now active participants of the Jugantar movement. Even though Jugantar was an autonomous wing, the British suspected its connection with the Anushilan Samiti.

Sitting in Dehradun, Rash Behari told Amarendra, 'The imperial intelligence is combing the country to eliminate any threat. What will happen to all our efforts? Jatin Mukherjee and you have done so much to establish the countrywide network and create awareness. How can you let everything get disintegrated?'

'We will not let that happen', replied Amarendra. 'It is true that Jatin and I will soon come under the radar of the British police. We will have to remain underground for the time being and cease all our activities. However, our mission, to keep the flames of freedom burning in the hearts of the people, will continue.'

Rash Behari looked blankly at Amarendra while he continued with zeal, 'You will be the torchbearer for that. From this moment, I induct you into this novel mission. Silently, you will establish the network between Bengal and the Northern Provinces. With your passion, you are the CHOSEN ONE! The British police will never suspect you. You don't have any records in their files. You shall be the bridge between Jatin Mukherjee and me. You will be the bridge between the East and the North.'

Rash Behari touched Amarendra's feet and said, 'I will dedicate myself completely to our goal of a free India.'

Looking at his passionate young face, Amarendra embraced him lovingly. However, he warned him to remain cautious and always be on his guard. Rash Behari could no longer afford to compromise his budding aspiration to fight against the ruthless domination of the colonial rule by venting his political opinions. He needed to keep his mouth shut. He needed to mature as a true political activist and revolutionary who would be able to lead a generation of youth to action. He could not become an enemy target and end his fledgling vision from blooming.

Rash Behari understood that he needed to keep far away from the Alipore trials and avoid drawing attention to himself. He was resolute in what he wanted to do in life and nothing could alter his determination anymore. The turns and twists in his life were now challenging his mettle and forging him in steel. Completely effacing himself for the greater interest of the motherland was Rash Behari's biggest test. He knew then, he could never take credit for the bombs that he made, the attacks on the colonial rulers he mounted or ever let himself get caught. He had to weave a convincing web of deceit around himself. This was a huge responsibility on the young man's shoulders – to keep the flame of armed struggle burning.

The next morning, he sent a telegram to his father, '*Dehradun and my work here is perfect. I shall stay in Dehradun. I love my job and my life over here.*'

When militant activities by the revolutionaries increased and attacks on the British began to see success, warrants for arrests were issued against many political activists suspected to have connections with the Anushilan Samiti, among them Jitendra Mohan. He was then left with the only option – to leave the country.

Before leaving his beloved India, Jitendra Mohan met Rash Behari one last time and said, 'Today, with a heavy heart, I am leaving behind my beloved country and countrymen. My brother, in your hands I place the priceless jewel of my life… my dream of Swaraj! Lead it ahead with your fearless valour! I pray to God… victory will be yours.'[3] Jitendra Mohan went completely underground after this and no one knew whether he was in India or abroad.

Chandannagore Calling

Rash Behari Bose sat inside the little outhouse of Prafulla Nath Tagore's vast estate. Girdled by large mango and litchi trees, the extensive garden of the Tagore Villa provided a natural camouflage of a small wood, within which the little one-storeyed caretaker's house was like a lone island.

'It is more than five years since I have been here', pondered Rash Behari. '1911 is almost at an end, yet so little has happened to our struggle for freedom. The British Raj has continued to strike at all the efforts of our revolutionary brotherhood of

3 *Chandernagore: From Bondage To Freedom, 1900-1955,* by Sailendra Nath Sen.

freedom fighters. Alas, even with the greatest determination, we have not been able to inflict any significant blow to the Raj nor retaliate against their oppression.'

Rash Behari did not know it, but one certain reason behind the Raj move to shift the capital from Bengal was the increasing militant attacks on British officials in Bengal. One such oppressive officer was the sub-divisional officer of Sylhet, G Gordon, who had in 1912 ordered a raid on the Jagatsi Ashram, run by the Arya Samaj, to capture and kill people he believed were nationalists, hiding in the ashram. Mahendra Nath De, the ex-Headmaster of Habibganj High School in Sylhet, a much-respected man of great knowledge, was one of the many innocent people killed in that raid.[4]

Sitting helplessly in Dehradun, Rash Behari could only mourn the loss of innocent lives and vowed to teach Gordon a lesson. 'Gordon, you villain, your days will soon be over', Rash Behari told himself as he added Gordon on his hit list.

One morning, as the wind fluttered the leaves of the trees outside the outhouse, Ramu rushed inside the room where Rash Behari was seated on his wooden chair. Ramu was the son of the gardener, Balaram Singh, and lived with his father within the Tagore Villa Estate. As the little boy entered the room, he hurriedly handed over a telegrammed message to Rash Behari and stood quietly.

Rash Behari looked at the memo that read... *Mother seriously ill. Come to Chandannagore immediately.*

---

4 Historical fact from: *Two Great Indian Revolutionaries-Rash Behari Bose & Jyotindra Nath Mukherjee* by Uma Mukherjee, page number 111.

A distraught Rash Behari understood the urgency in the little note and got up to pack his bag. Drops of tears appeared in his eyes and Ramu questioned him innocently, 'What happened? Is everything alright?'

'Maa is not well. I must go to Chandannagore', replied Rash Behari. 'Even though I was not born to her, she is a woman who always cast the gentle shadow of motherhood upon me. At this hour of urgency, I must be by her side. In her eyes, I am always her little Rasu, who is her ever-mischievous son for whom she has remained worried her entire life.'

That evening, Rash Behari boarded the train to Chandannagore and sat near the open window, while the gigantic locomotive gradually rolled out of the station. As he looked outside, the landscape of the township slowly faded away into the predominant greens of the wilderness.

Rash Behari closed his eyes while a bevy of emotions stirred in his heart. As he left Dehradun, thinking of his ailing mother, at the back of his mind was turmoil at the stagnation the freedom movement now faced. Rash Behari Bose had always been a desperate person. Even as a young man, he had secretly mastered the skills of making bombs.

His mind floated back to his early days at Chandannagore and how the entire world seemed to have come together to facilitate his journey into the universe of India's freedom struggle.

Rash Behari remembered the words of Jitendra Mohan, 'Punjab and United Provinces are important centers of Bengali revolutionary activities. The aspirations of Bengal's revolutionary spirit have gradually created an uproar within the youth of the North. I am glad that you, Rash Behari, are an able torchbearer for this mission.'

Shrish Chandra Ghosh (at an older age)

The dream came to an end with the sudden screeching noise of the metallic wheels, as the train came to a sudden stop at an unknown station. Rash Behari wiped his eyes as the wonderful vision faded. 'It has been almost a year since I last met Jatindra Mohan. Yet, so much time has gone by, without…', with these disturbed thoughts, he sat blankly, looking out.

In Chandannagore, Rash Behari returned home and went straight to his mother's room. As the frail lady held his hands and kissed them softly, Rash Behari felt the chalice of love still brimming within her overflow, even though he understood that her remaining days were not many.

That evening, as the blanket of darkness enveloped the township, Rash Behari entered the little room within the local clubhouse where he had spent many fond years with his old pals.

Dressed in white kurta and pyjama, Shrish Ghosh came forward and hugged his old buddy. Rash Behari looked around and saw a small gathering of men within the room, whose windows had been shut tightly.

'Rasu, let me introduce you to Moti Lal Roy, the revolutionary leader of Chandannagore', said Shrish Ghosh. 'An ardent follower of Sri Aurobindo, he is a visionary.'

Moti Lal Roy

As the night progressed, Roy delivered a fiery speech on *Atma-Samarpan*, or self-surrender. His oration was soaked in the honey of patriotism that he aspired to ingrain within the hearts of the youth. Stirred to the core, Rash Behari stood up and pledged passionately, 'It is God's Will that I must submit myself. Indeed, *Atma-Samarpan* is what I must follow. I must move ahead with my mission, with my head held in my hand. Even if it calls for a supreme sacrifice, I am ready for it.'

That night, Rash Behari's now matured zeal consolidated with the brotherhood in Chandannagore. It established a fresh chapter in his life, defining him as the primary link between the revolutionary movement of Bengal and the United Provinces.

A few days later, his mother passed away and a crestfallen Rash Behari went back to Dehradun after performing the last rites. Even though temporarily, the jolt of the sudden loss created a vacuum in his life, and Rash Behari sought solace in seclusion. And he kept himself insulated from all the brouhaha related to the imperial decision to move the capital of British India from Calcutta and militant Bengal to Mughal Delhi.

REVOLUTION SHARPNEL ET AL

23 DECEMBER 1912

'It's a bomb! Run for your lives!', Screamed a man as he stumbled upon the maddening crowd that was trying to escape to a safe spot. An unforeseen stampede started as men, women and children shrieked at the top of their voices.

English men and women, dressed in exquisite attires were running madly across the streets while the native Indian populace bumped into one another as they too scattered in every direction. The deafening noise of the explosion, coupled with the gust of smoke and fire, had left the overcrowded street of the Old Delhi suburb in a state of complete mayhem.

Amidst this chaos, somebody shouted loudly, 'The Viceroy, Lord Hardinge, has been attacked... I think he is dead....'

With terrified horses and the petrified elephants of the British cavalry on show running hysterically across the Chandni Chowk, the merriments of a grand event the Raj had meticulously planned had just been marred.

With eyes red with anger, a British officer screamed

at his subordinates, 'Catch the criminals. I want them alive. I will skin them with my own hands.'

As the panic and horror of the scene filled the atmosphere, two young men slowly walked up a side alley and vanished inconspicuously.[1]

Delhi, December 1912. The British celebrating the move of the Raj capital from Calcutta to Delhi. A bomb is thrown at the Viceroy on his decorated elephant. (Photo: Creative Commons)

1 Rash Behari Bose: *The Father of The Indian National Army Vol-1* by Elizabeth Eston & Lexi Kawabe, page number 65-71.
Referenced from Japanese books: *Dokuritsu no Tōsō* by Rash Behari Bose, *Seinen Ajia no Shōri* by Rash Behari Bose (published in 1937).

A FEW MORE months had elapsed after Rash Behari returned to Dehradun. However, the urge to do something drastic kept mounting as an inner unrest within him. Atul Chandra Ghosh, the caretaker of Tagore Villa, understood this discomfort and remained a silent witness to the young man's angst.

One morning, at the end of summer, Atul entered Rash Behari's room with a cup of hot tea. Rash Behari was seated upon the wooden chair in front of his writing desk and Atul softly placed the cup of tea in front of him. It was a monsoon morning and in the dull daylight, Atul could see a glow on Rash Behari's face.

With a sudden eagerness, he asked, 'What is it? I can see excitement in your eyes.'

Rash Behari sprang up from his chair, picked up the newspaper from the table and held it in front of Atul. As the latter read the headlines with a perplexed face, Rash Behari shouted, 'The signal has been raised. I must reach Chandannagore immediately.'[2]

Thus, with lightning speed, a restless Rash Behari returned to Chandannagore to meet his comrades.

As soon as Rash Behari arrived in Chandannagore, Shrish Ghosh arranged a meeting for him with the elusive local revolutionary group. With dark clouds gathering in the dusky twilight and flashes of lightning, the streets of the French colony town soon became empty, as people hurried inside their

---

2 *Two Great Indian Revolutionaries-Rash BehariBose & Jyotindra Nath Mukherjee* by Uma Mukherjee, page numbers 105-125.
Cross-reference from the following in the above book: Letters of Amarendra Nath Chatterjee dated 4.8.54 and 4.9.54 in Jadugopal Mukherjee's book, *Biplobi Jiboner Smriti* and an unpublished manuscript, *Bharater Swadhinatar Itihas*, page 34.

homes, in anticipation of a storm. At the same time, in the secret room of the clubhouse, another blizzard was about to be unleashed. Across a large wooden table, Rash Behari sat with his group of comrades, including Moti Lal Roy, engrossed in a discussion that was destined to become historical.[3]

Shrish Ghosh started the conversation with, 'Time is running out. The suffering of our countrymen has reached beyond tolerance. We must act now. Alas… we are just sitting and deliberating. Mere inept assaults upon the British Raj will have no significant impact. We need to execute a major onslaught that will shake the foundation of the brutal colonial empire.'

A young Dhritiman said, 'We are ready to act. There is no fear in our hearts. However, the question that remains to be answered is… DO WHAT?'

He looked around and added, 'Yes… What can we do?'

Ashim, another young lad, stood up and continued, 'Yes. However, even if we find a target, another pertinent question that remains unanswered is… HOW?'

As a deathly silence fell upon the gathering, Rash Behari banged his fist on the wooden desk that served as a table, and exclaimed, 'Execute Lord Hardinge! The assassination of the Viceroy of India will prove our worth to the entire world. Our fireworks will define a new dawn for our struggle to free India.' Rash Behari's voice reverberated within the closed room and erased the despondency that enveloped the young people gathered there.

---

3 Historical fact from: *Two Great Indian Revolutionaries-Rash Behari Bose & Jyotindra Nath Mukherjee* by Uma Mukherjee, page numbers 105-125.
Creative licence has been adopted by author here to provide continuity to this section of the lifestory.

Shrish Ghosh sat speechless while the others looked at one another. With great enthusiasm, Rash Behari took out a newspaper and placed it upon the table. The headlines clearly spelled out the grand ceremony that was being planned to shift the colonial capital from Bengal to Delhi. The Viceroy of India, Charles Hardinge, was bestowed the prestigious duty to formally complete this move with a grand gala.

As the others digested the idea that had just been put forth, Rash Behari added in a heavy baritone, 'It is a significant occasion for the British Raj and an act of defiance will certainly resonate countrywide and an attempt on the Viceroy's life will unquestionably be worth the effort.'

Moti Lal absorbed the import of Rash Behari's proposal with eyes wide open and then shot a question back, 'One challenge still remains unsolved. The idea to attack the Viceroy while he is engrossed in an extravagant procession is good. But one needs a watertight modus operandi for the operation to succeed. How will we execute such a daredevil plan? What shall we do?'

The answer again came from Rash Behari Bose, 'Let's blow him up!'

As the young men assembled in the room toyed with this bombastic idea and began to visualise it slowly, Rash Behari looked at Shrish Ghosh and said, 'This is an audacious scheme that needs meticulous planning. With only a couple of months at hand, we have a lot of work to do. The primary task is to find the right person to execute such an attack. Secondly, we need to be extremely cautious while organising everything.'

With a pause to let his words sink in, he continued, 'I volunteer to make the weapon. I am confident that I shall be able to make the perfect bomb.'

Shrish Ghosh responded, 'We can supply you with whatever is required to prepare the bomb. You can make it here in Chandannagore. It will be perfectly safe.'

Rash Behari replied, 'No.'

'Tomorrow, I must return to Dehradun. The barren grounds of the Forest Research Institute and the secluded garden of Tagore Villa are ideal for me to prepare the bomb. Procure the materials for the bomb. I will take them with me to Dehradun. If I make the bomb here in Chandannagore and the secret gets leaked, then the entire brotherhood of revolutionaries here will be in jeopardy. I cannot afford to do so.'

Rash Behari continued confidently, 'In Chandannagore, in our underground den, I have trained myself in the art of making explosives. I knew that a day would come when this knowledge will be useful. The radical thinking of revolutionaries like Jatin Mukherjee inspired me to be a part of Jugantar. The word means "epochal transformation". Today, that seed of change has been planted.'

Shrish Ghosh was elated and hugged his friend tightly. The little room was charged with enthusiasm and the tight little group of revolutionaries were excited at the thought that now they would at last get a chance to retaliate against the colonial rulers in a big way.

Rash Behari looked at everyone and said, 'This will be our most daring work till date. Yet, it is just the beginning. We cannot afford to lose our unity and our lives. The struggle for *Swaraj* needs to remain alive. For that, we need to stay alive. With utmost secrecy, we will keep in touch and execute our plan.'

'The day is 23 December', declared Shrish Ghosh.

The Nuts and Bolts of an Attack

In Dehradun, Rash Behari met the man in whom he had an enormous degree of faith. He was Amarendra Nath Chatterjee, the key individual responsible for keeping Jugantar alive following the government crackdown on Anushilan Samiti. Amarendra had not left the country yet. Amarendra was like his lifeline and Rash Behari's confidante. Rash Behari was sure that Amarendra would be proud of his plan.

Soon Rash Behari was all set to begin his mammoth task. In his secluded room in the garden of the Tagore Villa, Rash Behari collected all the ingredients needed to make his bomb. One afternoon, when Amarendra visited Rash Behari, he showed off his stash of deadly acids and chemicals. Earlier, Rash Behari had briefed Amarendra about the plan to kill Hardinge and Amarendra had pledged his support.[4]

Sitting in Rash Behari's room, Amarendra asked worriedly, 'A bomb attack is a perfect idea. However, it needs proper planning and infallible execution. Everything looks good. But Rash Behari, where are the shells that you will use? During the present repressive times, procuring shells for making bombs will be nearly impossible, without raising eyebrows.'

Rash Behari stared fixedly at his table. The question had already crossed his mind and he had been thinking about it. Suddenly an idea struck him. Rash Behari stood up excitedly

---

4 *Two Great Indian Revolutionaries-Rash Behari Bose & Jyotindra Nath Mukherjee* by Uma Mukherjee, page numbers 105-125.
Cross-reference from the following in the above book: Letters of Amarendra Nath Chatterjee dated 4.8.54 and 4.9.54 in Jadugopal Mukherjee's book, *Biplobi Jiboner Smriti* and an unpublished manuscript, *Bharater Swadhinatar Itihas*, page 34.

and looking at Amarendra, said, 'We will use inkpots. Yes... nobody will suspect anything if we use them.'

The two appeared content with the brilliant solution. But something else worried Rash Behari. Rash Behari turned towards Amarendra and said, 'Amarendra, I need a volunteer to execute this plan.'

He then continued, 'It has to be a person who has never been under the radar of the British intelligence services and who is fearless and precise enough to accomplish the attack successfully. This is the biggest gap now that needs to be plugged.'

Amarendra Nath had always been an intelligent man. He thought for a while and then patted Rash Behari on the shoulders. Then, with a slight smile, he replied, 'Don't worry. The solution is right in front of me. However, to get that, you must visit Chandannagore one more time.'

'Really?' replied an elated Rash Behari. 'Who is it? I will definitely travel to Chandannagore again, but what is your plan?'

Amarendra sat down on the wooden chair and said, 'Meet Moti Lal Roy in Chandannagore and ask him to bring the two brothers, Basanta Biswas and Manmatha Biswas, to you. Originally from Nadia, these two brothers now work at a Swadeshi workshop in Kolkata. They are the latest recruits of our movement and are completely beyond the grasps of the British Intelligence.'

An excited Rash Behari sat down beside Amarendra, while the latter continued, 'I will now write a letter to Moti Lal. You personally hand over this letter to him and ask him to burn it after reading it. We cannot afford to send such confidential messages over post. Once you have selected your candidate from the Biswas brothers, bring him to Dehradun as your personal attendant and cook. This will avoid all suspicion.'

Rash Behari stood up to hug Amarendra and replied, 'Thank you so much. Indeed, with the arrival of our prime executor in Dehradun, we will be able to utilise the two remaining months to train him and refine our plan before the final day arrives.'

The days moved fast and Rash Behari was thrilled masterminding his first major act of defiance against the British.

In Chandannagore, Moti Lal read the letter from Amarendra and then held it against the flame of the candle. With a sparkle in his eyes, he looked at Rash Behari and said, 'Tomorrow morning, I shall go to Kolkata.'

One more day passed and the following morning, Rash Behari and Shrish Ghosh arrived at the huge playground beside the Hooghly River. The two friends sat down on a concrete bench on the banks of the river, girdled with coconut trees whose long shadows provided a soothing seclusion. Soon, three people walked up to them and a voice said, 'We have come.'

Rash Behari and Shrish Ghosh turned around and saw Moti Lal standing behind them, along with two young boys. Rash Behari stared at the two visitors and then asked hesitantly, 'Did Amarendra refer to these young boys? Are you sure they will be able to...?'

One of the boys stood before Rash Behari and said, 'Don't judge us by our appearance.'

With skepticism writ large on his face, Rash Behari said, 'It is easy to speak with valour. The real test is not that of words....' He turned around to look at the river.

As a cool breeze rose, the boy held Rash Behari's hand resolutely and added, 'I am ready to take that test.'

Rash Behari turned back, picked up a medium sized stone

Basanta Biswas

from the ground and said, 'Take this and aim at that coconut atop that tree. Show me if you can hit it.'

The other lad came up to the first and spoke something in his ears. The brother listened carefully and then, after looking at the target carefully, he threw the stone at the nut on the tree with all his might. Rash Behari and the others watched as the stone struck the target and the dislodged coconut fell to the ground with a thud.

Rash Behari came up and patted the youngster on the shoulder and said, 'Good job. What is your name? And I must say, you have a great aim. Welcome on board.'

'My name is Basanta Biswas. This is my brother Manmatha', replied the boy.

'I have never aimed like this before. However, when you asked me to throw this stone at the coconut, my brother whispered in my ears that I should imagine the enemy at which I was throwing this stone. Then, in my mind, I saw the face of the oppressive British officers. In the coconut I saw their rotten faces. With my blood boiling, I threw the stone and it hit my target.'

'Amarendra was correct', replied a happy Rash Behari. 'You are indeed special. Now I am confident that you are the perfect candidate to throw a bomb. Tomorrow we will travel to Dehradun.' Thus, Basanta Biswas, dressed as cook and personal attendant of Rash Behari, reached Dehradun and started to live with him in the outhouse of the Tagore Villa.[5]

At a meeting inside the outhouse, in the presence of Amarendra, Rash Behari told Basanta, 'Basanta, your task is of great significance and of great sacrifice. The consequences will be drastic and might lead you to death. You might get arrested and even face the death penalty. Do you still agree to be a part of our plan?'

Basanta smiled and replied, 'Yes. My decision is final. My brother and I have dedicated our lives for Swaraj.'

Rash Behari replied, 'Then, from tomorrow, you will practice every day in the empty lawn of the Forest Research Institute and here, within the secluded garden of Tagore Villa. Your aim has to be perfect. Only one and a half month remains in between.'

Looking at Amarendra, Rash Behari continued, 'Viceroy Hardinge will be atop an elephant while leading the procession to formally shift the imperial capital to Delhi. Basanta and I will arrive in Delhi a day before. We will disguise ourselves. We will scout the Chandni Chowk area and fix the location of our assault.'

A perturbed Amarendra pointed out, 'Rash Behari, there will be heavy security presence at the venue on that day, the place will be impenetrable that day. You will need a watertight plan and a foolproof cover-up. What will be your disguise?'

Rash Behari smiled and answered, 'I will only reveal that plan… on that Day!'

---

5 *Two Great Indian Revolutionaries-Rash Behari Bose & Jyotindra Nath Mukherjee* by Uma Mukherjee, page numbers 105-140.
Cross-reference from the following in the above book: Delhi Lahore Conspiracy Case, 5th October 1914.

Ms Luxmee Bai Goes to See the Viceroy's Parade

Sitting inside a dingy room in Old Delhi's Chandni Chowk area, Rash Behari Bose, a master of disguise, diligently began his work in the afternoon of 22 December. The room belonged to Amir Chand, another elusive revolutionary from the United Provinces, who supported Rash Behari wholeheartedly.

A day before, a nondescript young lad had arrived in Delhi from Lahore. Rash Behari had completed all his regular work at the Forest Research Institute for the next few days so that his absence would not be felt and had reached Delhi, just in time to meet his lionhearted accomplice. Through the bustling lanes and alleys of Delhi, the two had arrived at the congested locality, where their single-room accommodation had been arranged by Amir Chand. Holed up inside the room, with closed windows, Rash Behari first tried his hands at the disguise he had devised for Basanta and himself.

'It's perfect!' commented Amir Chand. 'Now, we need to do a trial run.'[6]

'Yes indeed. Shall we go on a little trip Ms Luxmee Bai?' Rash Behari asked and held up a mirror in front of Basanta, who exclaimed on seeing his own new avatar as a pretty *Desi* damsel.

That evening, Rash Behari (disguised as a typical Indian Babu) and Basanta (disguised as a young Indian woman) took a *tonga*[7] for a ride across the busy streets of Chandni Chowk. The extra number of security personnel and the ramped-up

---

6 The scene has been imagined for the storyline. Historical fact from: *Two Great Indian Revolutionaries-Rash Behari Bose & Jyotindra Nath Mukherjee* by Uma Mukherjee, page numbers 105-140.

7 Tonga in Indian languages is a traditional horse-cart.
Desi: Local, native, Indian.

An old photo of Chandni Chowk

surveillance clearly displayed the importance of the historic event that was to take place the following day.

'We are all set', said a satisfied Rash Behari.

Next day, early in the morning, the two young men came out from their room and quietly headed out into the streets. With a heavy moustache and high-powered spectacles, Rash Behari looked the perfect Babu, while Basanta looked like an innocent young woman, whose face had an indisputable purity.

'Now take the bomb and hide it inside the folds of the saree.'

LORD CHARLES HARDINGE stood inside the sprawling lawn of the Viceroy's Lodge and beamed in front of the assemblage of his elite guests.[8] High-ranking British officers and their families had gathered around him. At a corner of the lawn, beside the palm trees, stood a decorated elephant. The mahout, dressed in an equally resplendent attire, sat in front of the grandly ornamented howdah, atop the elephant.

Viceroy, Lord Hardinge

Beaming with confidence, Lord Hardinge declared in that private assemblage, that the 23rd of December 1912, would be a memorable day in the history of the British Raj in India. He, on behalf of the British empire, would formally declare the transfer of British India's capital from Kolkata to Delhi. He reminded his audience of the converted that the iron fist of British rule in India must continue to establish law and order across the country so that the imperial rule over the subcontinent could continue beyond the century. He then invited his guests to proceed to the grand ceremony.

8 The British had just moved their capital to the Mughal city of Delhi. They had yet to start building assets here. 'He (Hardinge) made the Circuit House, a not-so-impressive building, north of the Ridge, his official residence.' Hindustan Times Report https://www.hindustantimes.com/delhi/a-temporary-fixture-of-permanence/story-onlBSOWqNQGA4t7T5YFf4M.html

Lord and Lady Hardinge then mounted the decorated elephant and sat under the canopy, while a personal attendant stood behind them. The mahout nudged the animal and the elephant sluggishly, yet majestically, moved out of the Circuit House premises and proceeded towards Chandni Chowk, the biggest plaza in Old Delhi.

A separate group of decorated elephants were waiting outside the Viceroy's Lodge. Other eminent guests mounted these waiting animals and then the grandiose procession began its journey. As the procession reached the main Chandni Chowk plaza, both sides of the main street teemed with spectators. The native guards of the British Army used their batons to keep the discipline and the crowd under control.

No one noticed in particular the unsuspecting Babu and his saree-clad young companion, who stood among the multitude, their eyes fixed upon the arriving entourage. Rash Behari's heart was beating fast. One last time, he looked at Basanta and together they closed their eyes in prayer and stood firm in their resolve to carry out the bombing of the Viceroy's howdah. The grand procession, comprising a parade of cavalry and marching officials and several flamboyantly dressed elephants carrying important dignitaries, moved down the street to the chowk. A row of native policemen and guards formed an impenetrable wall in front of the swarming crowd of spectators.

As the elephant carrying the Viceroy came in sight, Rash Behari moved behind the crowd and signalled to Basanta. Basanta disappeared behind a group of overenthusiastic men and women and arrived at an isolated corner. Then, with the speed of lightning, he took out the bomb and hurled it towards the Viceroy. The bomb, in the shell of an inkpot, containing deadly picric acid among other lethal explosive ingredients, took a parabolic arch and moved towards the place where Lord Hardinge was seated. The moment seemed like ages as Rash Behari and Basanta watched the bomb taking flight.

The bomb landed atop the elephant with perfect accuracy. With a flash of light and a deafening sound, the bomb burst like an active volcano and filled the entire area in a shroud of white smoke.

The personal attendant of Lord Hardinge, standing behind the Viceroy and holding his parasole, bore the brunt of the bomb blast and was flung from the elephant, while Lord Hardinge screamed in pain as the blazing fragments of the bomb injured his back, legs and head and tore away the flesh from his shoulder. Lady Hardinge's elegant dress caught fire and the elephant became restive. Neither Lady Hardinge, nor the mahout or the elephant were actually hurt. The baffled mahout struggled to keep the animal under control as the Viceroy and Lady Hardinge were flung to the ground. The multitude of spectators panicked and scrambled to get away from the spot. Chaos reigned all around.

In seconds, the Raj's grandest event, the magnificent procession that displayed its power, turned into a pandemonium while smoke and dust filled the air.

While nobody understood what had just happened, there was complete disarray and high-ranking officials quickly escorted a Viceroy in great pain to the circuit house which served as the Viceroy's Lodge.

With an equal dexterity and speed, Basanta and Rash Behari quickly discarded their disguise and melted in the perplexed crowd, dissolving in the distressed multitude. When they saw an officer struggling to quell the panic, Rash Behari timidly asked, 'Sir, what just happened?'

The British officer shouted back, 'Some radical native bloke has just hurled a bomb at the Viceroy! Thank God, his life is saved, even though he has been seriously injured. Our officers have taken him to safety. Now get lost from here or else....'[9]

Leaving behind the panic-stricken crowd, Rash Behari and Basanta exited from Chandni Chowk and reached the railway station. Before boarding the train to Lahore, Basanta spoke with a heavy heart and tears in his eyes, 'I failed in completing the mission. I couldn't kill my target.'

Rash Behari placed his hand upon Basanta's shoulder and said, 'My brother, you have done an excellent job. His life was spared perhaps because God didn't want him to die today. However, our work and our mission has succeeded. The bomb has shaken the very foundation of the British Raj in India and has shown what the true sons of the motherland can do for her. We have inflicted a huge insult on the Raj and this time it truly hurt their ego.'

As the train to Lahore departed from the station, Rash Behari Bose boarded the train to Dehradun. Already, the station was being combed by the British troops as they searched for the miscreants frantically.

Rash Behari sat by a window inside the compartment, wore a pair of dark-rimmed glasses and clasped his hands. He told himself, 'Perhaps the moment of glory rests on the fate of another day.'

---

9 Author interpretation based on historical facts from: *Rash Behari Bose: The Father of The Indian National Army Vol-1* by Elizabeth Eston & Lexi Kawabe, page number 68.

The next morning, he was back in Dehradun and quickly rejoined office to establish an alibi. As the news about the attack on the Viceroy soon reached Dehradun, Amarendra rushed to meet Rash Behari, to personally verify his safety. He was met with an astonishing sight as he entered the gates of the Forest Research Institute.

On the open lawn of the Forest Research Institute, Rash Behari stood on a small podium. In front of the podium were gathered a group of faithful native servants of the British Raj. 'My fellow citizens of the British Raj, we have assembled here today to organise a private conclave to condemn the attack upon the Viceroy, Lord Charles Hardinge', Rash Behari was saying. 'It is a heinous and cowardly act that the radical elements have perpetrated upon the ceremonial procession of shifting the capital of India to Delhi. I personally condemn the attack while I wish a speedy recovery for the Viceroy….'

A few native police officers stood at a corner and clapped in appreciation. Amarendra looked at Rash Behari who smiled in recognition and a satisfied Amarendra turned back and went away with a smile on his face.

PLAYING WITH FIRE

YES, AN ASSAULT on the Viceroy was an audacious act of outrage. The British Raj was bound to take revenge. Thus, in the aftermath of the attack on the Viceroy, the British government in India began a series of covert operations to capture and execute Indian revolutionaries.

Rash Behari Bose remained under cover in Dehradun.

Rash Behari knew the outcomes of his act of defiance and told himself, 'Many of the devoted sons of Mother India will perish. Perhaps, my beloved Basanta will go to the gallows. With that thought, my heart writhes in pain. I will grieve their deaths but salute their sacrifices. Their sacrifices will lead the way ahead for the children of India to unchain her from the shackles of captivity.'

The failure of the attack on Lord Hardinge and its aftershock was a setback for India's revolutionaries and their radical nationalist plans. All eyes were on French Chandannagore, already marked as a hub of anti-British activity in Bengal. Rash Behari's friends in Chandannagore, including his friend Shrish Ghosh, went underground and a great silence enveloped militant nationalism in the following years. Literally, a blackhole was created everywhere, so that the British Intelligence could not trace the involvements of the radicals in any anti-British operation.

Rash Behari Bose was not a person to be weighed down by this. He remained strong in his intentions to act against British interests in India. He knew the time was not yet ripe for yet another daring operation. First, he needed to ensure that his future strategies remained safe. 'For the British Raj, this Christmas and the New Year will remain memorable forever', Rash Behari smiled to himself.

'The purpose of the attack on Lord Hardinge was not just to kill an individual, but to inflict a blow to the overconfident colonial tyrants. It will open their eyes and show them that Indians abhor the imperial rule, and the children of this nation will do anything to set her free from bondage.'[1]

Amarendra sat quietly and with a concerned countenance listened to Rash Behari. 'True. However, they are not going to take the matter lightly. Extreme caution needs to be adopted. Their moles will now be super active, trying to sniff out the perpetrators. I feel worried about you', he said.

The two friends were sitting in Amarendra's house. The wintry winds blew freely and carried a chill that added to their discomfort. Rash Behari looked at Amarendra and said in a soothing tone, 'Don't worry Amarendra. I have faith in our ultimate mission. Trust me, I will not let them kill my dreams so easily.'

Amarendra felt a bit relaxed on hearing Rash Behari's reassuring words. Over the last one week, the police had been

---

1 *Two Great Indian Revolutionaries-Rash Behari Bose & Jyotindra Nath Mukherjee* by Uma Mukherjee, page numbers 105-140.

combing every corner of the Northern Provinces and Bengal to find the masterminds of the attack on Lord Hardinge.

Rash Behari was a shrewd man and his experiences had made him a meticulous planner. Hence, for the next two weeks, Rash Behari attended almost every social gathering or public meeting and executed a fantastic strategy to hoodwink his opponents. Very cleverly, he ensured that his pro-government banters reached the right ears. With time, the strategy started to show success and within the spheres of native supporters of the British Raj, the name of Rash Behari Bose gained credence.

During one such gathering of the Bengali community in Dehradun, Rash Behari spoke openly in front of the others, 'Many people are blind towards the good things that the British Raj has brought for us. The good jobs and the prosperity of the civil servants cannot be ignored. Alas, the failed attack upon the honorable Viceroy of India is such a heinous act. Nothing can be attained through violence....'[2]

Amarendra sat in a corner and listened to his exaggerated blabbering and chuckled. He felt amazed by Rash Behari's ability to hide his real intent. He said to himself, 'This man is like a chameleon. He is a master of disguise not just physically, but also psychologically. So adept is he in gradually convincing people around him that he is a Raj fan. The British moles are sure to get fooled.'

However, one mole was not so easy to deceive. He was a shrewd Bengali police officer, Sushil Chandra Ghosh. He was in Dehradun on a very special mission.

---

2 Historical fact from: *Two Great Indian Revolutionaries-Rash Behari Bose & Jyotindra Nath Mukherjee* by Uma Mukherjee, page numbers 105-140.

As Rash Behari finished speaking and sat down to sip his tea, Sushil came and sat beside him. He introduced himself and said, 'My name is Sushil Chandra Ghosh. I am an officer of the British Raj. I was listening to your words. Indeed, you are a very good speaker.'

Amarendra had felt uncomfortable seeing Sushil at the gathering. He tried to alert Rash Behari but was surprised to see that the latter refused to pay any heed and continued to chitchat with Sushil enthusiastically. At one point, Amarendra felt that perhaps there was a reason why Rash Behari was behaving in this peculiar manner.

'I think, we have a common connection…', Sushil told Rash Behari.

'Really? What is that?' replied Rash Behari innocently.

'It is Chandannagore!' said Sushil Ghosh.

'Even though I don't visit the place very frequently, I still have a good association with the beautiful town. My relative, Shrish Chandra Ghosh, lives there. He studied at the Dupleix College and lives in Chandannagore with his family.'

Sushil was a smart officer. He had done his homework. He knew that Rash Behari and Shrish Ghosh were childhood friends and that was the chord he struck. His intention was to extract information about Shrish Ghosh and his involvement in radical activities, including what was by then being called the 'Delhi Conspiracy Case'. The words of his commanding officer rang in his ears, 'Mr Shrish Chandra Ghosh is a revolutionary nationalist who lives in Chandannagore. Even though we don't have any solid evidence against his active participation, I strongly believe that he is one of the masterminds of various radical activities. Your prime duty is to uncover as much information as possible about Shrish Ghosh and his closest associates, so that we can arrest them.'

Rash Behari realised that Sushil Ghosh was looking for information on his friend Shrish Ghose and knew of his own connection to Shrish. 'He has come to uncover us. He intends to extract information on Shrish from me. However, I shall show him, what I can do.'

'Shrish Ghosh!' exclaimed Rash Behari animatedly. 'Really? He is my childhood friend. Even when I visit Chandannagore nowadays, I don't miss an opportunity to meet him. Wow, that makes us connected. I am sure, we will spend many interesting hours together.'

Thus began a series of meetings between the two that spanned over a month. It was a strange cat-and-mouse game where it was difficult to guess who the cat was and who was the mouse. Sushil Ghosh, suspecting Rash Behari and Shrish, tried his best to extract evidence that they were involved in anti-British activities while Rash Behari played at making Sushil believe that he was an ardent supporter of the British rule. The dangerous game continued, and time remained witness to their trysts. At last, a powerful influencer though very cunning, Rash Behari succeeded, and Sushil was finally convinced of Rash Behari's innocence.

Sushil Ghosh's report to his Commanding Officer said, 'It is the general belief amongst the Bengali community here in Dehradun and the Northern Provinces that Rash Behari is a staunch British supporter. Some people even believe that he is a spy for the police who supplies information to the CID.'

'He is not associated with the revolutionary elements of Chandannagore. Even though he is a friend of Shrish Ghosh, the two are poles apart in their political views. I traced the social activities of Shrish through Rash Behari and have come to a conclusion. Through my interactions with Rash Behari, I can assure (you) that Shrish Ghosh was not an active participant in the recent incidents', added Sushil Ghosh.

'However, I will continue with my efforts to extract more information through my other sources. I think, Rash Behari can be tagged with a green signal', finished Sushil.[3]

Soon, fate provided an added opportunity for Rash Behari to prove his loyalty to the Raj when the grapevine in Dehradun said, the hill station would soon have an important visitor. Viceroy Lord Hardinge was arriving in town to spend a few days in the local Circuit House, where visiting government officials stayed. He was coming to recuperate while he was recovering from his bomb blast injuries. Amarendra was the bearer of the news and Rash Behari's eyes flashed like jewels.

'The Viceroy will pass by the gates of Tagore Villa', said Rash Behari with glee. 'Let us show him some respect. Before that, let us create a convincing background.'

Soon, Lord Hardinge arrived in Dehradun by train, surrounded by a fence of tight security. He was still nursing his wounds. The frail Viceroy boarded his car and the vehicle started to move towards the Circuit House bungalow. As the car dashed past the scenic surroundings of Dehradun, a tall young man, along with a group of other Indians, stood in front

---

3 Historical fact from: *Two Great Indian Revolutionaries-Rash Behari Bose & Jyotindra Nath Mukherjee* by Uma Mukherjee, page numbers 105-110.

of the gates of a huge estate. As Hardinge's vehicle went by, the man along with his companions, offered a ceremonial salute to the passing dignitary.[4]

Lord Hardinge stared at the gathering, especially at the attractive young man who seemed to be the leader of the group, and enquired from his aide, 'Who is that man?'

The aide replied, 'Sir, he is an Indian who has immense faith on the British Raj. Two days ago, he even presided over a meeting here in Dehradun. In that meeting, he had proposed and carried a vote of condemnation of the heinous attack on you. I was present at that meeting. He works at the Forest Institute and is very vocal against the radical activities of natives.'

Lord Hardinge felt pleased and shut his eyes in relief. The pleasant impression the Viceroy had of the local opinion-maker was further augmented by Sushil Ghosh's assurances. Thus, as a reward for his loyalty, Rash Behari received an invitation to visit the convalescing Viceroy in the Circuit House bungalow.

One evening, in the presence of high-ranking officials and the Viceroy himself, Rash Behari stepped inside the decorated hall of the Circuit House. Escorted by Sushil, he got introduced to the British elite and was soon charming them with his excellent ability to speak well.

Rash Behari's eyes gleamed with mischief as he finally stood before the Viceroy and said, 'Sir, it is my greatest honour to be in your exalted company. I pray for your speedy recovery.' While

---

4 Historical fact from: *Two Great Indian Revolutionaries-Rash Behari Bose & Jyotindra Nath Mukherjee* by Uma Mukherjee, page number 111.
Cross-referenced from Lord Hardinge's book, *My Indian Years 1910-1916* (published London, 1948), page 83.

his lips uttered honeyed words, his mind was racing; his next target, G Gordon who had killed Headmaster Mahendra De.

Next Came Gordon Saheb

In the next few months, Rash Behari was back in Delhi with more bombs he continued to make quietly in Dehradun, having convinced the authorities that he was a loyalist of the empire. Inside a dilapidated room somewhere in old Delhi, Rash Behari Bose stood talking to his co-conspirators. The dimly lit interiors held two more people. With only a portable suitcase in hand, Rash Behari had reached Delhi by the morning train, disguised as a Sikh gentleman.

The glow of the flickering candlelight illuminated their faces. Among them, the youngest was none other than Basanta Biswas. The other was a man who Rash Behari had met many times in the last two years. With this person's help, Rash Behari published an anonymous English leaflet with the object of fomenting discontent against the atrocities of the British Raj among the local population. He was the brave Abad Behari.

As the three of them stood quietly, the door opened slightly, and two more men came into the room. They were Balmukund[5] and Dina Nath. The five men sat across a wooden table. Rash Behari spoke. 'The supreme sacrifice of Jogendra Chakravarty of Anushilan Samiti will not go in vain. He was martyred while trying to avenge the brutal murder of Mahendra Nath De, the Headmaster of Habibganj High School.'

---

5 Bhai Balmukund (1889 – 8 May 1915) was a freedom fighter. He was sentenced to death and hanged by the British Raj for his role in the Delhi conspiracy case. He was a cousin of another revolutionary, Bhai Parmanand, who was a founder member of the Ghadar Party.

Abad Behari

Balmukund

After a brief pause, he continued, 'Mr Gordon, the ex-Sub-Divisional Officer of Sylhet, is now the Assistant Commissioner of Punjab. Time is ripe to end his tyranny. We must mete out justice to him for all his villainy.'

With eyes that glowed like burning charcoal, Rash Behari added, 'My brothers, we are revolutionaries on a mission. Yet, revolution is not an act of man. It is the act of God. Brave martyrs like Khudiram Bose and Prafulla Chaki could sacrifice their lives, because God entered their bodies and overwhelmed their human spirits. We owe a debt to these brave men for their supreme sacrifices… It is time to repay that debt.'[6]

Abad Behari looked at the others and said, 'Rash Behari, *The Liberty* is ready for printing. Our voices will now reach every person in the Northern Provinces. It will be printed at Kapurthala and distributed from Lahore, with the help of Dina Nath.'

---

6 Historical fact from: *Two Great Indian Revolutionaries-Rash Behari Bose & Jyotindra Nath Mukherjee* by Uma Mukherjee, page number 112. Creative license has been used here to flesh out the facts.

Rash Behari replied in a solemn voice, 'That is a wonderful news. However, today, I have convened this meeting here for another reason. Just as *The Liberty* begins to propagate our voice among the masses, our actions must show them our zeal. The attack on Lord Hardinge has left a lasting impact. The fireworks must continue.'

Rash Behari then produced a deadly bomb from his bag and placed it on top of the table. His glanced at each one and then his gaze stopped at Basanta. He smiled and continued, 'Basanta… this is a sister bomb of the one we used in Delhi. Now, it's time to create some noise in Lahore. A long-overdue justice needs to be meted. We have to blow up the tyrant… Gordon. He has no right to live.'[7]

'With Manindra Nath Naik, I mastered the art of making these bombs in Chandannagore. Take this, it is your supreme honour to be chosen again for this task. With Abad Behari as your accomplice, you now have another golden opportunity to serve our motherland.'

The group continued its discussion in the dead of the night. As dawn broke, each of them dispersed from the hideout and evaporated into thin air. Dina Nath had arranged for a fresh disguise for Rash Behari. This time he was a Yogi and headed out of Delhi quickly. Alas, every meticulous planner also makes small mistakes that can lead to grave outcomes. Amid the hustle bustle of their flight, Rash Behari had left behind the portable suitcase inside the Delhi room.

---

7 Historical fact from: Home Political Proceedings of the Government of India, Part B No. 379, March 1915.
File No. 1/14 of the I.B. Records, Government of West Bengal.

In the second week of May 1913, Rash Behari arrived in Lahore. Secretly, he slipped into a secluded house in a residential locality. The house belonged to Dina Nath.

That evening, Rash Behari wrote a letter and handed it over to Dina Nath.

> *Dear Compatriots*
>
> *On 14 May, Gordon will be at the bar in Lawrence Garden. This is where you must perform your act. I am sure that your guests will enjoy the performance!*[8]
>
> *Dina Nath will purchase the railway tickets for you. After your show, you must immediately head back to Delhi and Kolkata respectively. You must vanish from public sight and go underground, until the ripples settle. Burn this letter after reading it.*
>
> *May God's blessings be always your escorts. I might not be with you physically, but my heart and soul remain as your companion forever.*

Dina Nath took the letter and replied, 'I will meet them tonight. Both Abad Behari and Basanta have already arrived and are holed up inside their respective hideouts. You must leave by the night's train. There must be no evidence. We must abandon this hideout immediately.'

That night, Dina Nath handed over the letter to the two activists. Abad Behari looked at Basanta and said, 'The countdown has begun.'

---

8 Historical fact from: *Two Great Indian Revolutionaries-Rash Behari Bose & Jyotindra Nath Mukherjee* by Uma Mukherjee, page number 112.

On the evening of 14 May, Abad Behari and Basanta arrived at the gates of the Lawrence Garden house. Dina Nath was supposed to stay at the railway station with their respective tickets. At the entrance, the two escaped the notice of the guards and entered the sprawling lawn. Near the eastern corner of the lawn, was the upscale bar.

The eyes of Abad Behari and Basanta sparkled as they saw Gordon seated on a lavish sofa and enjoying his drink. The two nationalists stood in a dark shadowy corner and waited for the right moment. Basanta took out the bomb and held it in his hand.

As Abad Behari signaled to him, Basanta was about to throw the lethal object, when an alarmed shriek rent the air, 'Stop! Who is there? What are you doing inside? What is there in your hand? Stop! Guards, come quickly!'

Abad Behari screamed, 'Oh no! It's the *chaprasi*[9]... we have been spotted. Basanta... quick... throw the bomb right now!' A bewildered Basanta swung his fist and tossed the bomb, but the chaprasi jumped in between and caught the bomb like a cricket ball and it exploded. Before anyone spotted them, Basanta and Abad Behari rushed out across the open lawns. They dodged the security guards, who were rushing towards the spot of the explosion, and headed out into the street. The confused guards could only see the shadows of the two men dashing out into the dark road. Gordon and his pals too rushed to the spot where the explosion had occurred. One of his companions shouted, 'Sir, it was a conspiracy to murder you.' Nobody, other than

9 *Chaprasi*: A houseboy in a large establishment. An odd-jobs man.

the dead chaprasi, had seen the two assailants. Shock and fear showed on Gordon's face.

Abad and Basanta were lucky to escape. At the railway station, Abad Behari and Basanta met Dina Nath. Basanta's eyes were full of tears. A perplexed Dina Nath looked at them while Abad Behari said with remorse, 'The plan failed. Despite all precautions, we were intercepted before Basanta could throw the bomb at Gordon. It exploded and killed a native servant who raised an alarm. However, we managed to escape unnoticed.'

Dina Nath shook his head and consoled them, 'Destiny was not in our favour tonight. Fear not, we will soon meet success. Now quickly take your tickets and board the trains. You must leave immediately.'

Abad Behari and Basanta ran up to their respective trains after bidding farewell, while Dina Nath waved at them with trembling hands and then disappeared in the crowd. In the busy premise of the Lahore railway station, their brief meeting went unnoticed but one man was suspicious. He was a intelligence mole stationed at the station and had noted the agitated meeting of three men on the platform. Even though he couldn't hear their conversations, he headed out to meet his senior officer.

The news about the failed attempt on the life of the Assistant Commissioner of Punjab was flashed in every newspaper. In Dehradun, Rash Behari read the news and in frustration thumped his fist upon his writing desk. There were tears in his eyes. Amarendra touched his shoulder, sat down beside him and said, 'In your own words… revolution is an act of God through the hands of man. His chosen legionnaires are destined to carry out his crusade. Perhaps for you, God has designed a path that is difficult and treacherous. But I am sure that you will attain what your heart truly desires. That is God's will.'

Over the next one week, the officers of the intelligence services combed the country for the rebel nationalists with a fine-toothed comb. The attempts on Hardinge's life and Gordon's were clubbed together in a case historically known as the 'Delhi-Lahore Conspiracy'. The two attempts had severely dented the prestige of the Raj and there was a deep sense of outrage in the colonial government. The intelligence services intensified their search for the perpetrators of these audacious attempts and would not concede defeat.

Abad Behari went underground in Delhi, while Basanta disappeared in Kolkata. In Lahore, Dina Nath remained inconspicuous. Rash Behari Bose, the mastermind behind the attacks continued his serene life in Dehradun and did everything possible to safeguard his alibi and remain in the good books of the intelligence services.

The mole who had seen Dina Nath at the Lahore station, however, reported to his superiors that he could certainly recognise the three men on the platform on the night of the blast if he saw them again. 'One of those suspicious men boarded a train to Delhi, while the other younger one boarded the train to Kolkata. The third, a middle-aged one, went back to Lahore city. For the next three days, I have kept vigil at the station, but he never reappeared at the railway station. Even though I don't know their identities, their faces are crystal clear in my mind.'

Officer Sushil Chandra had been summoned to that meeting in Lahore. He asked in an inquisitive tone, 'Can you describe them? If so, we can perhaps get their sketches done to help in the investigation.' Sushil's proposal was a promising one and was unanimously accepted. Thus, within a few days, the sketches of the three suspects were secretly prepared and distributed among the police. It did not take long for the police to identify the men with the help of these sketches.

BREWING MUTINY UNDER THE TEMPLE TREE

IN 1913, THE floods in Bengal overwhelmed the lives of the poor in the province.

In Dehradun, Rash Behari fretted at his inactivity and forced seclusion. The years 1913 and 1914 were turbulent times for Rash Behari, he had to take great precautions to keep a low profile and not draw the smallest attention of the intelligence services. Meanwhile, all around, his comrades in arms and his revolutionary friends were being arrested. The Anushilan Samiti was in complete disarray, Jugantar was in deep sleep, everyone was underground, non-existent in public view.

But Rash Behari, being Rash Behari, could no longer remain dormant. Finding an opportune moment, Rash Behari Bose again started commuting between hometown Chandannagore and work station Dehradun. This time, he dedicated himself ostensibly to the flood relief work in his native Bengal. Here, once again, destiny took Rash Behari's life in hand. It was during this flood relief work that Rash Behari Bose came in direct contact with Jatin Mukherjee, Bagha Jatin, the man he had idolised all his life.

Jatin Mukherjee was the leader of Jugantar, the fledgling wing of the Anushilan Samiti. Mukherjee's magnetic personality

Jatin Mukherjee

attracted Rash Behari. In Rash Behari, Jatin saw the makings of a master revolutionary. In Bagha Jatin, Rash Behari found his new 'Leader' and under his guidance Rash Behari recovered his enthusiasm for armed nationalism. Soon, Rash Behari was travelling frequently from Chandannagore to Kolkata to meet Bagha Jatin, with Amarendra Nath, his friend as a go-between.[1]

In September 1913, Rash Behari accompanied Pratul Chandra Ganguly to Kolkata. Pratul was an active member of the Bengal revolutionaries and was on a dangerous mission. The two arrived in Kolkata by the morning train and headed to a mess in the Badur Bagan locality. It was a top-secret hideout for a specific operation and Pratul wanted Rash Behari to see the plan in progress. The place was a mini storehouse of arms

---

1 Bagha Jatin, Jatinendra Mukherjee (7 December 1879 – 10 September 1915) was a revolutionary accused of smuggling arms into India and was on top of the British rebels' list. He had acquired the sobriquet 'Bagha' when he had killed a tiger with a dagger in a ferocious confrontation near his village.
In college, he became a disciple of Swami Vivekananda, whose social thought, and especially his vision of a politically independent India – indispensabable for the spiritual progress of humanity – had a great influence on Jatin.
In 1899, Jatin became a secretary to barrister Pringle Kennedy, founder and editor of the *Trihoot Courrier*, who advocated the urgency of having an Indian National Army and retaliating against the British. Several police reports with the British say, he was a close associate of Arubindo Ghosh, a founder of Anushilan Samiti and was in contact with Indian soldiers in the British Army.
Jatin, together with Barindra Ghosh, set up a bomb factory near Deoghar.

and ammunitions that these freedom fighters planned to use. Rash Behari was thrilled by all that he saw in this small hideout and said with enthusiasm, 'My heart swells with pride as I see my brothers in Bengal pour their brave hearts into the fire of supreme sacrifice.'

Pratul picked up a revolver and said, 'These revolvers are from Dhaka. Biren Chatterjee smuggled them here, taking an enormous risk. This stash of weapons will be extremely useful for my mission to kill Head Constable Haripada Deb.'

'Before the end of this month, I will accomplish this', Pratul told Rash Behari. The two inspected the weapons, but to everyone's surprise, in the small space a pistol suddenly went off. The bullet badly injured the third finger of Rash Behari's left hand. He crouched up in pain and sat down on the floor as blood oozed profusely from his hand.

The sound of the exploding bullet had already raised an alarm. A perplexed Pratul said, 'Oh my God! Rash Behari, your finger is badly bruised. It needs the attention of a doctor immediately.'[2]

Rash Behari lifted his head and looked at Pratul. 'No. Give me that bed cover. I will wrap the finger up and stop the bleeding. The sound of the bullet has already created an alarm. Pack up all the ammunitions and let us quickly abandon this place. Let us go to the Rajabazaar center and secure the arms first. I will get first-aid there', Rash Behari said.

---

2 Historical facts referenced from: *Two Great Indian Revolutionaries-Rash Behari Bose & Jyotindra Nath Mukherjee* by Uma Mukherjee, page numbers 116.
Cross-referenced from Moti Lal Roy's, *Amar Dekha Biplab O Biplobi* (published 1957), page number 101.

Pratul tore a portion of the bed cover and Rash Behari tied it tightly around his wounded finger. As the others collected all the weapons, Pratul said with respect, 'Even with a serious injury, your heart and mind is concerned about the safety of our mission. I salute you.'

Rash Behari smiled and replied, 'Don't salute me. I am just a soldier. Salute our Mother India, whose blood flows in all of our veins and has made us strong.' The brave men then abandoned the hideout and hurried away to safety. This was, however, a single example of Rash Behari's valour.

Amarendra Chatterjee's association with Jatin Mukherjee had grown stronger over the years. The two of them collaborated in forming the Chhatra Bhandar (Student's Association), which would be transformed later into the Shramajibi Samabaya. Under the canopy of this organisation, Rash Behari furthered his struggle to free India through militant nationalism.

One fateful day, a secret meeting of three men took place under the Panchabati trees of the Dakshineswar Kali temple, where Vivekanada once sat. They were Rash Behari, Amarendra and Jatin. Across the country the police had started arresting suspected revolutionaries and executing them.

Rash Behari said in a despondent voice, 'Soon, Basanta, Abad Behari and many of my beloved brothers will be arrested and sent to the gallows. We will witness the death of these brave souls as mute spectators. I just cannot tolerate the ordeal. I am sitting idle, holed up in Chandannagore, doing nothing. All our efforts are failing, and the children of our nation are dying.'

Jatin told him, 'Rash Behari, you have a huge responsibility on your shoulders. Don't become defeated by the failures. Yes, our brothers are dying, and it is an unbearable thought. Yet,

Dakshineswar Temple

you must remain strong, because you have to lead and be the torchbearer of our freedom struggle so that millions of others can join us and we can strike back with even greater strength.'

Amarendra looked at his two companions and said, 'Jatin, I understand your point, but I don't see how we can accomplish this dream.'

In the fading crimson twilight, Rash Behari tried to guess what Jatin was indicating. Hypnotised by the gravity of the moment, he announced, 'An armed uprising against the enemy…. Yes, that is going to be our clarion call. This is my biggest dream.'

Jatin's eyes sparkled as he looked at them and he continued, 'Excellent. Let us recreate the Rising of 1857. Let us create a revolution among our brothers in the British Army. Let us kill them with their own weapons.'

Rebellion of 1857 (Bengal Army)
Photo Credit: https://hmn.wiki/lv/Siege_of_Lucknow

Rash Behari replied, 'Ever since I was a child, I have had just one dream. It is to strike back at the Raj with a military uprising. That is why I even tried to join the army but failed repeatedly. I agree with you completely. Yes, Jatin, let us plan for a big Diwali. It will be a festival of light for the entire nation.'

Amarendra was a bit skeptical and asked, 'I don't know how we will be able to do it. Moreover, I don't see why the native soldiers of the British Army would join hands with us. Nevertheless, I support you wholeheartedly.'

'This will be a huge task to undertake, and we must create the background for it. Even I don't know how we will achieve this. Yet, time will reveal destiny's plans. I can only say… we must traverse the entire length and breadth of India and unite the masses. Punjab, Northern Provinces and Bengal needs to join their hearts and their hands. We must act to make that happen', Jatin responded.

Rash Behari replied, 'Yes… I agree. I will do my job with full fervour. Over the years, I have created a delicate network of like-minded nationalists in the Northern Provinces, Punjab, Lahore and Dehradun. Now is the time to connect them with the brave sons and daughters of Bengal.' The shooting star of their hope whizzed across a golden sky as the sun went down.[3]

Back in Chandannagore, Rash Behari told his friend Shrish Ghosh, 'A brewing pot of fire is about to be set upon the furnace. The path is long and dangerous. Nevertheless, the goal must be attained.'

Shrish Ghosh replied with a smile, 'I have not seen the future, but Rasu, my brother, I know that my instinct is never wrong. With you at the helm of the battle, the children of this country will see a new dawn… the Dawn of Freedom.'

Anushilan Samiti's Rajabazaar Center

A visibly restless Sachindra Nath Sanyal sat in front of Pratul Chandra Ganguly and said, 'The innermost circle of The Young Men's Association of Benares yearns to plunge into action. However, our frustration keeps growing, as the days pass without our being able to do anything.'

---

3 Historical facts referenced from: *Two Great Indian Revolutionaries-Rash Behari Bose & Jyotindra Nath Mukherjee* by Uma Mukherjee, page numbers 116-120.
While several sources record the fact that these revolutionaries met at the temple campus, creative license has been adopted by the author for a visual representation of the story of Rash Behari's activities in the years 1913, 1914 and 1915. The author's imagination has connected the various revolutionary activities undertaken by different like-minded organisations across North India to facilitate comprehension for the modern reader, keeping in mind all these liaisons were secret and all conversations unrecorded.

Sachindra Nath Sanyal

Pratul looked at him and listened to him keenly. In a secret room of the Rajabazaar Center, the two had been discussing a serious plan. Soon, Amrita Lal Hazra, another frontrunner of the Anushilan Samiti, entered the room and joined the meeting.

'From 1908, I have nurtured a Anushilan Samiti society in Benares', continued Sachindra Nath. 'Ever since its inception, our prime aim has been to work towards liberating our nation from British domination. After the Anushilan Samiti of Dhaka got banned, we renamed our organisation as The Young Men's Association. The core group of this organisation continues to strive for the liberation of our country.'

Sachindra Nath finished his words and looked at the other two. Then, he said in an earnest voice, 'Without the support of the Bengal nationalists, the aspirations of the revolutionaries in Benares cannot be realised. Please extend to us your support.'

'Together, we will be victorious…', he added.

Pratul replied in a gratified tone, 'I believe that the time is ripe for us to work together. You are right. However, the person who is the torchbearer of our efforts, is not here. We will meet him tomorrow. His zeal and his acumen make him an able leader of our grand plan.'

Amrita Lal added, 'Tomorrow, in Chandannagore, we will unify our efforts to redefine history.'

The following day, according to plan, the three young men

arrived in Chandannagore and reached a top-secret hideout of rebel nationalists. Within the solitary quarters of the shack, Sachindra Nath, Amrita Lal and Pratul waited to meet Rash Behari and Shrish Ghosh. This was not the first time Sachindra Nath was meeting Rash Behari. In early 1912, Rash Behari had visited Benares to consolidate his efforts to unite the Northern Provinces. Sachindra Nath was still struggling to establish his group and the talks with Rash Behari hadn't resulted in anything fruitful. Both the brave men had their own specific visions; however a roadmap was still in its nascent stage.

A while later, Ras Behari, Shrish Ghosh and Moti Lal Roy came in and the meeting commenced. Rash Behari spoke with a confident air, 'I am happy that Sachindra Nath is here with us today. It gives me immense pleasure when I see that the brave lions of Benares are now ready to unite with the tigers of Bengal.'

He turned towards Sachindra Nath and said, 'More than a year ago, our visions were fledglings, but now their wings have matured for the long flight. Under Jatin Mukherjee's able leadership, I can assure you that our plans are constructive enough to fulfil our dreams.'[4]

Sachindra Nath was elated and hugged Rash Behari. 'Today comes with the greatest blessing. Together, Bengal, Benares and the United Provinces will be a massive force that can strike against the British Raj.'

Rash Behari smiled and replied, 'Your restlessness is addictive. It tempts me to name you *Lattu*, the universal top.

---

4 Historical facts referenced from: *Two Great Indian Revolutionaries-Rash Behari Bose & Jyotindra Nath Mukherjee* by Uma Mukherjee, page numbers 117-120.

The day is not far when the brave sons of India will wage the war for Freedom with this addictive zeal.'

Moti Lal said with great fervor, 'Under the able guidance of Bagha Jatin and with Rash Behari's execution strategy, our Masterplan is destined to succeed.'

'What is the Masterplan? How can we unite with it from Benares?' asked Sachindra Nath eagerly.

'Let us recreate the Uprising of 1857', responded Shrish Ghosh. The next one hour went in discussing the particulars of the Masterplan.

Finally, Rash Behari looked at Moti Lal and said, 'You must immediately head out and reach Pondicherry. Meet Sri Aurobindo and get his blessings for the Masterplan! Meanwhile, we have a huge task at hand. The native soldiers of the British Raj have to dream our vision of a free India. We must begin our journey and traverse the expanses of the country to win their confidence.'

Sachindra Nath went back to Benares while Rash Behari focused his energies on making the plan materialise. Shrish Ghosh remained in Chandannagore to work on the support services. Jatin Mukherjee remained the prime inspiration for the entire plot and engaged himself in making the blueprint into a foolproof one.

As a first step, Rash Behari visited Fort William to covertly win the allegiances of the native Sepoys and Havildars. He arranged a secret meeting and deliberated with a small group of soldiers. The idea was bold, and it required the trust of these soldiers.

Rash Behari told them, 'In this struggle, perhaps many of our brothers will have to sacrifice their lives. However, their martyrdom will not go in vain. The generations to come in this country will sing about their heroism. The Indian soldiers of the British Raj are our biggest hope. Only with your support can the Uprising of 1857 become a reality today.'

For the soldiers, HOW was a big question, although what Rash Behari said, resonated in their hearts. Every Indian soldier knew the story of 1857.

One of the soldiers commented, 'My words come from the hearts of every soldier here and I am speaking on all our behalf. Your plan is wonderful, and it definitely raises a deep sense of patriotism. However, the probability of success seems little. With the mighty British Army on the other side and with their sophisticated weaponry and well-trained army, the Sepoys of Indian origin will not stand a chance of success. Moreover, we still don't know how many of the native soldiers will swear allegiance to this proposal. Can you assure us a number? However valiant we might be, the revolution will get crushed. Our children will be orphaned, and our widows will weep. Alas, the country will remain in shackles despite all the bloodbaths. It is unfortunate that we are still a weaker minority in front of the enemy. What will happen if we fail? What will happen if the Sepoys are captured? Can we save them from the torture?'[5]

The questions were harrowing and Rash Behari didn't have any answers. He understood the gravity of the concern. He replied, 'I can sense the concern in your voices but I can also sense the spark within your hearts about this Masterplan. Today, I shall leave. However, soon I shall return when I have all the answers to your questions.'

The soldier replied with a smile, 'Sir, that day, the Indian

---

5 Historical Cross-reference from: Letters of Amarendra Nath Chatterjee dated 4.8.54 and 4.9.54 in Jadugopal Mukherjee's book, *Biplobi Jiboner Smriti* and an unpublished manuscript, *Bharater Swadhinatar Itihas*, page 34.

Sepoys will stand ready for action and will die for their motherland.'

The failure of the talks at Fort William was a setback but it made Rash Behari and Jatin sit at the drawing board to rethink their next steps. Jatin commented, 'I shall join you in the efforts. Together, we will traverse the United Provinces, Benares and Dehradun. Let us judge the pulse of our countrymen, while we work towards our dream.'

Teaming up with Bagha Jatin made Rash Behari's resolve firmer. Using his social skills and extensive reach, Rash Behari started to propagate the ideology of revolutionary patriotism in various regions of Northern India, including Benares, Lahore, United Provinces and Punjab. Despite the continued cat-and-mouse chase with the police, he successfully strengthened Jatin Mukherjee's and Jugantar's philosophy of armed struggle.

February 1914 and Onwards...

By the middle of 1913, the police investigations into the Delhi-Lahore Conspiracy had progressed far and a lot of rebel nationalists were arrested and executed. By the beginning of 1914, the police had gathered some incriminating evidence against Rash Behari too.

In February 1914, with utmost secrecy, CID officers had stormed the house of Abad Behari in Delhi. Abad Behari was captured in that raid. As the officers searched his house and his belongings, the portable briefcase Rash Behari had left behind in their secret rendezvous fell into their hands. The officer commanding the operation skimmed through the papers they had found in Abad Behari's possession and discovered a letter from Dina Nath.

At the Police Headquarters, the Commanding Officer told his Chief, 'The letter, from a person named Dina Nath, clearly shows that he and Abad Behari are active participants in revolutionary activities and are the prime perpetrators of the Lahore attack on Gordon. Moreover, from the other evidences, I conclude that a man named Rash Behari Bose, who lives in Dehradun, is also involved. As per our intelligence, at present, this man is with Dina Nath in Lahore. Even though there is no direct evidence, I suspect that he is one of the conspirators.'

The police Chief replied, 'In Bengal, a young radical by the name of Basanta Biswas has been arrested today. From the sketches of the culprits and other evidences from eyewitnesses, it is crystal clear that this man is one of the prime suspects in both the Delhi and the Lahore Conspiracy.'

The Commanding Officer asked, 'Sir… does it mean that both the incidents are related and carried out by the same group?'

The Chief replied dryly, 'Yes. The forensic reports show that even the composition of both the bombs were similar. It further proves that they were prepared by the same person. I think, our men in Lahore are going to arrest Dina Nath tonight. They have also been instructed to arrest Rash Behari, if they find him. Even though we cannot find real evidence against him, I guess we can torture him and make him accept his offence.'[6]

Indeed, that night Rash Behari was in Lahore. God saved him that day. Before he met Dina Nath, a stealthy messenger had informed him, 'Please be careful. Right now, Dina Nath's

---

6 Historical facts from: Judgement Records of M Harisson, Additional Judge in the Delhi-Lahore Conspiracy Case, dated 5 October 1914.

house is being searched and poor Dina Nath has been arrested.' The timely message saved Rash Behari by a whisker. He dashed out from his hideout, took the first train to Dehradun, reached Tagore Villa with lightning speed and established an alibi.

However, when Amarendra heard the entire story, he was very worried. 'Rash Behari, you must leave Dehradun immediately', he said.

'Go to Chandannagore and remain holed up there. It will be difficult for the British Police to capture you directly in the French dominion. That will buy you some time to plan an escape. Time is precious. The situation is boiling now, the passage of time will buy you safety', he advised.

Rash Behari understood the gravity of the situation. The next morning, he wrote an application of leave due to illness and submitted it at the Forest Research Institute. Then, evading the watch of the police and the CID, he boarded the train to Chandannagore.

As a final adieu, he said to Amarendra, 'This is not my last fight. I am a fighter and I will be so forever. God knows, I will return soon with an even stronger attack.'

At the Chandannagore station Shrish Ghosh received his friend. Rash Behari whispered, 'Nobody must know that I am here. I will remain within the inner quarters of my house and go underground for a couple of days. I cannot jeopardise the fate of my revolution. Keep me informed, I trust nobody else but you my brother.'

The colonial government had filed criminal offense cases against many people they suspected of revolutionary activities, among them Lala Hanumant Sahai, Basanta Biswas, Bhai Balmukund, Amir Chand and Abad Behari. In the next

Amir Chand

couple of weeks, many of the accused were sentenced to life-imprisonment, while some were meted out death sentences. The fate of Abad Behari, Balmukund and Basanta Biswas wavered under the guillotine.

Rash Behari was marked 'Wanted for the Delhi-Lahore Conspiracy' and the colonial government tried its best to find him. Secretly, Rash Behari Bose continued to strengthen the links between the revolutionaries of Bengal, Benares, United Provinces and Punjab. He knew, the day would come soon, when he would be able to use these connections to fulfill his objective of a free India.

Calling him 'The Most Dangerous Man' among the militant revolutionaries, the British Raj even placed an award of one lakh rupees for his capture. However, Rash Behari was smart and shrewd. He escaped their every effort and the authorities failed to establish his active involvement in the Delhi-Lahore assassination attempts. Yet, the period of silence was unbearable and Rash Behari suffered from the wounds of not doing anything and having to stay hidden.

Rash Behari remained holed up within the bounds of a single room in his home in Chandanogore. His mother was no more, his father was posted in Shimla. To avoid all suspicions, even food and water were supplied to him inside the room. Rash Behari ensured that the room remained under lock and key throughout the day and night. In this time of ordeal, only

Shrish Ghosh remained his confidante.[7]

However, the hunt for the Viceroy's attackers was on even two years later and the British were extremely suspicious. Where could Rash Behari have vanished? Their senses pointed at French Chandannagore, his home. Under the strict supervision of an Irish officer, Charles Tegart, the Kolkata police mounted a top-secret mission to capture Rash Behari.

Rash Behari was unaware of the development and remained within the confines of his room. However, a few hours past midnight of one fateful day, 8 March 1914, a sudden knock on the door woke him up. The door opened and Shrish Ghosh rushed inside with a haggard countenance. As a confused Rash Behari sat up on his bed, Shrish said excitedly, 'Rasu, hurry up. We must abandon this hideout immediately. The Kolkata police have got a hint of this place and are on their way here. You must escape at once.'

Rash Behari understood the impending danger but kept calm. He deliberated over the situation and said, 'It is not safe for me to leave Chandannagore now. I must hide somewhere in the vicinity, until the raid is over. I cannot hide inside a house, because they will look inside every suspicious dwelling. The best and the safest place is... our own mango orchard.'

'Go back home Shrish. While I hide behind the mango trees, you must remain within your house. If the police come to enquire, you must get a clean chit for yourself. This is important for your own safety', Rash Behari told him.

---

7 Historical facts referenced from: *Two Great Indian Revolutionaries-Rash Behari Bose & Jyotindra Nath Mukherjee* by Uma Mukherjee, page numbers 119-120.

Rash Behari then collected all his belongings and with lightning speed, the two fled from the room and into the sheltering darkness of the familiar garden. Shrish Ghosh returned home with his heart in his mouth.

At the break of dawn, the British Police, led by Godfrey Denham and Charles Tegart, stormed Rash Behari's home. Like vultures scavenging for prey, they searched every room and every corner within each of the rooms. Away from their notice, Rash Behari stood behind the mango trees, a witness to the drama.[8]

After hours of desperate search, the policemen were left red-faced as their suspect had again managed to escape capture. In a fit of frustration, Denham banged his fist on a wooden table and screeched, 'The sly fox has escaped. I can't believe that he has managed to hoodwink us.'

A visibly frustrated Tegart added, 'All our efforts to convince the French dominion authorities and carry out this search has gone in vain. Nevertheless, he cannot have gone far away. We must hunt him down. Let us do so at all exit points and within possible hideouts in Kolkata. This time, he won't be able to escape.'

As the dejected policemen made their exit from Chandannagore, away from everyone's eyes Shrish Ghosh entered the mango garden and met Rash Behari. They were both traumatised by the raid. Shrish Ghosh said in a weak tone, 'We can trust nobody. We still don't know who the traitor was. He is still roaming around freely and we need to be extremely cautious.'

The fading hues of the setting sun washed them in crimson. Rash Behari said thoughtfully, 'Let us return to the same room.

8 https://en.wikipedia.org/wiki/Anushilan_Samiti

It is the safest place now. Nobody will suspect a place that has just been raided.'

'Excellent', said Shrish.

'Yes, let us do that. The darkness is settling in and it will be easier for you to sneak into the room from the garden. Stay there for a couple of days. Meanwhile, I will arrange for a new hideout for you. In Hatkhola, under the care of Narendra Nath Banerjee, where you will be able to spend some days of safety.'

WORLD WAR AND SAYING GOODBYE

AS THE DAYS passed, Rash Behari was again forced into a prolonged period of indefinite concealment. Yet, the valiant and restless soul nudged himself towards the perils of adventure and bravery. During a meeting with Shrish Ghosh, Rash Behari announced, 'I will leave Bengal and head to Benares. Nobody will know about this journey. From the secret retreat at Benares, with Sachindra Nath as my lieutenant and under the tutelage of Jatin, I shall carry on with my mission. The Masterplan cannot be abandoned.'

'Soon, I will leave', he continued.

'However, before I do so, I must send my final words to Baba. I know, he is always worried about my safety. Before I fully dedicate myself to this battle for India's freedom as a fierce soldier, I must do my bit as a son. Baba must know what his son has devoted himself to.'

Before he left Bengal, Rash Behari wrote a parting letter to his father. With the help of Shrish Ghosh, it was sent to Shimla, where Binod Behari Bose was posted. In April 1914, the old man received the message from his beloved son and he read it with eyes full of tears and a heart full of pride…

Dear Baba

After crores of salutations, my submission is this that you have surely heard by this time that I am now entangled in a net of dangers of the most terrible nature. Though God knows that I am wholly innocent, yet through the influence of my stars, I am today in the eyes of all, an accused in the Delhi case.

This is perhaps my last letter. But I trust you will never look upon me as faithless and guilty. I say in the name of God that I am wholly innocent. Be that as it may, everything is happening through the influence of stars, and I too am being carried along in their revolutions.

What can I do? Man can never alter fate. Besides, when the mightiest government is my antagonist, it will be extremely difficult (for me) to obtain justice in the Court (of law). However, whatever is decreed by fate, will happen.

I have been dreaming of how you might get happiness in the end of your life, when the terrible bolt from heaven fell. Don't waste money for nothing by engaging a pleader for me, for it is almost an impossibility to fight against the government… I resign everything into the hands of God; Do pray to Him for my welfare.

The flight to Benares was a daring one, but Rash Behari accomplished the impossible task with utmost dexterity and without leaving behind any clue of his movement across the country. In Benares, Sachindra Nath received him with equal amount of caution and took him to a nondescript house inside a busy locality of Misir Pokhara, on the banks of the river Ganga.

As the two entered the shabby living-room, they were greeted by an aged man. There was a serene expression on the man's face that attracted Rash Behari. Sachindra introduced the man as the owner of the house. He was a retired health officer and an ardent supporter of the Freedom Struggle.

For the next few months, during daytime, Rash Behari remained within the inner quarters of the house. Only after the canopy of darkness covered the skyline, Rash Behari ventured out and headed to the Ghats. The secluded banks of River Ganga were the safest place to meet in this holy city. Therefore, the revolutionaries in Benares congregated at pre-selected spots on the river bank and discussed their plans and progress in utmost secrecy. This way, Rash Behari managed to survive right under the nose of the British Intelligence and they remained oblivious of his whereabout.

As soon as he arrived in Benares, Rash Behari took charge of the revolutionary efforts across the United Provinces, Bengal and Punjab. The Misir Pokhara residence was soon the haunt of prominent nationalists like Nalini Mohan Mukherjee, Preo Nath Bhattacharya, Ashutosh Roy, Manmatha Biswas and Narendra Nath Banerjee. With Sachindra Nath as his able commander, Rash Behari kept the flames of his Masterplan alive for many months in the beginning of 1914. The young men's nationalist sentiments were high, but something was still lacking.[1]

During one such covert assembly, Rash Behari sighed, 'All our efforts are perfectly channelised. Yet, something is missing.

---

1 Historical fact from: *Two Great Indian Revolutionaries-Rash Behari Bose & Jyotindra Nath Mukherjee* by Uma Mukherjee, Pages 122-125.

The X-factor that can create a moment of glory which will transform this flame into a wildfire. However, my intuition tells me that the day is not far. That moment… that special spark, will happen soon.'

Rash Behari's intuition was not deceptive. What happened was an event that rewrote world history. On 28 June 1914, a Yugoslav nationalist and member of the Serbian Black Hand Military Society, assassinated the Austro-Hungarian prince Archduke Franz Ferdinand in Sarajevo. In response, Austria-Hungary invaded Serbia on 23 July. By November 1914, Europe was divided into two camps, and they started fighting each other in what the world knows as World War One. It churned the various forces of anti-imperial rebellion in all corners of the world, including the Ghadar movement that took root in the USA and Canada and the Bolshevik revolution in Russia.

By every measurable scale, this was one of the most devastating wars in modern history. Over a million Indian soldiers were inducted in the British Army, among whom over sixty-two thousand were destined to die a grotesque death in lands far away from their motherland, serving a cause that they were never meant to fight for. The prelude and the interlude of this horrible dirge united many revolutionaries and formed an invisible bridge. Fate plunged the destinies of Rash Behari Bose and Jatin Mukherjee into this scheme of ferment brewing freedom for India.

During a meeting at yet another secret location, Jatin Mukherjee said in an excited tone, 'Fate has provided us with a golden opportunity. This is the moment that will unite our brotherhood with the common people as well as the native

Indian soldiers in World War

soldiers of the British Army. We must act to make this happen.'

He turned towards Rash Behari and said, 'Destiny itself has answered the intriguing questions that the Sepoys had asked you at Fort William several years ago. That day, you were at loss for reply. However, today the answers are floating in the wind.'

After listening to Jatin patiently, Rash Behari replied, 'I think I understand the point you are making and agree with you. A huge segment of the native Indian soldiers has been commissioned to fight on behalf of the British. Even though reluctant, these men have to travel to unknown foreign lands and even die in hostile conditions. Far away from their families and their homes, they will bite the bullet and combat an enemy whom they have never even imagined to be their rivals. Then, their corpses will rot in distant lands and will perhaps be denied a proper funeral.'

Rash Behari stared at the others present in the meeting and continued, 'This entire situation is bound to create a sense of dissent and dissatisfaction amongst the community of native soldiers, who were till now reluctant to oppose their mighty employer. Their anger and the angst is likely to give rise to a sense of rebellion that will melt their hesitancy and can forge their allegiances towards nationalist processes. It is always a greater honour to die for one's own nation rather than for an alien cause.'[2]

Jatin added in quick response, 'Additionally, with majority of the British Indian soldiers engaged in a battle far away from India, the strength of the enemy will be very curtailed. Hence, the second most important concern of the Sepoys, about the might of the opponent, also finds an answer. The time is ripe for action.'

Rash Behari added again, 'The number of British soldiers will be miniscule and nothing in comparison to the native army that might assault them. In such an Uprising, we will be able to overthrow the imperial regime. It will be such a great and glorious victory.'

Patting Rash Behari on the back, Jatin added, 'Yes, let's create an uproar that history will remember.'

Amidst the global crisis and mayhem of the World War, another invisible pot of fire began to burn bright on the

---

2 Historical facts from: Atul Krishna Ghose's statement as recorded in *Banglay Biplabbad*, Page 320, by Nalini Kishore Guha.
Taken from: *Two Great Indian Revolutionaries-Rash Behari Bose & Jyotindra Nath Mukherjee* by Uma Mukherjee, Pages 135-137.
The unrecorded conversations have been created by the author using his creative liense to formulate the essence of the meeting.

other side of the globe. It was a chapter in history that was being written by the Ghadar Party in the United States and the Berlin Committee in Germany. Members of the Punjabi Sikh community in the United States and Canada were among the most prominent participants of this secret scheme. Even though the plot was relevant in the context of the world war, the foundation of the upheaval had been laid many years ago.

The Ghadar Movement

Looking back in history, the story of yet another uprising surfaces.

During the late nineteenth century, to alleviate their financial difficulties and to overcome the economic downturn in India, many Indians emigrated to foreign lands in search of employment and livelihood. Many of these emigrants settled in Canada and North America. A significant part of that demography comprised people from the region known as the Punjab in undivided India.

The communities from Punjab had been loyal legions behind the British Raj since the 1860s. Hence, they expected equal rights and warmth for their communities across the British and Commonwealth countries. However, when Canada promulgated strict laws against the emigrants, the Punjabi communities faced the harsh reality of racism and discrimination for the first time. Some of the members migrated from Canada to the United States, but the same humiliation followed them there. The enraged Punjabis felt cheated and tricked.

Hungry for justice, they swore retribution.

The party they set up in 1913 in the USA was initially named the 'Pacific Coast Hindustan Association'. The prime

Ghadar di Goonj Cover

focus of the party and its members was to wage war against the British Raj in India. Under the able leadership of Lala Har Dayal, Santokh Singh, Baba Jawala Singh, Sant Baba Wasakha Singh Dadehar and Sohan Singh Bhakna, who was its president, the fledgling organisation first started to spread its wings with a popular newsletter, *Ghadar di Goonj*.

The organisation quickly gained popularity among Indian expats, particularly in the United States, Canada, East Africa and Asia. The prime members of the Hindustan Association were Indian immigrant students, largely from the Punjab. Many of them were students at the University of California at Berkeley. A few important individuals were VG Pingle, Har Dayal Singh, Kartar Singh, Tarak Nath Das. Within them, the sense of betrayal metamorphosed into a deep sentiment of patriotism. Far away from home, these young and valiant men felt the call of nationalism and the urge to uphold the honour of their motherland.

In the charged atmosphere of the initial meetings, the words of Sohan Singh Bhakna reverberated, 'We are not Sikhs or Punjabis. Our religion is patriotism!'

Ghadar Party members

Sohan Singh Bhakna Kartar Singh

Their strong sense of patriotism exhibited itself in their weekly paper, *Ghadar*, that the party circulated. Using the Arabic word *Ghadar*, meaning revolt, as its name, this audacious publication carried the caption on the masthead: *Angrezi Raj Ka Dushman* (an enemy of British rule).

In bold words, the weekly paper propagated…

Wanted - brave soldiers to stir up rebellion in India.
Pay - death;
Price - martyrdom;
Pension - liberty;
Field of Battle - India

In the first issue of the fearless paper, Kartar Singh wrote…

Today there begins 'Ghadar' in foreign lands, but in our country's tongue, a war against the British Raj.
What is our name? Ghadar.
What is our work? Ghadar.

Where will be the Revolution? In India.
The time will soon come when rifles and blood will take the place of pens and ink!

During a high-level meeting of the prominent members, Hal Dayal noted, 'Shyamji Krishna Varma founded the India House in London with the objective of propagating nationalist opinion and pro-independence work. I was a privileged member of that society and am fortunate that my personal opinion has been deeply influenced by the ideologies of the association. Alas, after India House was subdued, I had to abandon London and find asylum in Paris and then in the United States. However, now seeing the zeal of the Ghadar Party, I feel that my blood is again boiling to fight for my mother nation.'

Kartar Singh echoed Har Dayal's words, 'Yes, let us return to India to fulfil this mission. Let us unite our brothers across the globe and create a revolution.'

Shyamji Krishna Varma

Har Dayal added, 'In September 1913, the brave Mathra Singh visited Shanghai and promoted our cause within the Indian community there. In January 1914, he visited India and circulated our pro-independence literature amongst Indian soldiers, before leaving for Hong Kong. In our confidential discussion, Singh has reported that the situation in India is extremely favourable for a revolution. Our literature has already reached our motherland. Now, it is time for us to do so.'

Sohan Singh added, 'The efforts of the Congress-led mainstream movements for dominion status is a soft approach and we do not adhere to it. Victory must be attained valorously, and we must bring it in through an armed rebellion.'

Har Dayal pointed out, 'The British Raj is wary of the Ghadar Party. They are pressing the Government of United States to suppress Indian revolutionary activities and Ghadar literature. We must be very careful. Let us connect with our brotherhood and then congregate once again, after we reach India.'[3]

As an aftermath of the meeting, thousands of members of the party returned to India with their audacious intentions. Significant people among them included Har Dayal Singh, Sohan Singh Bhakna, Tarak Nath Das, Vishnu Ganesh Pingle, Kartar Singh and Harman Singh. United with their families and the fuming brotherhood of Punjab, the Ghadar members were ready to plunge into action.

A number of failed attempts at isolated mutinies opened the eyes of the primary members of the Ghadar Party to what

---

3 The Ghadar Movement has been mentioned in various books and accounts. Some of the information mentioned in this book have been taken from: *Two Great Indian Revolutionaries-Rash Behari Bose & Jyotindra Nath Mukherjee* by Uma Mukherjee.
Atul Krishna Ghose's statement as recorded in *Banglay Biplabbad*, Page 320, by Nalini Kishore Guha.
Agni Diner Katha, by Satis Pakrasi, 1947.
India as I Knew It by Michael O' Dwyer.
[O' Dwyer was Lieutenant Governor of Punjab between 1913 and 1919. It was during O'Dwyer's tenure that the Jallianwala Bagh massacre occurred. He was killed by Udham Singh in 1940.]
Ghadar Movement: ideology, organisation, and strategy by Harish K Puri (1993).

Tarak Nath Das

the flaw in their plan was. The fact was that none of their assaults were properly planned or executed. They were all disparate attempts without finesse. These were defeats that made them introspect on how to succeed.

With deep concern, the members assembled to discuss the steps ahead. Considering their failures, they concluded, 'We don't have a Leader under whom our sense of patriotism can be consolidated. We desperately need a Leader to lead us to revolution.'

Destiny now played its card once more.

With Bengal and Punjab, the most notorious opponents of the British Raj, the eyes of the Ghadar Party fell upon the two brightest jewels of revolution from Bengal – Bagha Jatin and Rash Behari. In the backdrop of the World War I, thus began yet another chapter in India's bid for freedom.

Jatin Mukherjee was a well-connected man. Despite being a devoted Indian Freedom Fighter, he continued to remain associated with global student movements and international politics. The charged environment and the restlessness of the rebels of Punjab didn't escape his notice and he foresaw a more strategic alliance between Punjab and Bengal's revolutionaries.

Soon, Amarendra received a letter from Jatin and he discussed it with Rash Behari in Benares. Eagerly he pointed out,

'The world is becoming favourable towards our endeavours. We are getting noticed. I just received a letter from Jatin. He seems hopeful about the developments. The arrival of members of the rebellious Ghadar Party in India is a fresh opportunity for us.'[4]

Rash Behari asked with enthusiasm, 'What does Jatin foresee?'

Amarendra replied, 'He didn't mention the details in the letter. His only hint is that an alliance with the brotherhood of the North will soon become a reality for our brothers in Bengal. I hope to receive some positive news from him soon….'

Rash Behari replied, 'Moti Lal had visited Sri Aurobindo last year, just as we had planned. Dressed as an Englishman, he had disguised himself to reach French Pondicherry. After three months, he has returned with Rishi Aurobindo's blessings. Everything seems to be slowly moving towards the path of success. The day is not far, when we shall overthrow our colonial masters.'

Rash Behari's Misir Pokhara hideout was also a haven for collecting explosives and ammunitions for their plans. Rash Behari used to regularly examine them personally. On 8 November 1914, Rash Behari was routinely checking out a few bombs. As he scrutinised the arsenal, he explained to Sachindra Nath, 'These bombs have the typical characteristics of the ones made in Chandannagore. Look carefully. The caps of the bombs are intentionally detached from the main body. Just before these lethal objects are thrown, the cap is attached

---

4 The conversation was created by the author under creative license. Historical facts were taken from: *Two Great Indian Revolutionaries-Rash Behari Bose & Jyotindra Nath Mukherjee* by Uma Mukherjee. Pages 118-125.

to the body, to create percussion. This is the mechanism behind the bombs…', just as the conversation was happening, two bombs exploded with deafening noise.

Even though the explosions were not fatal, it was severe and coupled with the jolt of the discharges, created an alarmingly loud noise. A few devoted followers of Rash Behari were standing outside the premises of the house. The sudden blast unnerved them momentarily. However, after the few initial moments of confusion, when the thunderstruck men rushed inside, they confronted a scene of horror.

The smoke and fire from the blasts had flung Rash Behari and Sachindra Nath into the air and then on to the floor with great impact, resulting in severe injuries to both of them. Due to the shock, both Rash Behari and Sachindra Nath had lost consciousness; blood oozed from their injuries. The blast created quite a panic in the vicinity of the house, drawing attention to it. Rash Behari's followers rushed the two injured revolutionaries to another safehouse.

Even as he was being taken away, a semi-conscious Rash Behari feebly ordered, 'Remove every suspicious thing from here. We must not leave behind any clue'. Stunned by their leader's vigilance, three of the men cleaned up the mess and removed the remaining bombs and ammunitions. The safety of the Misir Pokhara residence had been severely compromised and the nationalists could not afford to leave behind any traces. Even though the blasts caused a bit of unrest and alarm in Benares, the police were unable to trace any direct link of the people involved to any militant activity. No evidence could be submitted with the investigation report.

Amarendra received the shocking news and rushed to the

rescue. Within a few days, Rash Behari and Sachindra Nath recovered from their injuries. Yet, they were still somewhat weak. In a worried tone, Amarendra said, 'Both of you are still very weak. The police have submitted their report but I am sure their moles are still active and are looking for answeres. The place was cleaned before the police arrived. I am sure that they will lay a trap to capture the men behind the explosion.'

Rash Behari too felt concerned and thought for a while. Then, he replied, 'You are correct. We must immediately shift to a different hideout. It must be a place where we will be completely untraceable. Only a few trusted members need know that address. Yet, this time, my residence need not be a single refuge. A revolutionary is like a vagabond. I need to change my address frequently. The Brits must never be able to capture me.'

Sachindra Nath looked at the others and added, 'I know just the place to hide. Bangalitola. Yes, it is the perfect place where you can take refuge in multiple places. I have my people there and I can definitely arrange it.' Within the next few days, Rash Behari and Sachindra Nath were disguised in the attire of women and moved to a new address in Madanpura, located in Bangalitola. As a trusted assistant of Sachin opened the door, Rash Behari said mischievously, 'Sir, your much awaited madam is here. Is her accommodation ready?'[5]

The three of them looked at each other and then broke out in laughter.

It was well known that the aim of the Ghadar Party was to overthrow the British Raj in India through an armed revolution,

---

5 The historical facts have been referenced from: *Two Great Indian Revolutionaries-Rash Behari Bose & Jyotindra Nath Mukherjee* by Uma Mukherjee, Page number 123.

in a manner similar to the Sepoy Mutiny of 1857. Across the Americas, effort had been underway among the desperate and valiant Ghadar members to make this feasible. Tarak Nath Das, the man behind the *Free Hindustan* journal, along with VG Pingle, Kartar Singh and others of the University of California at Berkley, were successful in planting the seed of the movement across the USA and Asia. In India, they had begun their search in earnest for a man who could make their dream a reality. Canada's exclusion laws, formulated to prevent non-Europeans from entering Canada, had triggered a set of events in that distant land that had global implications. A faceoff became the flashpoint.

The Komagata Maru

In April 1914, a Japanese steamship named *Komagata Maru* was chartered by Gurdit Singh Sandhu of Sarhali, to ferry Indians to Canada for jobs. The ship, filled with Indians, began its journey in the British port of Hong Kong and made her way towards Canada. Among all its passengers, 337 were Sikhs while the rest were Hindus and Muslims.

After a long and arduous journey, hope rose high among its passengers as the port of Vancouver loomed in sight. The passengers had left a resource-drained motherland under colonial rule to earn a decent living elsewhere in the world, far away from home. The declining economic opportunities within India for the natives was the biggest driving force behind this migration. Nevertheless, they carried with them the patriotic dream that India would one day be a free nation and they would be able to return to their motherland and lead a life of honour and prosperity once again.

On board the *Komagata Maru*

The Canadian government was apparently aware of the intent of the passengers of the incoming *Komagata Maru.* A segment within the Canadian bureaucracy was apprehensive about these men and they did not want what they called 'native settlers' in Canada.

After a long voyage, when the *Komagata Maru* sailed into Burrard Inlet, near Vancouver on 13 May, one of the Sikh passengers was Jagat Singh Thind, the brother of Bhagat Singh Thind, an Indian-American Sikh writer and lecturer who had been active in his legal battle over the rights of Indians to obtain citizenship in the United States. As the ship stood in the shallow waters, awaiting clearance from the Customs Department, away from the eyes of the authorities, two revolutionary nationalists, Maulana Barkatullah and Bhagwan Singh Giani, established a contact with the ship and distributed Ghadar literature among the passengers. The weary passengers were already homesick. The nationalistic sentiment in the pamphlets they read augmented the sense of patriotism in them.[6]

The ship was yet to dock at a harbour and the passengers were sick of the monotony of the voyage. The Ghadar literature distributed on board raised their spirits and the slogan, *Angrez Raj Ka Dushman,* reverberated among the patriotic meetings that were held on the ship. These were anti-British, not anti-Canadian or anti-White or anti-West. A sublime sense of freedom prevailed on board.

Passenger on board *Komagata Maru*

6 The Historical facts of the Komagata Maru incident were taken in exerpts from books: *The Voyage of the Komagata Maru: The Sikh Challenge to Canada's Colour Bar* by Hugh J M Johnston.
Voices of Komagata Maru – Imperial Surveillance and Workers from Punjab in Bengal by Suchetana Chattopadhyay.
Official Website of Canada Government: https://www.canada.ca/en/parks-canada/news/2016/08/the-komagata-maru-incident-of-1914.html
Maulana Barkatullah and Bhagwan Singh: Barkatullah was a professor in a Japanese university who was in Canada in 1914 and Bhagwan Singh was a Gurudwara priest from Hong Kong; both the men had extensive connections in Asia.

However, as the *Komagata Maru* slowly entered Canadian waters, first at the Coal Harbours in Burrard Inlet, the steamship was not granted permission to dock. The frustrations of the passengers mounted as their wait for permission began.

Immigration Officer, Frederick Wellington Taylor, was the first one to enter the vessel. He calmly announced, 'The *Komagata Maru* will not be allowed to dock right away. A diplomatic decision is under consideration. I urge all of you to keep calm while the issue gets resolved.'

One of the infuriated passengers screamed in frustration, 'This is a lie. We are being denied entry because the British Raj is skeptical about us. They are the real villains.'

Taylor was a compassionate man. He replied, 'My sympathy is with everyone. I understand the ordeal that you are going through after such a prolonged voyage. However, refrain from unsolicited allegations. I will do my best to establish a connect between you and the personnel on shore.'

Frederick Wellington Taylor

Another passenger angrily added, 'This ship belongs to the whole of India, this is a symbol of Indian honour. If the ship gets detained, there will be rebellion in the armies.'

Taylor was alien to the cultural and regional values of the passengers. Yet, he remained complacent and said politely before leaving ship, 'I will not start a debate that will create unrest. The fate of this ship is not in my hand. I am a facilitator, and I will ensure that peace and harmony is maintained.' Yet, as the days passed, the agony of the passengers continued to mount while the bureaucrats took their own sweet time to resolve their troubles.

At a high-profile meeting, Richard McBride, founder of the British Columbian Conservative Party, said in a stern voice, 'I strongly oppose the entry of those suspicious men in Canada. The ship's travelers must not be allowed to disembark. This is my firm belief.'

Sir Robert Borden, the Prime Minister, replied, 'Do you understand the consequences? The Indian natives in Canada are at the verge of a massive protest. If we decide to stop their entry, then we must have a solid reason behind it.'

McBride replied with determination, 'We are ready to do our bit. The Indians must not enter at any cost. The Canadian Law is very clear in its verdicts. Every opposition will face a fitting reply. We must remain firm in our decision.'

Richard McBride

Sir Robert Borden

Borden was yet to declare a decision. However, the sentiments prevalent amongst his own countrymen influenced his verdict. He just needed to remain politically correct to avoid all speculations and counter every opposition.

Another member of the Canadian parliament from the British Columbian Conservative Party, Henry Herbert Stevens, organised a public meeting and announced loudly, 'The non-European immigrants aboard the Japanese steamship *Komagata Maru* must not be allowed to disembark at Vancouver. The infiltration of these doubtful men in our lands will only create an environment of disharmony and unrest. The extremist sentiment prevalent in India must not touch the soil of Canada. We must protest against it.'[7]

Away from the eyes of the common people, Stevens met Immigration Officer Malcolm R J Reid. In a secret conversation, he influenced Reid's stubborn temperament and instructed him, 'These men must not step foot on Canadian shores. Ensure a watertight policy. Let them rot inside the vessel until the government proclaims its decision and the ship is sent back.'

Reid was a hardheaded man, and his allegiances were easily sold to those orders. He used all his powers to make the lives of the passengers aboard the *Komagata Maru* miserable. The mistreatment and prolonged delay in arriving at a decision further fueled the frustrations of the men. The *Komagata* issue soon breached the tolerance levels of the masses on-shore and a wildfire of protests commenced.

---

7 http://komagatamarujourney.ca
https://en.wikipedia.org/wiki/Komagata_Maru_incident
https://en.wikipedia.org/wiki/Henry_Herbert_Stevens

Officer Malcolm R J Reid on board *Komagata Maru*

Among the Indians residing in Canada, a 'Shore Committee' was formed with Husain Rahim and Sohan Lal Pathak at the helm. Across the United States and Canada, protest meetings were held criticising the behavior of the Canadian government. This behaviour was again a blow to the honour of the emigrant Indian community. At the Dominion Hall in Vancouver, during a heated convention, the assembly erupted with echoes of, 'If the passengers are denied entry, then the entire Indo-Canadian community will follow them back to India to start a rebellion against the racial atrocities.'[8]

8 The Historical facts of the *Komagata Maru* incident were taken in exerpts from books: *The Voyage of the Komagata Maru: The Sikh Challenge to Canada's Colour Bar* by Hugh J M Johnston.
Voices of Komagata Maru – Imperial Surveillance and Workers from Punjab in Bengal by Suchetana Chattopadhyay.
Official Website of Canada Government: https://www.canada.ca/en/parks-canada/news/2016/08/the-komagata-maru-incident-of-1914.html
https://www.newwestrecord.ca/local-news/new-west-district-gets-set-to-rename-richard-mcbride-school-3125606

The screams resounded across the streets, 'Ghadar is the call of duty. Rebellion is the only answer to this gross injustice towards Indians.' A secret agent of the British Raj infiltrated the meeting and then hurriedly wired the government officials in London and Ottawa, 'Supporters of the Ghadar Party are probably aboard the *Komagata Maru*. The steamship is a sitting time bomb.'

To desperately save the passengers from their continued suffering, the Shore Committee raised funds to keep the steamship chartered as the prolonged delay meant that the ship would have to remain stranded. As their last hope for justice, the Shore Committee appealed at the court of law. However, on 6 July 1914, the British Columbia Court of Appeal passed an undisputed judgement that under the new 'Orders-in-Council', it had no authority to interfere with the decisions of the Department of Immigration and Colonisation. Thus, the appeals suffered a miserable demise. It was the death knell for all hopes and the sentiments of the Punjabi community which witnessed firsthand the harsh reality of White colonial rule.

At the zenith of the torment, the angry passengers raised a rebellion and relieved the Japanese captain of *Komagata Maru* of the control of the ship. As a result, an apprehensive Canadian government ordered that the ship be pushed off to sea, after allowing only twenty passengers to enter Canada. With every level of tolerance breached, the passengers resorted to an angry attack on the mediating immigration officers. It was a complete chaos, and the bitter brawl ended every scope of further dialogue.

Leading newspapers in Canada flashed the news as: *Howling masses of Hindus showered policemen with lumps of coal and bricks... it was like standing underneath a coal chute!* The situation had now gone out of hand and the agitated Canadian government finally declared that since the ship had violated the exclusion laws, the passengers did not have the necessary clearance, and as they had not sailed directly from India, the *Komagata Maru* must return from where it came. It was the final nail in the coffin of hope. On 23 July 1914, the *Komagata Maru* was turned around and forced to depart for Asia. Alas, finally the disgraced and disappointed passengers returned to India, to Kolkata Port, after a two-month-long legal tussle. However, their humiliation was yet to be over.

In Kolkata, the colonial government again detained the passengers under the new Defense of India Act at Budge-Budge, and forcible tried to send them back to Punjab. The news of this detention spread far and wide and led to further unrest within India and among the Punjabi community abroad.

Komagata Maru being escorted away from Canadian waters

The Commanding Officer at Budge-Budge said in a skeptical tone, 'The men aboard the *Komagata Maru* are not only proven lawbreakers but also dangerous political agitators. We cannot let them roam around freely.'

A police inspector, who was a staunch supporter of the colonial rule, declared, 'I will go aboard the ship and arrest Gurdit Singh Sandhu and a few other leaders who are primary threats. No one must disembark from the ship, before these radical elements are captured.' The British police then entered the *Komagata Maru*, docked at Budge Budge.

The Commander of the force asked sternly, 'Where is Gurdit Singh Sandhu? We are here to arrest him.'

A group of angry supporters came forward and said unanimously, 'We are all Gurdit Singh! Arrest us, if you dare.' Another group of passengers then attacked the police party. A bitter struggle ensued while the entire steamship transformed into a battleship, within moment.

Unable to control the situation, the ambushed Commander of the police party then screamed, 'Fire! Kill the scoundrels!'[9]

---

9 The Historical facts of the *Komagata Maru* incident were taken in exerpts from books:
The Voyage of the Komagata Maru: The Sikh Challenge to Canada's Colour Bar by Hugh J M Johnston.
Voices of Komagata Maru – Imperial Surveillance and Workers from Punjab in Bengal by Suchetana Chattopadhyay.
Official Website of Canada Government: https://www.canada.ca/en/parks-canada/news/2016/08/the-komagata-maru-incident-of-1914.html
Newspaper clips: https://www.thehindu.com/opinion/open-page/saga-of-indian-immigration-and-komagata-maru/article8637876.ece
Exerpts from the Canadian Excyclopaedia: https://web.archive.org/web/20210405043204/https://www.thecanadianencyclopedia.ca/en/article/komagata-maru
Journals from House of Commons, Canada: https://www.ourcommons.ca/DocumentViewer/en/39-2/house/sitting-70/journals

Gurdit Singh Sandhu

The unarmed passengers grappled with the police to save their lives. Bullets showered on them and the pungent smell of gunpowder filled the air. The riot left nineteen passengers dead and many others wounded. Gurdit Singh and a few others had jumped from the ship and managed to save their lives. The rest of the passengers were arrested. With broken legs, fractured bones and oozing gore, the bloodbath on *Komagata Maru* was complete, leaving a permanent scar in the hearts of all Indians. Some of the arrested men were imprisoned while the rest were forcibly sent back to their respective villages and kept under harsh police scanner.[10]

From the Cradle of American Universities

The Budge-Budge incident was a momentary victory for the British authorities, but it created a gaping wound in the hearts

10 The Historical facts of the *Komagata Maru* incident were taken in exerpts from: Official Website of Canada Government: https://www.canada.ca/en/parks-canada/news/2016/08/the-komagata-maru-incident-of-1914.html
Newspaper clips: https://www.thehindu.com/opinion/open-page/saga-of-indian-immigration-and-komagata-maru/article8637876.ece
Exerpts from the Canadian Excyclopaedia: https://web.archive.org/web/20210405043204/https://www.thecanadianencyclopedia.ca/en/article/komagata-maru
Journals from House of Commons, Canada: https://www.ourcommons.ca/DocumentViewer/en/39-2/house/sitting-70/journals

of the Ghadar Party members across the world. Men and women from Punjab and the United Provinces were devastated by the incident.

Vishnu Ganesh Pingle was a Marathi young man from Telegaon, of the Poona district. Early in 1911, he had migrated to the United States as a student to join the University at Seattle. However, luck had other plans for this brave youth. Attracted by the ideologies of the Ghadar Party, he had joined the group and in the next three years emerged as a sworn Ghadarite.

Vishnu Ganesh Pingle

At the University of Berkley, Pingle had got familiar with Satyen Bhushan Sen. Sen was a staunch follower of Jatin Mukherjee and his ideologies.[11] The connection came into play just at the right time. Following the *Komagata Maru* episode, Pingle was convinced that he should return home to India and devote himself to India's freedom as an ardent Ghadarite.

---

11 Bagha Jatin leased from Sir Daniel Hamilton lands in the Sundarbans to shelter revolutionaries. With Atul Krishna Ghosh, Jatin Mukherjee founded the Pathuriaghata Byam Samity which was an important centre of armed revolution of the Indian national movement. It is, therefore, natural to assume that many families living in Pathuriaghata, including the Tagore family, helped those involved in armed struggle for a free India. Since 1906, with the help of Sir Daniel, Jatin had been sending meritorious students abroad for higher studies as well as for learning military craft. Thus, Jatin had a wide international network of supporters.

Satyen Sen told Pingle, 'Jatin Mukherjee from Bengal is not just a leader. He is a living idol of freedom struggle in India. Even in the absence of his physical presence, his thoughts can keep the flames of revolution alive. An association of the Ghadar Party with Jatin would be like a fiery union of two volcanoes.'[12]

Pingle listened to him with great attention as Satyen continued, 'Take this letter and meet my nephew Bejoy Krishna Roy. He is an active member of Jatin's party. Bejoy will be able to arrange a meeting with Jatin. Trust me… you will not be disappointed.'

By the end of November 1914, Pingle was on Indian soil headed to Kolkata. Here he met a lanky young man with an unassuming appearance. The young man was initially skeptical. Pingle greeted him and handed over a hand-written letter. The man received the letter from Satyen Sen, read it and then said, 'Yes, I am Bejoy. Please come and meet me tomorrow.'

With a heart full of expectation, Pingle returned to the same address the following day. However, this time, there were many people in the little room. After the initial greetings, a man came forward and stood before Pingle. He had a majestic personality. The man said, 'I am Jatin Mukherjee. Bejoy has told me about you and the letter from Satyen Sen. Please tell me how I can assist you.'

---

12 Historical facts taken from: *Two Great Indian Revolutionaries-Rash Behari Bose & Jyotindra Nath Mukherjee* by Uma Mukherjee, page numbers 123-124, 125.
Cross-referenced from Moti Lal Roy's, *Amar Dekha Biplab O Biplobi* (published 1957).
Rash Behari Bose by Satyavrata Ghosh & Luis Fernandes.
Judgement in the Lahore Conspiracy Case, as delivered by AA Irvine and TP Ellis and Sheo Narain, Special Commissioners on 13 September 1915.
The conversations were secret, with no records but referred to in the documents above.

Pingle had already heard about Jatin and now he was ecstatic at meeting him in person. With his dreams soaring high, Pingle replied, 'I have come here with the desire to unite the two major frontiers of the country whose purposes are the same. You must be aware of the gross injustice meted out to the people of Punjab, primarily, across Canada, United States and in India. We, the unfortunate children of this country, who had traveled far away from their motherland with the hope of employment or education, have been greatly humiliated.'

Pingle paused and then continued, 'I am a member of the Ghadar Party that aims to liberate our country from the shackles of the British Raj. The active members of the Ghadar movement are already back in India and masses are joining us in our efforts. However, we lack a leader in the Northern Provinces. We desperately need a strong personality who will be able to consolidate the efforts of the brave sons of the soil to raise a revolt. We need somebody, who will be the bridge between Bengal and the Northern Provinces.'

Pingle spoke his heart out for the next thirty minutes and said everything that had been going on with the Ghadarites. There was anguish in his voice and an honesty in his persona that perhaps touched the hearts of the others present within the room.

Chosen Leader of Ghadar Party

Jatin listened to him keenly and then told him, 'Mr Pingle, I know of just the person whom you're seeking. Perhaps destiny forged his birth to become the leader you are looking for.'

Pingle's eyes lit up like burning charcoals while Jatin continued, 'He is the very valiant and able Rash Behari Bose. The fearless man now lives in Benares and is currently in a hideout to evade the clutches of the British police. By the biggest stroke of destiny, Rash Behari is the perfect person to become your leader. He dreams a majestic dream that is a mirror replica of what the Ghadar Party aspires to attain. I believe that there can be no other person who can make this dream a reality.'

Jatin sat down near a wooden desk and said, 'I will now write a letter for you. It will be my personal message to him. Please reach Benares with haste. With an open mind and heart, go and meet him. Give him this letter. I am sure, you will find your leader in him.'

Having written the letter, Jatin folded it and handed it over to Pingle. The latter got up to leave and Jatin added, 'The dreams of the Ghadar Party, the dreams of the Northern Provinces and the dreams of Bengal will soon become united.'

Evading the eyes of British moles, Pingle reached Benares and began his search for Rash Behari. Despite the fact that the intelligence services and the imperial police were completely unaware of his existence, the revolutionaries in Benares did know of Rash Behari's whereabouts. Three days later, Pingle knocked on the wooden door of a dilapidated house in Bangalitola. After a few minutes, a man opened the door and looked at him with suspicion. Pingle understood the unease and remembered the instructions from Jatin. He said with a smile, 'I want to meet Narendra Nath Sen.'

The man who had opened the door was Sachindra Nath Sanyal. He replied in a stern, dry voice, 'There is nobody here by that name. Who has sent you here?'

'Jatin Mukherjee', replied Pingle with a smile. 'I have a letter from him but I cannot give it to anyone else other than Sen.'

Sachindra Nath went inside and returned after a few minutes. He said, 'Please come with me'.

Inside the nondescript interiors of the house, Pingle waited for a couple of minutes, and then, a man entered the room. He was dressed in a crimson-coloured kurta, wore a pair of dark-rimmed glasses and flaunted a thick beard. The man greeted Pingle and took the letter from him. He read it with utmost keenness and then, with a sudden jolt, pulled down his beard and glasses to reveal his cleanly-shaven countenance that had a dash of a smart moustache.

Pingle was puzzled. The man smiled at him and said, 'Mr Pingle, I am Rash Behari Bose, aka, Narendra Nath Sen.'

Pingle said with awe, 'You are a master of disguise. It is impossible to know how you really look.'[13]

'It is the fateful need of the hour that the sons of this nation have to remain disguised to escape the eyes of the foreign enemies!' replied Rash Behari and asked Pingle to take a seat.

Thus began a historic meeting of the three men, within the silent quarters of the house in Bangalitola. Pingle spoke vivaciously and told his new allies everything about the background of the Ghadar movement, the formation of the Ghadar Party and the audacious plans of the Ghadarites. Rash Behari and Sachindra Nath listened to him eagerly and deliberated over what they understood of the aspiration of the Sikhs and others abroad.

---

13 Historical facts taken from: *Two Great Indian Revolutionaries-Rash Behari Bose & Jyotindra Nath Mukherjee* by Uma Mukherjee, page numbers 123-124.
Judgement in the Lahore Conspiracy Case, as delivered by AA Irvine and TP Ellis and Sheo Narain, Special Commissioners on 13 September 1915.

Finally, Pingle said, 'The latest blow has come from the *Komagata Maru* incident. The loss of life and blood of the innocent passengers is a stark example of the brutality of the British Raj.'

Pingle looked at Rash Behari for a moment and then said, 'Four thousand men of the Ghadar Movement have already arrived in India and thousands of others from Punjab have sworn their allegiances. Hundreds of Sikhs are arriving soon, and an equal number of men are waiting to join, as soon as the revolution begins.'

Rash Behari's eyes sparkled on hearing this, He had a vision of a dream that he had dreamt for ages. United with the Ghadar movement, his dreams were now destined to come true. While Rash Behari was ecstatic at the turn of events, a shadow loomed large on his visitor's face. Pingle continued to speak. 'In October, we had sailed from America to India. Midway, we halted in China to meet Ghadar leader Tahal Singh, who was tasked to carry forward the movement in Bangkok. In the last two months, thousands of men from the Ghadar Party, including significant members like Udham Singh, Nidhon Singh, Mula Singh and Nawab Khan, have set foot in Punjab with the flaming desire to create an uprising. Throughout these two months, these men have attempted several acts of rebellion but unfortunately, not one of these acts of dissent have succeeded. Many attempts have been aborted. Alas, all our efforts are simply proving fruitless.'

Rash Behari sat listening to Pingle with great attention. Pingle continued, 'The reason for this is not a lack of valour. I have studied the causes of our failure, along with the prime members of the party. Honestly, our conclusions are two. First, we do not have proper arms and ammunitions against the sophisticated weaponry of the mighty enemy. Secondly, the Ghadar movement in India needs the guidance of a LEADER. Yes, we need a leader who can consolidate the sentiments of the masses and lay out the road for our revolution. Please give us the strength of your authority and... please become our leader.'

Pingle's touching words pierced Rash Behari's heart. His eyes became moist and his determination firmer. He held Pingle's hands and said, 'From today, the Ghadar movement is my life's greatest purpose! From today, I promise to become one among you. I swear, Bengal and the Northern Provinces will fight together and create the Ghadar Revolution. Our united efforts will strike the British Raj like a great storm.'

Pingle was elated by his success. At last, the leadership issue plaguing the Ghadar movement had been solved. Instead of the scattered acts of violence, their efforts would be collated and channelised. The meeting had been a grand success.

He said with a smile, 'Jatin Mukherjee was correct. You are a magnificent person. Under your magical guidance, the Ghadar movement will become successful. The time is ripe. The British Army is busy in foreign lands while a worldwide war is raging. We must strike at this precise moment.'

Rash Behari replied thoughtfully, 'With Sachindra, you must travel to Punjab. Meet the Ghadar Party members and discuss my proposal of associating with the Bengal revolutionaries. Talk to them about the dream that I have been dreaming, along with Jatin Mukherjee. It begins with an armed uprising among the native soldiers of the British Army to overthrow the British soldiers in their respective cantonments. The entire nation will join in that revolution. With the downfall of the British Army at the hands of the native soldiers, the British Raj will not get a chance to retaliate and will be forced to accept defeat.'

This was a dream that took another thirty years to become real. But a realistic beginning had been made with the pooling of rebellious nationalist streams in different parts of the country.

Pingle's heart swelled with hope, and he stood up. Rash Behari said again, 'I, and the Bengal revolutionaries will supply the arms and ammunitions. Tomorrow, we must meet again and deliberate on exactly what you need to discuss with the men in Punjab.'

Then Rash Behari stood up too and added, 'Tomorrow I shall give you a flower. You must take it as my gift. Let my brothers in Punjab enjoy the fragrance of my creation and judge my abilities.'

With a heart full of anticipation, the next morning, Pingle arrived at Rash Behari's Bangalitola residence. Rash Behari was waiting for him, along with Sachindra Nath and a few other supporters. As Pingle joined the group, they silently went out towards a secluded section of the ghat of the Ganges River that flowed through this holy city. To Pingle's surprise, it was at a decrepit shack within a deserted wood beside the Ghat that the party of young men stopped.

Rash Behari and Pingle entered the shack while the others stood outside to guard the place. Pingle was fascinated, as if he was watching the unfolding of a fairytale. Inside the empty shack, there was nothing. However, Rash Behari sat down near a particular spot on the earthen floor and started to dig. As Pingle stood quietly, Rash Behari dug deeper for a couple of minutes and then, suddenly, he pulled out a metal-box. Carefully, he placed the box in front of Pingle and opened it with equal caution. Then, he took out something and held it in front of Pingle. The spherical earthen pot, of the dimension of an oversized cricket ball, stole Pingle's heart.

With eyes full of excitement, Rash Behari proclaimed, 'Behold… it's the FLOWER. It is my prized creation. She is a beauty. Take this with you. Don't panic, nothing will happen until the cap is placed properly on the top. You must take it with you to Punjab. Sachindra knows everything about it. To win the confidence of the Ghadar Party and its members, they must be convinced about my capabilities. Only then can I become an able leader for their revolution.'[14]

After this fantastic display, Rash Behari and the others quickly returned to the Bangalitola residence. Within the safe quarters of the house, they again congregated to discuss their plan. Rash Behari instructed Pingle and Sachindra in detail about what all needed to be discussed and finalised in Punjab. Hours went by and the planning continued.

Finally, Rash Behari said, 'While the two of you are in Punjab, I shall use my connections in Benares, Dehradun and Bengal to sensitise the native troops of the British Army. At the first opportunity, I will personally address them too. The success of our mission will depend on their confidence in us. Remember, the Uprising of 1857 can only be re-created, if, and only if, the Indian soldiers of the British Army participate in the revolution.'

14Historical facts taken from: *Two Great Indian Revolutionaries-Rash Behari Bose & Jyotindra Nath Mukherjee* by Uma Mukherjee, page numbers 125-127.
Judgement in the Benares Conspiracy Case, as reported in *The Statesman* newspaper on 15 February 1916.
The dramatisation is by the author. No written records exist for such a secret meeting.

UNITED WE STAND

SOON, SACHINDRA NATH and Pingle left for their mission. Rash Behari remained hidden in Bangalitola. However, with his secret network of faithful nationalists, he remained in touch with Amarendra and Jatin and carried out the objective of convincing the troops within the fraternity of native soldiers of the British Army.

Sometimes dressed as a Pathan, or sometimes disguised as a woman, Rash Behari attended secret meetings to motivate the youth to join hands in the armed struggle for India's freedom. The prying eyes of the intelligence services were always searching for him and the atmosphere was too hostile for Rash Behari to take the risk of getting caught. He had to be extra vigilant now, as the success of the Ghadar Party too depended on him.

As time passed, the combing efforts of the police too increased. This was a result of the growing frustration of the imperial rule at their failure to capture just one man. At one point, to ensure greater security, Rash Behari had to even abandon his Bangalitola hideout and move to a safe house in Harish Chandra Ghat Road.

In Punjab, events were moving at a pretty fast pace. In Kapurthala, Pingle convened a meeting with some important leaders of the Ghadar Party. He knew what he had to tell them. Prominent members like Amar Singh, Nidhon Singh, Kartar Singh, Ram Saran Das and Bhai Parmanand attended the top-secret meeting.

Pingle told a room full of emotionally charged and ambitious men, 'The time has arrived to unite the radical efforts of Bengal and Punjab. Our objective is the same. Our valiance is the same. So why are we not united? The Ghadar Party and its goal is sky high. However, it is true that we lack organisation and a leader who can plan and lead us forward. Joining hands with Bengal and with their proven record of success, I can foresee the fruition of our dreams. We lack arms and arsenal. They have that strength. They need to reach out to Northern Provinces and willing fighters. We have that strength. Together, it will be a unique cooperation of the two frontiers against one opponent. They have a man with unparalleled capability, who can lead us forward.'

One of the men eagerly said, 'I feel motivated by your words. I have faith in what you believe. However, who is this man?'

Pingle beamed with pride and said, 'He a valiant Tiger from Bengal. He has the fire within his heart and his eyes, that can miraculously take our revolution towards its victory.'[1]

---

1 Historical facts taken from: *Two Great Indian Revolutionaries-Rash Behari Bose & Jyotindra Nath Mukherjee* by Uma Mukherjee, page numbers 126-127.
Cross-referenced from: Atul Krishna Ghose's statement as recorded in *Banglay Biplab-bad*, Page 320, by Nalini Kishore Guha.
Agni Diner Katha by Satis Pakrasi, 1947.
India as I Knew It by Michael O' Dwyer.

Members of Ghadar Party

Another man said, 'Can you tell us his name?'

Pingle knew that Rash Behari Bose's name had to be kept a secret during the entire course of events. So he smiled and only said, 'I can only say, a Bengali Babu has agreed to help us. He is our messiah now.' Though many took this at face value, Pingle knew people needed to be really convinced. Satisfied with the first meeting, Pingle went ahead to conduct many more. He knew, time was short, and he had to do things fast.

Rash Behari felt heaven's doors to his dream had opened. Collaborating with Bagha Jatin, he secretly started to draw up the plans for the pan-India uprising. The political scenario was volatile and Rash Behari Bose was now permanently based in Benares, from where he was constantly in touch with Jatin Mukherjee, Amarendra Chatterjee and Aurobindo Ghosh. At the same time, he also continued his experiments with making improvised explosives that would be useful in their future struggles against the British.

Time was running out and the ground for revolution needed to be set. On the 31st day of December 1914, another significant meeting was held at Virpali Dharamshala, Amritsar. Important members like Kartar Singh, Harman Singh, Paramanand, Balwant Singh, Nidhon Singh, Mula Singh and many others were present. Pingle still didn't want to reveal Rash Behari's identity. However, the abilities of the Bengali revolutionaries were unchallenged and proof enough to convince the Ghadar Party members.

Pingle spoke in a sober tone, 'I assure you about the efficacy of the plan. The Bengali Babu is a man of enormous competence. For the last few weeks, we have been able to gain the confidence of a significant number of native soldiers of the British Army.

The involvement of the British soldiers in the World War and their scanty presenc in India is a boon in disguise. This is the perfect time to assault them. The Uprising of the Indian Sepoys now will result in a massive victory. The Ghadar Revolution will bring valour and dignity to our countrymen.' Time moved on and a consensus was attained and the members felt elated as their nascent ideas gradually took shape. Pingle was happy about the results of his meetings. He had been diligently doing all that Rash Behari had instructed him to do and say.

Enthusiastically, Kartar Singh said, 'We are always prepared for Ghadar. We are prepared to die for our motherland. Yet, for the success of this mission, we need to contemplate a few important things. One such significant factor is finance. We will have to loot treasuries and have to consider contribution from the masses. Next, we will have to convince more and more troops and win their full allegiance.'[2]

Balwant Singh came with the last question, anxiously he asked, 'We have all the plans in place. However, we lack arms and ammunitions. How are we going to overcome this barrier? How will your Bengali Babu help us in this?'

Pingle stood up and replied, 'I have brought a gift from our Bengali Babu and I want to show that to all of you. It's a beautiful flower and it has mesmerised me. I am sure, it will do the same to you as well. Once you see this gift, all your doubts will be answered.'

---

2 Historical facts taken from: *Two Great Indian Revolutionaries-Rash Behari Bose & Jyotindra Nath Mukherjee* by Uma Mukherjee, page numbers 129-130.
Cross-referenced from: Atul Krishna Ghose's statement as recorded in *Banglay Biplabbad*, Page 330, by Nalini Kishore Guha.
Agni Diner Katha, by Satis Pakrasi, 1947.
India as I Knew It by Michael O' Dwyer.

Pingle looked at everyone present in the meeting and finished, 'Tomorrow, at Sant Gulab Singh's Dharamshala, I shall show you this rare flower.'

The next morning, at dawn, the group congregated at a secluded spot near Sant Gulab Singh's Dharamshala. Along with Pingle was Sachindra Nath, who had been touring the Northern Provinces, especially Punjab, and meeting Ghadar party members regarding the possible association between Bengal revolutionaries and the Ghadarites. Pingle addressed the group and said, 'Today, with me is a special person. He is a representative of the Bengali Babu and a man who has been active in carrying forward the torch of the Bengal revolutionaries in the Northern frontiers. Now, in the auspicious presence of all of you valiant people, let me showcase the prized gift… the flower.'

Pingle then took out a spherical earthen pot from a box and held it high. The group looked at it with awe, while Pingle handed over a ball-like object to Sachindra Nath. It had a cap. Sachindra removed the cap and inserted it in the right position, on the bomb. Then, waiting awhile and taking a deep breath, he lobbed the bomb towards an empty spot. The group stood spellbound as the bomb zoomed across space and landed on the ground with a thud. Then… with an enormous dazzle of fire and sound, it exploded like an active volcano.

The jolt of the blast broke the silence as the men shuddered at the power of the bomb. A collective murmur arose, 'Perfect! This is perfect! The FLOWER is indeed most precious.' The mood was joyous. Pingle and Sachindra Nath looked at one another and smiled a satisfied smile. The exhibition had made a significant impact on the members of the Ghadar Party and it was enough to win their confidence on Rash Behari Bose's behalf.

Flag of the Ghadar Party

A gratified Pingle announced, 'I think we don't have any further doubts. Let me reiterate the assurance that is reverberating within everyone's heart… We must bring the Bengali Babu here to Punjab. He is our messiah now.'

The Amritsar meeting was a grand success and sealed the fate of Rash Behari with that of the Ghadar Revolution. On 12 January 1915, Pingle secretly received an amount of five hundred rupees from the Ghadar Party, on behalf of Mula Singh. Pingle handed over the five hundred rupees to Sachindra Nath. A safe house was secretly secured at Mussalman Attari (an Amritsar suburb, now closest to the Wagha border) for Rash Behari to hide in. Sachindra then returned to Benares and met Rash Behari.

With a world war raging, British soldiers were engaged in various fronts, providing the Ghadar movement opportunity to create a chain of mutinies among the existing British Indian forces stationed in India that comprised numerous Indian soldiers. Rash Behari Bose was now an active leader of the entire movement along with the other prominent members of the Ghadar Party in India.

Around early January 1915, a top-secret meeting was called at Rash Behari's residence at the Harish Chandra Ghat Road in Benares. Prominent revolutionaries like Sachindra Nath,

British and Indian Soldiers in World War I

VG Pingle, Damodar Swarup, Narendra Nath Banerjee, Jamna Das, Vinayak Rao Kaple and Bibhuti Bhushan Halder attended the urgent meeting.[3]

Inside a closed room, the men assembled sat around a table. Rash Behari presided over the meeting. Several secret meetings had already been conducted to plan out a coordinated and synchronous attack. Numerous suggestions and ideas had been generated about the nature of the revolution. Yet, the final blueprint was kept a secret.

Rash Behari addressed the gathering and started the conversation, 'The much-appreciated association of the

3 Historical facts taken from: *Two Great Indian Revolutionaries-Rash Behari Bose & Jyotindra Nath Mukherjee* by Uma Mukherjee, page numbers 126-127.
Cross-referenced from: Atul Krishna Ghose's statement as recorded in *Banglay Biplab-bad*, by Nalini Kishore Guha.
Sedition Committee of 1918.

Narendra Nath Banerjee

Ghadar Party and the Bengal revolutionaries have opened the doorway that leads to paradise. Vishnu Ganesh Pingle has returned with the fantastic news about a successful vote of confidence from the members of the Ghadar Party. Yes, the amalgamation is complete. Now, I can gladly declare that the country-wide coordinated Uprising is scheduled for February 1915.'

A murmur filled the room and Rash Behari felt positive vibes all around. He continued, 'We must be fully prepared now. I will personally travel to Punjab, along with Pingle and Sachindra Nath and meet the members of the Ghadar Party. Along with Pingle, I shall visit the Indian troops and try to win their complete confidence in this Uprising. Moreover, my biggest duty in Punjab will be to prepare the weapons for carrying out this mammoth revolution. Yes, I will personally oversee the manufacturing of the bombs.'

Rash Behari took a pause and then announced, 'The time has come when we are finally ready to die for our country. Today, we have congregated here for an important decision. Everyone present in this room, and a few others who are not here now, have a huge duty to fulfil and I am sure we will do so with all our beings.'

As a long night began, he stared at everyone and said with a great deal of conviction, 'This revolution is going to be unlike any other. It will be a countrywide explosion that will uproot the foundation of the British Raj. I have chalked out a meticulous plan that needs to be carried out with utmost precision. Damodar will be the leader at Allahabad. Bibhuti and Preo Nath will travel to Benares and win the confidence of the native soldiers. Nalini Mohan will be responsible for carrying out the mission at Jabalpur. Narendra Nath and Preo Nath will be vested with the phenomenal task of bringing the weapons from Bengal to UP, while Vinayak Rao and Hem Chandra will transport them to Punjab. This is again a critical task and nobody must get a hint of what is conspiring. Thereafter, Vinayak will go to Kanpur to take charge locally.'

Taking a quick look at everyone, Rash Behari added, 'Pingle will be primarily responsible for winning the confidence of the troops in the Northern Provinces and act as the pivotal bridge between the Ghadar Party and the Bengal revolutionaries. Two members, Kalipada Mukherjee and Ananda Charan Bhattacharya, will remain as reserves in Benares.'

The gathering was astonished by Rash Behari's meticulous planning. The latter continued with full energy, 'I have requested Jatin Mukherjee and Atul Krishna Ghosh to come to Benares at the earliest, so that we can get their expert guidance and I am able to bestow upon them the commands of Bengal, before I leave for Punjab.'

As the night grew deeper, under the flickering light of the earthen lamps, Rash Behari took out a huge stack of handwritten papers and said, 'These are the plans that I have formed, and they are extremely important for the success of this mission.'

'Remember, apart from the assault that we will carry out,

it is particularly important to disrupt the communication lines of the enemy. Only by doing so, can we ensure that any contingency plans of the mighty British Army do not work. This will impair all their efforts to retaliate. Look, these are the plans of how we can blow up bridges, cut telegraph wires and destroy railway lines. Doing these at the relevant places will ensure the safety of our brotherhood of nationalists. Moreover, let us contemplate the looting[4] of treasuries to gather funds for our work. My friends, time is less, and we must act in haste. I urge all of you to study these hard, so that we can do the needful within the little time at hand. We need to act with full force at every location. Lahore, Rawalpindi, Dhaka, Benares Jabalpur and all other prime locations where Indian soldiers are stationed must create an earthquake to shake the pillars of the imperial rule.'

As the atmosphere became charged with excitement, a shadow passed across one of the closed windows. Instinct made Rash Behari wary, and he turned his attention towards the closed shutters of the window. Sachindra Nath saw this and went out stealthily, while Rash Behari carefully opened the window.[5] However, there was no trace of anybody outside that window.

---

4 By the middle of 1914, the militant freedom fighters in India had begun to network with what is known as the German Plot, or the Hindu–German Conspiracy, or the Zimmermann Plan. One part of it was funds collection for armed revolution.
Jugantar started to collect funds by organising a series of *dacoities* (armed robberies) known as Taxicab dacoities and Boat dacoities, says Charles Tegart, in his Report No. V on the seditious organisations. He mentions 'certain amount of success' in the contact that exists between the revolutionaries and the Sikh soldiers posted at Dakshineshwar gunpowder making factory.

5 The historical facts have been referenced from: *Two Great Indian Revolutionaries-Rash Behari Bose & Jyotindra Nath Mukherjee* by Uma Mukherjee, page number 141.
Information as per The Judgement in the Benares Conspiracy Case, as reported in *The Statesman* on 15 February 1916.

As Sachindra returned and nodded an okay, Rash Behari looked at the other members and said, 'Let us keep away all our suspicions and focus on our dream. We shall now disperse and must go ahead with full fervour to complete our individual duties.'

Yet, away from everyone's eyes, a shadow had emerged from the darkness of the dimly lit lane and vanished into the night's obscurity. Only destiny knew what it held for the future. As the final day came closer, Rash Behari worked hard to ensure that all aspects of his megaplan was completed safely. Within the next few hasty days, another series of meetings were organised. Jatin Mukherjee and Atul Krishna Ghosh had arrived in Benares and met him. This was another significant meeting where Rash Behari spoke his heart out to the man whom he had idolised.

Rash Behari looked at Jatin and said, 'In your eyes and because of your valorous temperament, I have gathered the strength to dedicate myself to this WAR. Bless me, so that I may succeed in my endeavours. I don't know what the future holds for me, but I am confident that my fight will not be an ordinary one.'

Sitting inside a dingy hideout, Rash Behari explained the details of his plans. He told his visitors about the progress that had happened in uniting the Bengal revolutionaries and the Ghadarites. He revealed the entire blueprint in front of his guests and then added, 'My plans are right in front of you. However, I have not invited you here to merely reveal my plans. I have an earnest request that I want to put forth to you....'

Jatin smiled and replied, 'Yes, my brother. Tell me whatever is there in your heart. Be fearless in revealing what you desire.'

Rash Behari retorted, 'I want you to take command of Bengal. Yes, this is my earnest desire. While I dedicate myself in Punjab to formalise the last steps, I want to bestow the

Atulkrishna Ghosh

responsibility of the Bengal revolutionaries in your able hands. As the revolution explodes in Rangoon, Singapore, Amritsar, Lahore, Danapur, Benares and the entire Northern Provinces, the brave sons of Bengal must plunge into the war... with you as their leader.'

Rash Behari paused a while and then exclaimed, 'The time has arrived when we are finally ready to die for our country.'

Jatin Mukherjee pondered a bit and then asked, 'You have my full support. However, should we not wait for two more months for the arrival of firearms from Germany?'[6]

---

6 In 1912, Jatin Mukherjee had met the German Crown Prince during his visit to Calcutta and received a promise about firearm supply in India. Following this, he was allegedly involved in masterminding two plots, called the Christmas Day plots, supposed to precipitate armed rebellion among the British Indian soldiers. The uprising Rash Bihari and Jatin were planning was a good ten months before the second Christmas plot.
The Germans in Berlin, the Ghadar Party in North America, and the German Foreign office in India is said to have set up an Indian independence committee.
After Rash Behari's cantonment rebellions in February failed, the Jugantar activists planned another uprising across the country in December.
Scheduled for Christmas Day 1915, the plan was for an uprising in Indian cantonments, to be coordinated with simultaneous uprising in the British colony of Burma and Kingdom of Siam (Indo-China) under direction of the Ghadar Party, along with a German raid on the South Indian city of Madras and the British penal colony in Andaman Islands. The alleged aim of the plot was to seize the Fort William, isolate Bengal and capture the capital city of Calcutta, which was then to be used as a staging ground for a pan-Indian revolution.
The plot was ultimately thwarted after British intelligence uncovered the plot through German and Indian double agents in Europe and Southeast Asia.

Rash Behari knew that this subject would surface. He replied with confidence, 'No. We shall fight with our own ammunitions. When Naren Sen returned to Kolkata with definite information from Dhiren Sarkar about the formation of the Berlin-India Committee, I met him here in Benares. During a boat-ride over the Ganga at dusk, I discussed with him and received the letter that confirmed German readiness to help Indian revolutionaries. However, I was unsure about the uncertain element in the assurance. Hence, I have decided that we will proceed with our own indigenous plan. I have created the blueprint accordingly and I shall travel to Amritsar to begin setting up the secret bomb factory that will give us the weapons to carry out our fight.'

'Excellent decision', exclaimed Jatin, 'I admire your courage.'

Rash Behari smiled and said, 'The exact day of the uprising in February is yet to be decided. However, the plan is that the revolutionaries in Bengal will await the arrival of the *Punjab Mail*. It will be an apt signal telling you about the success of the first mutiny, since the newspaper will not arrive if the plans succeed. Soon, I shall disclose the date and together, we shall plunge into action.'

Jatin replied, 'I am hopeful, by that time, the arms from Germany will have arrived. The revolution will have an added grandeur with that firepower. My brother, Bengal is ready to plunge into battle.'

A few days before leaving for Amritsar in the end of 1914, Rash Behari met Anukul Chakraborty and Nagen Dutta. Within the secure setting of his Harish Chandra Ghat Road residence in Benares, Rash Behari told them, 'After another day, I shall leave for Amritsar. I have summoned the two of you here to reveal something very vital. In fact, I aspire to hand over a huge responsibility on your shoulders.'

In the presence of Kartar Singh, Sachindra Nath and Pingle, Rash Behari continued, 'Under the able leadership of Jatin Mukherjee, you must carry out the uprising in Kolkata. In Dhaka, you must seduce the Benares Regiment posted there and carry out the plans as per the blueprint. Remember, the outrage must spread like a wildfire across all corners of Bengal.'

Rash Behari arrived in Amritsar and reached the secret hideout at the Mussalman Attari house in Chowk Baba Atal sometime at the end of 1914. As he reached the den, he was greeted by members of the Ghadar Party. Despite being a top-secret meeting, it was perhaps a prophetic note in India's struggles for freedom.[7]

Mula Singh embraced Rash Behari with, 'Bengali Babu, today my heart is filled with hope and courage. Your charismatic personality, your somber baritone, your skillful hands and your valorous demeanor fill me with confidence that victory will be ours. Together, we shall bring freedom to our Mother India. Lead us ahead into revolution.'

In front of them stood two young men. Rash Behari was not previously acquainted with them, but he was told that they would be his assistants. Rash Behari said with a confident smile, 'Without wasting time, I shall begin the bomb-making process at the Sant Gulab Singh Dharamshala. These two bright young

---

7 Historical facts taken from: *Two Great Indian Revolutionaries-Rash Behari Bose & Jyotindra Nath Mukherjee* by Uma Mukherjee, page numbers 130-133.

men, Amar Singh and Ram Saran Das, will be my assistants.'

Mula Singh told them, 'More men will join you tomorrow and the bomb factory will soon be fully operational. Meanwhile, I have made arrangements for you to meet the troops. Your encouraging words of valour will inspire them to join our mission.'[8]

Rash Behari replied 'Yes indeed. Emissaries are being sent to Benares to bring more bombs from there. Hidden in biscuit tins, the arsenal will soon be here.'

Rash Behari personally visited several cantonments and met the native soldiers in the Punjab and northern areas. Disguised as an Army Officer, Rash Behari convinced them, using his magnetic words, 'This is the golden opportunity that destiny has provided us with. With a war on in the West, the British Raj is most vulnerable no. We have prepared ourselves with everything, starting from a foolproof plan to acquiring the necessary weaponry. Let us overthrow the foreign rule and bring freedom to our nation.' The eyes of his audience sparkled with hope and courage, as roars of enthusiastic voices rend the air with, 'We are with you. Yes, we are ready to even die for our country now.'

In Amritsar, Rash Behari ensured that the bomb manufacturing units were safeguarded. A second unit was set up at Jhabewal, but it was later transferred to Lohatbadi to ensure complete safety.

---

8 Historical facts taken from: *Two Great Indian Revolutionaries-Rash Behari Bose & Jyotindra Nath Mukherjee* by Uma Mukherjee, page numbers 126-127.
Cross-referenced from: Atul Krishna Ghose's statement as recorded in *Banglay Biplab-bad*, Page 320, by Nalini Kishore Guha.
India as I Knew It by Michael O' Dwyer.

BETRAYED

THE BEGINNING OF February 1915 was filled with anticipation. As Rash Behari sat with his accomplices, news arrived from Bengal that the police had intercepted several parties of revolutionaries engaged in the looting of arms and money from treasuries. An apprehensive Mula Singh said, 'Rash Behari, you must immediately abandon the hideouts in Amritsar. We cannot afford to compromise your security. The British Raj must never know about our Bengali Babu.' Sachindra Nath and Pingle were present in the meeting. A consensus was reached and Rash Behari agreed to leave Amritsar.

He said, 'Tomorrow, on 2 February, we shall relocate to Lahore. Indeed, this plan cannot be compromised. We must take separate routes and reach Lahore. Once there, we shall reassemble.'

Pingle added to the conversation, 'I will make all the arrangements. The parcel of biscuit tins will now arrive in Lahore.'

Rash Behari looked at his companions and said, 'Before we leave, send out emissaries across the Northern Provinces. They must reach every corner. Jalandhar, Peshawar, Rawalpindi, Kapurthala, Meerut, Ambala, Ferozepur, Kohath… every location must be covered to win the confidence of the troops. Remember, the success of this revolutionary uprising depends upon the mass participation from everywhere.'

According to plan, messengers of the revolution reached various army depots and regiments like the 16th Rajput Rifles at Fort William, 7th Rajputs of Benares and the 89th Punjabis at Danapur, while Rash Behari arrived in Lahore with his companions and took refuge in a top-secret den. Then Rash Behari convened an urgent meeting and summoned everyone.[1]

Soldiers of the 89th Punjabi Regiment

1 https://en.wikipedia.org/wiki/Ghadar_Mutiny#cite_note-35
The above link cross-references from: Ker, J C (1917), *Political Trouble in India 1907–1917, Calcutta*. Superintendent Government Printing, India, 1917. Republished 1973 by Delhi, Oriental Publishers, OCLC: 1208166.

In Lahore, inside the undisclosed hideout, yet another historic congregation took place on 12 February. While the principal members sat talking inside the room, others stood outside and guarded the den like a fortress. Within the room were present Rash Behari, Sachindra Nath Sanyal, VG Pingle, Mula Singh, Kartar Singh and few more important members of the Ghadar Party.

Rash Behari opened the discussion with, 'The Ghadar movement is about to make its mark on history. Twenty-six cantonments have sworn their allegiances to us. The native soldiers are ready to die for their motherland. Funds have been secured and the bombs have been made. Within our nation, the entire United Provinces, Punjab, Northern States and Bengal will fight in unison to overthrow the colonial rule.'

He looked at the sparkling eyes of the men within the room and continued, 'However, not just the regiments in India, but Indian soldiers in Singapore, Burma and many more colonial territories across Asia have joined hands with us to bring an end to imperialism.'

Taking a brief pause, Rash Behari added, 'And now I shall announce the date. Yes, the date that has remained hidden in my own mind so long. I will reveal that to all of you. Companions... the time has arrived.... The Great Uprising will take place on 21 February. On that day, we will have the first revolt in a cantonment against the British and unfurl a flag with three colours.'

An exuberant Pingle commented, 'Yes, a flag with three colours, the Red (signifying Hindu), Yellow (signifying Sikh) and Blue (signifying Muslim), will show our enemies that India is a united nation. Her sons have joined hands to oust their colonial masters.'[2]

Rash Behari continued with his high-voltage speech, 'My brothers, in the last few days, we must gather as much mass-confidence as possible. I will personally visit the villages and gain the confidence of the villagers. Secret emissaries will reach every location and inform the date. This is especially necessary for our brotherhood in Bengal, who are eagerly waiting for our signal.'

Mula Singh was beaming with confidence. He asked, 'What will be the trigger? How will we signal the commencement of the upheaval?'

Rash Behari looked at him and replied, 'At Mian-Mir cantonment, the first uprising in Lahore will serve as the signal. A chain reaction will begin, and revolt will break out at multiple locations, including in Rawalpindi, Ferozepur, Benares cantonments and subsequently trickle down to Bengal. As our comrades quickly uproot the telegraph lines and destroy railway tracks, the British Raj will lose all modes of communication. The 23rd Cavalry in Punjab is prepared to launch the first protest on 21 February, followed by that of the 26th Punjab, while the others will follow in sequence. The damage will be done swiftly, even before they realise what happened and we will be able to overthrow the imperial rulers.'[3]

2 Historical facts about the flags were taken from: *Two Great Indian Revolutionaries-Rash Behari Bose & Jyotindra Nath Mukherjee* by Uma Mukherjee, page number 130. Cross-referenced from: *India as I Knew It* by Michael O' Dwyer. He mentions that rebel flags were confiscated in police raids in Lahore on 19 February 1915. One of them, O' Dwyer claimed, he had and held as souvenir. Page 202.

3 Historical facts taken from: *Two Great Indian Revolutionaries-Rash Behari Bose & Jyotindra Nath Mukherjee* by Uma Mukherjee, page numbers 130-140. Cross-referenced from: *India as I Knew It* by Michael O' Dwyer.

As the entire room broke into cheers of joy, the names of the junior members were selected, who would act as the messengers for the entire plan. These junior members were not in the radar of the British Police and were thus the safest ones for the job.

Rash Behari closed the meeting with the electrifying words, 'The cyclone is about to strike. Let us welcome it. May this storm wipe away the shackles of captivity from our Mother Nation.'

The Traitors

Among the junior members of the Ghadar Party was a man called Kirpal Singh. He was not privy to any core group discussion but did odd jobs for the organisation and was often used as a guard for the premises where meetings were held. However, this was not his first appearance at Rash Behari's secret meetings. In January 1915, the shadowy figure who had eavesdropped on the meeting at Harish Chandra Ghat Road residence of Rash Behari, was none other than Kirpal Singh himself.[4]

Having heard the conversations of the party high command in January, a surprised Kirpal Singh had managed to escape the eyes of the revolutionaries and had rushed to meet his Commanding Officer in the British Intelligence.

---

4 The historical facts have been referenced from: *Two Great Indian Revolutionaries-Rash Behari Bose & Jyotindra Nath Mukherjee* by Uma Mukherjee, page number 132.
Derived from 'The Sedition Committee Report', 1916, page 110.
More reference: https://en.m.wikipedia.org/wiki/Kirpal_Singh_(spy)
This is cross-referenced from Popplewell, Richard J (1995), *Intelligence and Imperial Defence: British Intelligence and the Defence of the Indian Empire 1904-1924*, Routledge, ISBN 0-7146-4580-X.

Clad in an untidy dhoti and kurta,[5] he entered the room of the Commanding Officer, Liaqat Hayat Khan, and sat on a chair while panting for breath.

The Commanding Officer blew a puff from his cheroot and asked, 'What news do you bring?'

Kirpal Singh paused a while and then blurted out whatever he had heard. Then, he added, 'They are planning to bring down the entire British Army in India with a revolution like that of 1857. They plan to create a bloodbath when the British Army in India is the most vulnerable....'

'Never!' shouted the Commanding Officer, 'Those traitors will never succeed. Who is the mastermind behind this plan? What is his name?'

Kirpal Singh replied, 'Sir, I don't know his name. I am a junior member, and we are not told much. I am the brother of a faithful British soldier and I can never see this disaster. I have kept a low profile within the group and try to gather as much information as possible. I only know that this mastermind is a man from Eastern India, whom everyone calls Bengali Babu.'

Liaqat Hayat Khan

'A Bengal revolutionary', screeched the Commanding Officer, 'We will teach him a lesson. I will immediately alert the CID. However, we

5 Dhoti, kurta, pyjama: Indian wear, a wraparound and a top.

shall not act immediately. Let them go ahead with their plans. Kirpal, bring me more information. I want to know the dates. On the day of their dreams, their Day of Victory, we will crush all their hopes and their mortal existence.'

Almost a month later, on learning of the date of the uprising, Kirpal Sigh again rushed to his Commanding Officer. However, this time, he was in Lahore. So, he needed to inform a British Agent who would pass on his information to his Commanding Officer. Taking utmost precaution, Kirpal Singh sneaked out and reached Lahore Railway Station. At the gate, he met a British Officer dressed as a civilian. Kirpal knew him. He came close to the man and whispered in his ears, 'Tell Commanding Officer Liaqat Khan that the Day of the Uprising is on 21th February. Tell him to come here immediately and arrest the radicals. Wire him my message urgently.'

Destiny was playing a game. By a stroke of luck, a faithful member of Rash Behari's team saw Kirpal Singh at the station and speaking to a British official. He rushed back to the Mochi Gate hideout in Lahore and told the revolutionaries what he had seen and heard. A distressed Sachindra Nath arranged a hurried core group meeting. The news struck him like a cataclysm.

'We must call off the Uprising', exclaimed Sachindra Nath. 'Pingle is in Meerut, we must inform him too. The native troops across the country need to be alerted to halt their plans. Hundreds of bombs have already reached their hands. They must stop immediately. I am apprehensive about a strong retaliation from the British.'

Rash Behari stood up and thumped the table with his fist. His somber voice echoed, 'There is no looking back now. We cannot be cowards. If the Uprising doesn't happen now, then it will fail miserably and will destroy the morale of everyone nationwide. We cannot afford to do that.'

Rash Behari added, 'Kirpal Singh must never get to know that we have discovered his game. Let him continue to play his tricks. We shall fool him. His punishment will come after we have achieved our goals.'

A question came in an earnest voice, 'Then what should we do now? We have been betrayed.'

'Not yet', replied Rash Behari. 'The Uprising will happen... but on 19 February. The storm will strike two days earlier. The British will not get a hint of this change.'

He looked at Sachindra Nath and said, 'Send out emissaries to inform everyone that the Day of the first uprising is now 19 February'. However, Kirpal Singh was not the only mole

Public execution of mutineers in Singapore
Creative Commons

among the junior supporters of the revolutionaries. Kirpal Singh soon learnt of the new date and the news reached the British Intelligence officers.

The morning of 19 February was grim. Inside the secured quarter of the Mochi Gate house, Rash Behari sat with Sachindra Nath, VG Pingle, Kartar Singh and a few other Ghadar Party members. The atmosphere was overloaded with anxiety and apprehension. Rash Behari spoke with his accomplices in a worried tone. 'Four days ago, the mutinies at Rangoon and Singapore were crushed by the British with an iron fist. My heart is breaking, and my eyes are weeping tears of blood. The traitors among my countrymen have led to this unbearable defeat. Our brothers are being tortured and shot like dogs. I cannot bear this pain.'[6]

Sachindra Nath consoled him and touched his shoulders. Rash Behari continued, 'Today is Doomsday. Either we shall succeed or we shall fail. Such a golden opportunity may never come again. Yet, I feel a rising hope in my heart that a good news will soon arrive. Let us pray for the success of our Masterplan.' The dreams of the Master Planner soared high, but once again the winds of destiny blew them away like the flame of a candle in the wind.

---

6 Historical facts taken from: *Two Great Indian Revolutionaries-Rash Behari Bose & Jyotindra Nath Mukherjee* by Uma Mukherjee, page numbers 135-145.
Cross-referenced from: Letters of Amarendra Nath Chatterjee dated 4.8.54 and 4.9.54 in Jadugopal Mukherjee's book, *Biplobi Jiboner Smriti* and an unpublished manuscript, *Bharater Swadhinatar Itihas*, page 34.
Author interpretation based on historical facts from: *Rash Behari Bose: The Father of The Indian National Army Vol-2* by Elizabeth Eston & Lexi Kawabe.

At the 23rd Cavalry in Punjab, the 26th Punjab, 7th Rajput and the Jat Artillery, the native soldiers woke up with a new dream in their eyes. But their sleepy eyes soon saw that the entire Indian contingents of soldiers were surrounded by a heavily armed British Army who charged at them, overpowered them and captured them. They cried out in despair, 'Oh cruel destiny, what have you done? We won't be able to die in peace. This is unfair. This is injustice in the eyes of God.'[7]

At the cantonments of Ferozepur, Lahore and Agra, with bombs in their hands, the native Sepoys and soldiers attacked their outnumbered British counterparts. However, as they struck their assault, their hearts sank. Reinforcement poured in for the British, even as hand-to-hand skirmishes began and the rebellions were soon crushed, and the native soldiers were shot. Hundreds of Ghadar Party members across the Northern Provinces were waiting in their hideouts to hear the news of victory. Policemen from the CID and British soldiers stormed their bastions. The Gadhar Revolution now faced death.

At the Mochi Gate house, nobody was aware of the horrific scenes unfolding across North India. Nonetheless, something even more horrid was about to happen. As the leaders discussed various issues, a young member of the party rushed inside the room. His face was pale and his expression clearly fearful. 'The

---

7 The historical facts have been referenced from: *Two Great Indian Revolutionaries-Rash Behari Bose & Jyotindra Nath Mukherjee* by Uma Mukherjee, page number 140. Derived from 'The Judgement in Lahore Conspiracy Case'.
https://en.wikipedia.org/wiki/Ghadar_Mutiny#CITEREFKer1917
The above is cross-referenced from: Majumdar, Bimanbehari (1967), *Militant Nationalism in India and Its Socio-religious Background, 1897–1917*, General Printers & Publishers.

British… the British Army and the CID policemen are here. They have surrounded this house. We are all finished.'

Rash Behari replied quickly, 'So, that is why the traitor Kirpal Singh is sitting in the corridor from the morning. I guess the police is waiting for his signal. We must be quick now. Pingle, Sachindra Nath and Kartar, escape through the window behind the kitchen. You won't get noticed. I will stay here, and my voice will assure Kirpal that we are still indoors. Meanwhile, I shall use my biggest weapon… my disguise to fool those British soldiers.'

As Pingle, Sachindra Nath and Kartar Singh fled from the premises, Rash Behari went inside silently and took out his prized briefcase. However, a commotion started outside and Rash Behari heard the voice of a British Officer, ' Don't let anyone escape.' The police stormed the Mochi Gate house and began a thorough combing operation. They ransacked everything and arrested the revolutionaries still present in the Lahore house.

However, even as the grand dream of revolution crumbled, the police failed to notice a nondescript man, timidly carrying night soil on his head and leaving the house. The man nervously walked past the officers, who shoed away every passing spectator. This timid man was actually Rash Behari Bose in disguise. So skillful was his disguise that he was able to escape from the location and quickly reached a secluded lane. Then, he took out another set of disguises and like a chameleon, within a flash of a moment, he changed into a fierce Pathan.

At the Lahore railway station, the Pathan met with an accomplice and boarded a train to Benares. As the gigantic locomotive slowly moved out from the station, the Pathan looked at his companion and whispered, 'Pingle, you must get off at Meerut. You need to gauge the pulse....'

With tearful eyes, Pingle said, 'My heart is paining beyond all imagination. I cannot believe that a traitor has trampled our dreams to dust. I feel so much despair. This cannot happen. We cannot let this happen.'

Rash Behari looked at Pingle and said, 'We must not shed tears. Perhaps, today is not the day of glory. Perhaps, that is what destiny has ordained for us. However, we are fighters. We must never give up. I shall never surrender as long as I am alive. And the British will never be able to capture me. I promise you, we shall fight, strive and finally bring Freedom to our motherland.'

At the Meerut station, Pingle got off the train and vanished in the crowd. Within the relatively empty compartment, Rash Behari, dressed as a Pathan, folded his arms and dug his head within their hollow. Tears didn't come from his eyes. However, his heart wept tears of blood, as he knew that his biggest plot so far, his Masterplan, had failed to make a landfall. The Ghadar Movement had just been totally crushed.

In Kolkata and Chandannagor, the Bengal revolutionaries received the news of the failure and their hopes were washed away by a tsunami of despondency. Yet, it was the harsh truth. Across the Northern Provinces, within the next few days, thousands of Ghadar Party members were arrested. Their fates were already sealed. The gallows awaited their heads. Almost all major leaders of the Ghadar Party were chased out of India or arrested. However, despite every effort, the notorious Bengali Babu could not be found anywhere.

The British Raj was elated by its massive success in quelling

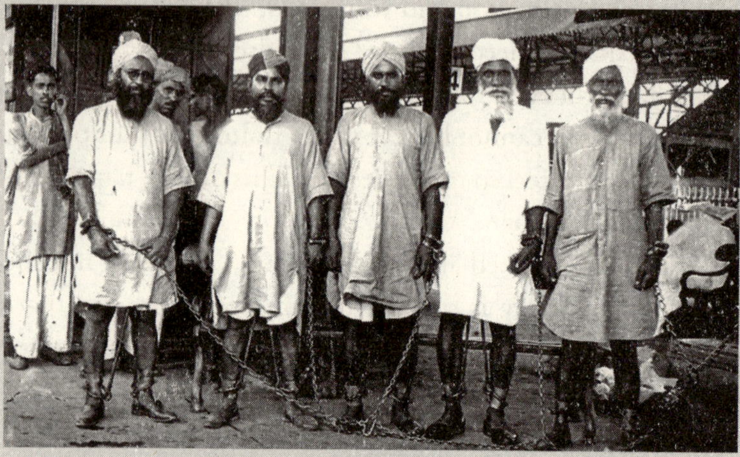

Arrested members of Ghadar Party

the rebellions. The buzz within the government was, 'If the mutiny had not been prevented, the damage would have been colossal. The coordination and the meticulousness of the plan was perfect. Had the CID not received the timely intelligence on the dates, the foundation of the British Raj in India would have been massively jolted.'

In Benares, Rash Behari returned to a top-secret hideout and remained holed up. Even though the intelligence services were still in dilemma about his name, slowly they began to zero in on a single name among the revolutionaries from Bengal.

During an urgent meeting, in the presence of Amarendra and Sachindra Nath, Rash Behari stated, 'The safety of the brotherhood in Benares and Bengal are of utmost importance to me. I urge all of you to become completely invisible. Sachindra Nath, you must immediately go to Chandannagore to seek refuge. My friend Shrish Ghosh, with the assistance of Moti Lal Roy, will be able to conceal you. I shall remain here until the British get tired of hunting for me. Amarendra, you must remain engrossed in your routine work and elude all suspicion.'

Amarendra asked anxiously, 'The British are searching for you desperately. They even have your name and identity on their shortlist. How do we ensure your safety?'

Rash Behari replied, 'They will not be able to find me. As soon as things begin to settle down, I shall go to Chandannagore.' Thus, according to plan, a complete void was created around Rash Behari and he cut off all personal contact with his other colleagues, leaving the intelligence services frustrated that they were unable to capture one notorious man.

A month later, a visitor arrived at Rash Behari's hideout. Cautiously, Rash Behari opened the door and saw Pingle standing in front of him, along with a man whose eyes were blindfolded.[8]

Pingle silently signalled Rash Behari, while he led the two men inside. Then, for the next one hour, a relentless discussion continued to verify the allegiance of the stranger whom Pingle had brought with him. Finally, when both Rash Behari and Pingle were decently satisfied, Pingle introduced the man, 'This is Nadir Khan, an Afghan Jamadar[9] who has a decent following. With his aide, I wish to take forward the rebellion among the soldiers in Meerut.'

---

8 Historical facts taken from: *Two Great Indian Revolutionaries-Rash Behari Bose & Jyotindra Nath Mukherjee* by Uma Mukherjee, page numbers 140-147.
Cross-referenced from: The Note of Mr Cleaveland, Director of Criminal Intelligence, I B Records.

9 Jamadar: An Indian title of a group leader who commanded a group of Indian soldiers of the British Indian Army.

A shocked Rash Behari replied, 'No. Pingle, don't be desperate. These are difficult times and we must be absolutely cautious. A mutiny in Meerut would be suicide. All our credible friends in the cause are lost. How can you carry out such a mammoth task alone?'

Pingle clutched Rash Behari's hands and pleaded, 'My entire existence is dedicated to this uprising. I cannot die in peace if the revolution doesn't happen. Please allow me. Please grant me the permission. Even if I have to sacrifice my life, I shall do so. However, the uprising must happen. I will do that in Meerut. I have full faith on the native troops of the British regiment.'

Finally, Rash Behari agreed. He sat with Nadir Khan and Pingle and explained how the earlier uprisings had been planned. He explained to Nadir Khan how the bombs worked and even revealed that he had prepared almost three hundred bombs for the 12th Cavalry. Rash Behari even handed over a hand-written formula for manufacturing more bombs, if required. Finally, Rash Behari gave ten bombs to Pingle and said, 'My brother, take these ten bombs and go to Meerut. I trust your faith in Nadir Khan and his associates. Even though our Masterplan has failed, may your deep perseverance yield you success.'

That night, Pingle and Nadir Khan returned to Meerut. Next morning, Pingle went back to his den, while away from everyone's notice, Nadir Khan arrived at the quarter of a Commanding Officer of the 12th Cavalry.

Two days later, on 23 March, as an unsuspecting Pingle sat in his hideout with the stash of ten picric acid bombs, the Commanding Officer of the 12th Cavalry stormed the den. Even before the suddenness of the attack sank in, soldiers pinned down Pingle and captured him red-handed along with the ten bombs in his custody. Behind the officer stood the Afghan traitor, Nadir Khan, while the soldiers dragged away Pingle. All that Pingle could do was mutter, 'Traitor! God will never forgive you. My motherland will never forgive you.'[10]

The Commanding Officer growled, 'Whatever you may scream, you are definitely going to the gallows.'

The news of Pingle's arrest struck Rash Behari like a final blow. The simultaneous arrest of Shrish Ghosh in Howrah was another unbearable blow. Amarendra, the bearer of the news, said in an apprehensive voice, 'The CID has identified that the bombs in Pringle's possession are of the same kind as those used in the Delhi Conspiracy case. They have even discovered the identity of the Bengali Babu... Rash Behari. The British are now aware of who you are and are on a wild hunt to catch you.'

After a brief pause, Amarendra said, 'You must immediately go to Chandannagore and seek refuge. At least for a couple of days, you will be able to get asylum. Then, you can decide the next course of action.' A visibly upset Rash Behari muttered, 'Yes....'

---

10 Historical facts taken from: *Two Great Indian Revolutionaries-Rash Behari Bose & Jyotindra Nath Mukherjee* by Uma Mukherjee, page numbers 135-147.
Cross-referenced from: The Note of Mr Cleaveland, Director of Criminal Intelligence, IB Records.

HUNTED

THE FLIGHT FROM Benares on a night train brought Rash Behari to Chandannagore. Dressed as a Brahmin Pujari, he had escaped the eyes of the British policemen. Along with Nalini Mohan Mukherjee, he arrived in a place called Mogra and from there, with the help of Jyotish Sinha, reached Chandannagore.

An important meeting was convened in Chandannagore by Moti Lal Roy and Sachindra Nath. Rash Behari sat silently, contemplating the turn of events. Sachindra Nath started the conversation and said, 'The police are desperately searching for you. Their ultimate objective is to capture you and make an example of you. Posters have been put up everywhere and their spies are scavenging every corner to find you.'

Moti Lal Roy added, 'Whatever happens, we cannot afford to lose you. If you get captured, it will be a fatal blow to our Movement for Freedom. Rasu, you are our only hope. We cannot let you perish. You are too precious for the future of this country.'

Rash Behari smiled dryly and said, 'For the first time, I am clueless about what to do. Where shall I seek refuge? I now feel the futility of my dream of an armed uprising to overthrow the British with the help of the native troops. Perhaps, I was wrong. Perhaps, this is not the way forward. The lack of proper arms, proper training and insufficient funds makes the foundation of our dream weak. Traitors are many and their greed cannot be quenched by the money and power we command. Neither do we have the skill and acumen to identify such soft targets. To fight the mighty opponent, we must be like a national army that has skill, ammunition and money. Alas, all that is still a distant dream. Can we indeed achieve it?'

Moti Lal Roy added, 'Yes Rasu. Remember, a year ago, you had contemplated international aid and their help in defeating the Raj rule. That time, we had even procured a ticket for you to travel abroad and tour foreign lands to seek support for our cause of both military and financial nature. However, you had torn the ticket because you believed that your work in India was still incomplete. My friend, the time has now finally arrived. You must leave India and head abroad. You must leave the soil of your beloved nation to fight for her freedom.'

With shattered dreams and a broken heart, Rash Behari Bose now knew he had no other option but to agree with Moti Lal's suggestion and go away from his beloved motherland. Roy paused a bit and then said with determination, 'You must go… so that your motherland can be free. And I know the place that is apt for you. You must go to Japan. Yes, Japan is the country where you can take refuge and also work towards your mission.'[1]

---

1 The historical facts have been referenced from: *Two Great Indian Revolutionaries-Rash Behari Bose & Jyotindra Nath Mukherjee* by Uma Mukherjee, page numbers 135 and 136.
Derived from 'The Judgement in Lahore Conspiracy Case'.
More reference: *Rash Beharir Atmakatha* published by *Prabartak* in a monthly issues of Bengali calendar year 1331.
With all the information available today, one can say, Japan as a country of choice was made by the group as a lot of Ghadar Party activists were refugeees there already.

An element of surprise filled the room while everyone contemplated the idea. Finally, Rash Behari said, 'Alright! With a shattered heart, I will abandon my beloved country so that I can protect her dignity from a faraway foreign land. Yes, I will go to Japan. I must forsake my country so that I can fulfil my mission.'

Rash Behari looked at everyone present in the room and continued, 'Over the years, I have dreamt of and planned for a cyclone to strike the mighty British Raj. The treachery of a few ignorant souls has destroyed my dream. But my confidence is strengthened by the faith of my countrymen. It can never be broken. Even if I am never able to see my country and my countrymen again, I shall remain happy and dedicate my life to realise my dream of a free India.' The setting sun left behind a crimson hue as it sank beyond the horizon. Perhaps, even the sky wept at the sacrifice and courage of this brave son of Mother India.

'It is not easy to live the life of a fugitive in the town where I have spent my entire teenage', sighed Rash Behari. 'Time is running out and the hands of the Raj are closing in fast to grab me.'

Posters had been put up everywhere and rewards had been announced for anybody who could provide any information regarding Rash Behari. Even in the streets of Chandannagore, policemen kept a strict vigil to catch any suspicious person and question him.

For almost a month, Rash Behari had remained confined within the secret hideout in Chandannagore, camouflaged as a Brahmin priest. Only his most trusted lieutenants met him secretly. Plans were underway and his colleagues were working hard to ensure a safe passage for Rash Behari out of India.

Moti Lal Roy told him, 'You will be able to leave in a month's time. Poet Rabindranath Tagore is scheduled to travel to Japan very soon. As planned, we have created a fake identity for you. You will travel in the name of Preo Nath Tagore, aka PN Tagore, at about the same time.'

Rash Behari looked at Moti Lal attentively, while the latter continued, 'You will travel as a distant relative of the bard. In everyone's eyes, you are a rich patron who is travelling to Japan to make arrangements for the poet's reception in the foreign land.'

Sachindra Nath added with enthusiasm, 'With a watertight identity, you will be able to embark on your journey. In Japan, you will be received properly and provided shelter, arranged through German help. Then, through their assistance, you will be able to supply arms and ammunitions to India. Even though far away, you will be able to keep the flames of our struggle alive.'[2]

Rash Behari listened to what they said and then replied, 'Yes indeed. Our fight must never cease. I shall not let that happen. Tomorrow, I will visit Nabadwip. I need to meet Anukul Chakravarty. I must cross the last hurdle, that is, collect funds for this strange journey. With the help of Nagen Dutta, aka Girija Babu, I will be able to get that from Dhaka.'

Rash Behari was a meticulous schemer, but he had to go through strange tests. His disguise as a Brahmin priest was so perfect that he was able to deceive everyone. That evening, as

---

2 Historical facts taken from: *Two Great Indian Revolutionaries-Rash Behari Bose & Jyotindra Nath Mukherjee* by Uma Mukherjee, page numbers 135-147.
Rash Beharir Atmakatha in Asar, 1331 B.S. issue of the monthly *Prabartak*.

Rash Behari stepped out into the streets, a native policeman came towards him. Looking at the fast pace of the constable, Rash Behari was wary, but he held his peace and continued walking. To his great surprise, the native policeman came up to him, touched his feet in the customary Pranam, and took his blessing. Rash Behari felt relieved. He understood that the policeman had identified him as an auspicious priest and was taking his blessings.

A day later, Rash Behari reached Nabadwip and met Anukul Chakravarty. With specific instructions, Chakravarty was sent to some financers. Soon, Nagen Dutta arrived in Nabadwip with the required funds from Dhaka and met Rash Behari. Rash Behari then returned to Chandannagore hastily, along with Nagen Dutta.

Then one day in the hot summer month of May, in a secret room at Chandannagore,, Moti Lal said in an apprehensive voice, 'Rasu, we have procured a Second-Class ticket for you aboard the steamship, *Sanuki Maru*. The ship will leave Kolkata on the twelfth of this month. We only have a week at hand.'

Rash Behari smiled sardonically and said, 'I don't know whether I will ever be able to come back. However, I must ensure that this journey must not go in vain. The disguise of PN Tagore, the rich patron, is foolproof. My intuition, however, tells me... I have one last task left to perform.'

A few days before the scheduled departure date, Rash Behari arrived in Kolkata, along with his companions. Dressed elegantly as PN Tagore, Rash Behari stood in front of his companions and said, 'Moti Lal, go ahead and change my ticket. PN Tagore will travel on a First-Class ticket. His social position will not be justified if he boards the ship with a Second-Class ticket. I have thought much about it. This modification will also restrict any unnecessary frisking by the British officials. Tomorrow, I shall visit the office of the Police Commissioner and collect the identity card of Preo Nath Tagore. Let's see if they can identify me.' The plan was daring but faultless and went perfectly.

Inside a dingy room on the second floor above the Dharmatala Post-Office, Rash Behari invited his companions for one last meeting before he departed. The most trusted associates who attended the meeting included Sachindra Nath, Nagen Dutta, Damodar Swarup, Bibhuti Bhushan and Jyotish Sinha, aka Pasupati. Shrish Ghosh, his best friend, was in jail as was Pingle, one of his closest comrades. Jatin Mukherjee was in hiding, masterminding arms import from Germany.[3]

With a heart full of emotion, Rash Behari said, 'Tomorrow, as the sun rises on a fresh new day, I shall leave my motherland

---

3 In April 1915, Jugantar decided that Jatin Mukherjee should move to Balasore on the Odisha coast, which was selected as a safe place, being very near the spot where German arms were to be landed for the Indian uprising. To facilitate transmission of information to Jatin, a business house under the name, Universal Emporium, was set up, as a branch of Harry & Sons in Calcutta, which had been created for keeping contacts with revolutionaries abroad.

Jatin had moved to a hideout outside Kaptipada village in the state of Mayurbhanj, more than thirty miles away from Balasore.

Jatin had sent one of his close associates, MN Roy, to Batavia, to make a deal with the German authorities concerning financial aid and the supply of arms.

A network of anti-German Slavs in the USA exposed this plot by providing information to the British.

By July, the British authorities tightened their surveillance on the east coast, and sealed off all the sea approaches from Noakhali-Chittagong side to Odisha. Harry & Sons was raided and searched, and the police found a clue which led them to Kaptipada village, where Jatin was staying. On 9 September 1915, a fleeing Jatin Mukherjee was killed by the British police in an encounter near the Balasore station, led by Charles Tegart. Rash Behari had fled to Japan in May.

forever. Only destiny knows what is in store for me as I venture into this unknown journey. Tonight, all of you must disperse from here and vanish into anonymity. Yet, I urge you with all my heart… the WAR must go on. The flame of our fight must remain ignited until India sees her Freedom. Upon the able shoulders of Sachindra Nath and Nagen Dutta, I bestow the duty of carrying forward this torch.'

He took a deep breath and said, 'In this life, we may never meet again. However, our hearts will remain joined for eternity. Goodbye my brothers… in the hope of a New Dawn.'

The next day, Rash Behari boarded the *Sanuki Maru*. He sailed through the security with elan and mingled with the First-Class travelers. Even as the ship was about to depart, a posse of policemen hurried on board with orders to search for a suspected fugitive… Rash Behari Bose. The police combed the ship but they had to spare the First-Class passengers, as this would violate their privacy and social status. Not finding their fugitive, the police left the ship, apologising to the captain. Rash Behari watched them leave, sitting among the privileged, making polite conversation.

LAND OF THE RISING SUN

AS THE SHIP set sail, Rash Behari stood at the deck and saw the coastline of his beloved motherland gradually disappear beyond the horizon. His eyes brimmed over, but he wiped away the tears valiantly and went into his cabin. The Land of the Rising Sun awaited his arrival and a novel beginning loomed across the vast ocean in anticipation of India's Disobedient Boy.

The *Sanuki Maru* touched the shores of Japan on 5 June 1915. With almost no acquaintances and a fake identity, Rash Behari set his feet upon the foreign land with a great deal of apprehension. Not only was the country alien, but so also was the weather, the social etiquettes and the demography. Everything was new to him. He also wondered if his escape to Japan had become known to the British police. With a great deal of caution and deep determination, he went past all the security and in the next few days established his identity as the distant relative and emissary of Rabindranath Tagore, who had arrived in Japan to ensure a smooth reception in Japan for the poet.[1]

---

1 *Two Great Indian Revolutionaries-Rash Behari Bose & Jyotindra Nath Mukherjee* by Uma Mukherjee, page numbers 144.
Rash Behari Bose by Satyavrata Ghosh & Luis Fernandes.

Japan was a kingdom made up of a long chain of islands. The weather was extreme. The people's food and clothing very different from British India. The initial months were extremely difficult, as Rash Behari struggled to acclimatise himself with the new climatic conditions, new cuisine and culture. The barrier of language was also massive and Rash Behari decided to overcome all these hurdles before he proceeded to return to his activities related to the movement for India's freedom.

Tokyo and her people seemed very different to the man who had never stepped out of his own country. Yet, in the contrasting climate, in the scenic diversity and in the distinct social behaviour of the citizens of Tokyo, Rash Behari tried to find solace. His mind and body were still grieving for his motherland but he controlled his grief and tried to embrace the beauty of this foreign land. Soon, destiny again came to his aid.

A few weeks later, Rash Behari came in contact with a man of Indian origin. This man was Bhagwan Singh Giani, a staunch supporter of the Ghadar Movement.[2]

Rash Behari felt happy at meeting Bhagwan Singh. He knew about Bhagwan Singh and of his whereabouts. This was the first time that the two were meeting. Dressed in English clothing, the two men sat at a breakfast table, chatting about India. Bhagwan Singh said in an animated tone, 'For many years I have led the life of a fugitive, despite being a loyal son of

---

2 Bhagwan Singh was a prominent member of Ghadar Movement who had been deported from Canada and had fled to Japan. This is the most important contact Rash Behari Bose had in Tokyo. After reaching Japan, Rash Behari met Herambalal Gupta and Bhagwan Singh of the Ghadar Party.
The historical facts have been referenced from: *Two Great Indian Revolutionaries-Rash Behari Bose & Jyotindra Nath Mukherjee* by Uma Mukherjee, page numbers 142 and 143.

my motherland. Here in Japan, under Maulvi Barkatullah's shelter,[3] I found a new zeal. Together with him, I even held a meeting on board the *Komagata Maru* two years ago. Alas, the Ghadar Movement has suffered a terrible defeat, just because of some traitors working for the British.' Rash Behari was filled with disbelief. He just could not believe that there was another fugitive in Japan, just like him.

Bhagwan Singh Giani

3 Mohamed Barakatullah Bhopali, known as Maulana Barkatullah (7 July 1854 – 20 September 1927), was an Indian revolutionary politically very vocal. In the first decade of the twentieth century, he was very active in the USA. An erudite man, he came to Japan in 1904, where he was appointed Professor of Hindustani at the University of Tokyo. He was back in the USA in 1906, taking part in anti-British forums. He associated with Vivekanada's brother Bhupendra Nath Datta, who in 1908 had been invited by George Freeman to edit the *Free Hindustan* from the Gaelic American newspaper office, Tarak Nath Das went to New York to join his old colleague Datta at the time. Tarak Nath was a Ghadar Party supporter and an acquaintance of Rash Behari.
In March 1909 Barakatullah returned to Japan. In 1914 his appointment at the university ended.
In May 1914, Prof Barakatullah returned to San Francisco with Bhagwan Singh (alias Natha Singh), who was the granthi (priestJ of the Sikh Gurudwara at Hong Kong and joined the Jugantar and worked with Tarak Nath Das. He soon became a close associate of the Ghadar Party in San Fransisco.
With the outbreak of the War in August 1914, the Maulana supported the Germans against the British and by December 1915, had helped establish a Government of Free India in Kabul. The Maulana's associate Bhagwan Singh was in Japan and met Rash Behari in Tokyo. These Ghadar Party activists had a secure and powerful network in Japan and other Asian countries.

Bhagwan Singh continued, 'Maulvi Barkatullah is a professor of languages at the Imperial University of Tokyo. Under his tutelage, I have accustomed myself with the culture of Japan. With his help, I have been able to get the protection of Mitsuru Tōyama, a Japanese ultra-nationalist. He is the founder of Gen'yōsha, or the Black Ocean Society and the Kokuryūkai, or Black Dragon Society. A true Samurai, Mitsuru Tōyama is a man whose firm support for Pan-Asianism has created strong allies for him across the continents.'

Bhagwan Singh held Rash Behari's hands and said, 'Now, today my fate has united me with the man who has been the torchbearer of the entire Ghadar Revolution. Rash Behari, I feel honoured to meet you. Be fearless, I will use all my powers to ensure that you are well established here in Japan. The tale of your ordeals and struggles are not unknown to me. I am in awe of the zeal and the optimism you carry.'

Maulvi Barkatullah

'Bhagwan, I need two favours from you. First, I need to be conversant in the local language to overcome the communication barrier. Second, I need to get in touch with the German Consulate. Even though I know where the offices are, yet, I need a strong connection to connect me with the right person', Rash Behari told Bhagwan.

Bhagwan Singh replied confidently, 'Done! Both your wishes are my command. However, how can the German

Bhagwan Singh and Rash Behari in Japan

Consulate help you?'

Rash Behari replied, 'The Germans have tried to smuggle big cargoes of arms into India for our nationalist brothers. However, every such occasion has failed. I want to convince them about a different plan. Rather than big cargoes, we can send small consignments via land, through China and Burma, and help these packages reach the hands of our revolutionary brothers. My companions are still active within the country and a successful receipt of arms now will lift their spirits immeasurably .'

Bhagwan Singh was amazed at Rash Behari's cleverness. He replied with joy, 'Fantastic. I bet that the Germans have been contemplating the idea... but your participation will certainly make things perfect. I shall get in touch with the German Consulate and their agents and introduce you. They will, in turn, connect you with the German Consulate in Shanghai.'

In a few weeks, a secret meeting at the German Consulate was arranged for Rash Behari. The officials connected Rash Behari with a seasoned secret agent in the German Intelligence service, one Mr Neilson. The latter was an expert in collecting arms and gathering materials for making explosives. He managed four hideouts in Shanghai, where loads of these bombs were kept, safely away from the prying eyes of the Shanghai authorities.

Neilson met Rash Behari and Bhagwan Singh and said, 'Go to Shanghai and meet me at my residence in Yangtsepoo Road. The next steps of our plan will be framed there.'[4]

The world was now calling the man from a small Indian village who had been peripatetic since a teenager, never resting at any one place even within his country. Even before he could settle down in Japan, revolution dragged him away to yet another unknown land, about which he was completely unaware.

Together with Bhagwan Singh, Rash Behari traveled to Shanghai and reached the designated destination. A meeting was arranged between the Indians and the German Consulate in Shanghai. At the meeting, Rash Behari expressed his views on arming the freedom movement in India. 'I need guns and ammunitions to send back home. With the idea that I have just put forward, I hope we can be successful. My companions in India will receive the stash, I can assure you that', he promised. Neilson was appointed the secret service agent who would mentor the plan. The course of action was discussed in detail.

In a somber tone Rash Behari said, 'My trusted companion Amarendra Chatterjee will receive the stash. As I told you, the consignment needs to be small so that it doesn't come under the radar of the British Intelligence. As the goods are smuggled into Kolkata, Amarendra, along with Manmohan Bhattacharya will take charge of them. I even plan to send a messenger to India, who will carry verbal messages for my companions.'

---

4 Historical facts taken from: *Two Great Indian Revolutionaries-Rash Behari Bose & Jyotindra Nath Mukherjee* by Uma Mukherjee.
Cross-referenced from: Home Political Proceedings of the Government of India, November 1916; No. 44 Deposit, for the statement of Abani Nath Mukherjee.

Neilson replied thoughtfully, 'Yes, that will be great. I have made the necessary arrangements here. Two Chinese men will carry the small consignment of arms via the route that you have suggested. Once they reach Bengal, your men will take charge. Hope, this time, everything works fine.'

Bhagwan Singh had now fully dedicated himself to Rash Behari's efforts. He selected a man, Abani Nath Mukherjee, for the job and brought him to Shanghai for an urgent meeting.

Rash Behari met Abani in Shanghai and satisfied himself about his allegiance to the cause of armed struggle for freedom. Then, he gave him an anonymous handwritten notebook. Finally, he said, 'Pass on my messages to the people whose names are written here. I have full faith in you.'

For Rash Behari and Bhagwan, there was a long wait in Shanghai while their plan was actually being executed. Meanwhile, Bhagwan Singh ensured that Rash Behari became a familiar face among the Indian community in Shanghai and his presence was felt among those who supported the movement for bringing freedom to India.

Two months later, the consignment finally reached Bengal. Alas, the British authorities became suspicious of the two Chinese men and the consignment for the revolutionaries was seized. The police arrested the two men and a tormenting interrogation yielded vital information. Luck was still unfavorable for Rash Behari and his companions. Yet, more bad luck followed them.

Even before the arrest of the Chinese men, Abani Nath was arrested in Singapore and the British Intelligence confiscated the notebook with names from him. Even though Rash Behari's name did not surface, it was quite clear that some radical

Abani Nath Mukherjee

nationalists in several Asian cities were working hard to remain in contact with the ones in India and were supplying them arms and ammunitions with the help of the Germans. The Indian authorities were on the alert, 'The Chinese men were carrying 129 pistols and almost 1,2000 rounds of ammunitions. These were being smuggled into India by the Germans. Two men, Amarendra Chatterjee and Manmohan Bhattacharya were supposed to receive them.'[5]

By this time, Rash Behari Bose was identified as the 'Chief Indian Revolutionary Leader' by the German Consulate. Apart from this small consignments, Rash Behari even managed to send two shipload of arms to India with the help of Neilson and the Germans. Alas, yet again, these two ships were intercepted by the British and the arms were confiscated even before they reached India. Rash Behari shed tears of frustration before his friends, 'Every effort is being marred by destiny. Why God? Why? Why am I always being awarded such a fate?'

5 Historical facts taken from: *Two Great Indian Revolutionaries-Rash Behari Bose & Jyotindra Nath Mukherjee* by Uma Mukherjee.
Cross-referenced from: Rash Behari's written statement entitled, 'Our Struggle'.
The letter of Mr Cleaveland, Director of Criminal Intelligence, Delhi to Police Commissioner, Bengal dated 21 October 1915.

As the plans to send arms back to India became unsuccessful, Rash Behari decided to return to Japan. Along with Bhagwan Singh, he came back to Tokyo and started to think about the next course of action. In his own mind, he told himself, 'Despite every setback, I shall not stop. I shall not give up. Destiny cannot remain unfavorable forever. I must strive, as long as I am alive'

'The smuggling of arms has failed. However, I have another idea. Here in Japan, I shall create a buzz! It will be a buzz across Asia that will reverberate globally...ASIA FOR ASIANS! This will not be a simple task. It will take time, perhaps years. However, an awareness amongst the Asian countries will get us friends. India needs strong friends and allies who will support her need for FREEDOM. Yes, this must be my next piece of work.'

During a solitary moment, Rash Behari told Bhagwan Singh, 'My friend, the tactic of the war needs to be redefined. We just cannot keep sending arms to India to create a revolution. The revolution against colonialism has to happen across the globe. We need to generate empathy amongst Asian countries, Europe and the USA to create pressure upon Britain. Here in Japan, I wish to begin that silent battle. Yes, and I need you by my side to create that buzz.'

In Tokyo and throughout Japan, thus began Rash Behari's campaign to sensitise the Japanese about the ordeals that India and her children had been suffering for decades. With the assistance of Bhagwan Singh and his contacts, Rash Behari continued to generate friendly sentiments amongst the Japanese as well as in the Indian society residing in Japan. Within six months of his arrival in a country where he was completely unknown, Rash Behari was able to organise a big meeting designed to be attended by top-ranking Japanese politicians, newspaper editors, writers and public figures. Rash Behari did not leave any stone unturned to create a buzz in Tokyo's society for his Asia for Asians event.

The historic congregation was held on 27 November in Astar Hotel at Ueno Park, Tokyo. The grand event in 1915 was attended by many important people including Indian leaders like Lala Lajpat Rai, Heramba Lal Gupta, and Japanese opinion-makers like Dr Shūmei Ōkawa.[6]

The meeting commenced with the unfurling of the Japanese National Flag, followed by the singing of the Japanese National Anthem. The attendees were overwhelmed by the opening ceremony and in their eyes, Rash Behari saw a rare understanding and empathy for India, the land of the Buddha, enlightenment, friendship, and freedom.

Lala Lajpat Rai

Lala Lajpat Rai delivered a fiery speech that went straight to the hearts of the people present in the room. He concluded his speech with, 'Ladies and gentlemen, we the children of Mother India

6 T*wo Great Indian Revolutionaries-Rash Behari Bose & Jyotindra Nath Mukherjee* by Uma Mukherjee, page numbers 135, and 143 and 145.
Cross-reference by Uma Mukherjee: JG Ohsawa's *The Two Great Indians in Japan* (published 1954).
Rash Behari's written statement entitled, 'Our Struggle'.

have just narrated to you the agony that we have suffered at the hands of the British Raj for a century. We urge you, the honourable men of the Land of The Rising Sun, to extend your hands of friendship towards us, so that we may end this colonial rule soon.'

In his speech, Rash Behari expressed his unrestrained frustration and said, 'We have suffered enough at the hands of the colonial rulers. It is now time to end this suffering. ASIA FOR ASIANS… this is my motto. The entire human race in Asia must stand beside each other and strive for their security and freedom. Tonight, I request that support from everyone present here.'

Dr Shūmei Ōkawa[7] was a staunch critic of the British Administration in India. He too delivered a powerful speech, loaded with facts and evidences and tales of misery of the people of India.

The meeting was a grand success and created an uproar in the entire Japanese community and Rash Behari's call reverberated in the neighbouring countries of Asia as well. However, the British did not like it at all. News of the anti-British gathering in Tokyo hit the Raj like a typhoon, denting its prestige. By this time, the Raj government was convinced about Rash Behari's involvement in the Delhi Conspiracy as well as the Ghadar Revolution.

At an urgently-convened closed-door high-profile meeting, the British ambassador in Japan flexed his diplomatic muscles

---

7 Shūmei Ōkawa was a Japanese nationalist and Pan-Asianist writer, known for his publications on Japanese history, philosophy of religion, Indian philosophy, and colonialism. It is believed that he even sheltered Rash Behari Bose for a brief while.

Dr Shūmei Ōkawa

before the government of Japan and reminded it, 'The Anglo-Japanese Alliance fosters mutual cooperation to maintain harmony.'

The envoy pointed out, 'The fugitive Indian radicals, especially Rash Behari Bose and Lala Lajpat Rai, are present in Tokyo and are spreading venom about the British administration. This is intolerable. We urge their immediate arrest and extradition.'

The envoy said, 'The British Government demands speedy action against these men.' The outcome was that the imperial government of Japan issued an Extradition Warrant against Rash Behari and Lala Lajpat Rai. This was a disastrous outcome for the two, but the news reached them early through reliable sources. Lala Lajpat Rai quickly fled across the Pacific to America while a destitute Rash Behari became a homeless fugitive in a foreign land.

A SAMURAI LIFELINE

WITH BOTH, THE British and the Japanese authorities, hounding him now, Rash Behari fled from one shelter to another, in search of safety. The bitter winter season was almost at the doorstep, and he was virtually homeless. He was cold, hopeless and frustrated when, as if by divine intervention, a messenger arrived at his temporary hideout and took Rash Behari to yet another unfamiliar location. The messenger was a trusted aide of his faithful ally Bhagwan Singh and the two drove down the streets of Tokyo and entered the premises of a spacious house with a big garden.

As they alighted from the car, the messenger said, 'This is the house of Mitsuru Tōyama, the leader of the Samurai. My duty ends here.'

As the man left, leaving their shoes outside, Rash Behari and his friend entered the house with some apprehension. The entrance hall was decorated in a typical Japanese style. Waiting for him was a traditionally dressed Japanese man, Mitsuru Tōyama, who greeted Rash Behari with open arms. All his apprehensions vanished with Tōyama's magical touch and Rash Behari felt as if he was familiar with the man for ages.

Mitsuru Tōyama

One of the most respected men in Japan, Mitsuru Tōyama, had a thin yet strong stature. The long white beard and his wise intelligent eyes lent him a divine appearance and Rash Behari was instantaneously attracted towards him. Tōyama welcomed Rash Behari in an amicable manner and said, 'You are completely safe here. As you already know, I have extremely high regards for the freedom movement of India and her brave people. I am aware of your own supreme sacrifices and the tremendous valour that you have displayed. I respect you and I promise you that I will extend you all my help'.

Rash Behari held his hands and said, 'Thank you so much. I pray to god that this union of our souls is as pure as heaven's bondage.'

Tōyama smiled in return and then said thoughtfully, 'The British Intelligence and the Japanese authorities are searching for you frantically. In this situation, you need to remain concealed in a place where nobody will be able to find you until the situation settles down. Hence, I have thought about an apt hideout for you.' Tōyama pointed towards an window, outside which stood another Japanese man. He was a relatively elderly man with a calm face and a decent appearance. His attire had the shine of a well-off Japanese citizen.

Aizō Sōma

Tōyama looked at Rash Behari and said, 'That is Aizō Sōma, founder of the popular Nakamuraya bakery in Tokyo. He is a man of honour and is highly respected.'

Tōyama beckoned the man in and introduced him to Rash Behari. Then, Tōyama said, 'Aizō Sōma is an entrepreneur, philanthropist and patron of Pan-Asian politics. Just like me, he has extremely high regard for you and your country.'

Tōyama added, 'Rash Behari, you must remain under his protection. He is fully aware of the situation and is genuinely concerned about your safety. This morning, he came to me and told me he was anxious to do anything to protect a destitute man whose bravery is of high esteem. As a true Samurai, it is our duty to protect brave men in distress. I am confident, Aizō Sōma San will fulfil that duty efficiently.'

Outside, the local police had already surrounded the house. However, the officers were not sure about entering the house of a highly respectable man like Mitsuru Tōyama. They saw Rash Behari's footwear outside the door and waited patiently for him to come out. Tōyama and his men knew that the police were waiting for Rash Behari. Tōyama instructed Aizō Sōma and Rash Behari to leave through the unguarded back entrance of the garden, 'Dr Sugiyama's car is waiting outside', said Tōyama, 'The two of you must leave immediately. Even before the police get to know, you shall be in a safe place, away from their gaze.'

The bird had flown and soon the British Intelligence realised that, though far away from his own country, Rash behari Bose had gone completely underground and was not an easy man to capture.

Nakamuraya Bakery

Dressed in a traditional Japanese Kimono and hat, Rash Behari entered Aizō Sōma's house in the dead of night. Thus began a new chapter in the life of Rash Behari Bose.

As the door shut behind them, Rash Behari looked at the perturbed face of a woman, who scrutinised him with scared eyes. She was Kokkō Sōma, Aizō Sōma's wife. The couple ran the business of a bakery and restaurant that was popularly called the Nakamuraya Bakery.

Kokkō Sōma

Aizō Sōma told his wife, 'This young man is in grave danger. The Japanese Foreign Affairs Minister, along with the British Authorities, are planning to deport him to India. Alas, that means… he will be brutally killed once he reaches India as a prisoner.'

The docile and motherly Kokkō Sōma was a strong woman. She too was a person who truly cared for human bravery and courage. She agreed to conceal Rash Behari in their premises.

The night was dark, and the atmosphere was grim. Rash Behari was a fugitive foreign revolutionary in the house of a stranger. Yet, compassion bound his courageous hosts to him and provided him his umbrella of safety.

The next morning, Aizō Sōma called all his household staff and said in a resolute tone, 'My people, today I have taken a big decision. It is perhaps the biggest risk that I have ever taken. Danger looms above our heads, but I shall still undertake this task because it is for the sake of humanity and the true Samurai spirit.'

He pointed at Rash Behari, standing before them with him, and continued, 'He is a poor Indian revolutionary in exile. He is a man of great valour who has sacrificed much to bring freedom to his country, India. Alas, the Japanese and British police are looking for him, to deport him. He will surely be killed by the British. I am going to hide him within my house, in the attic, and protect him.'

Aizō Sōma looked at everyone and said, 'This is now an international affair and brings great danger to us. The Nakamuraya Bakery and everyone associated with it will face the wrath of the authorities if they discover this secret. Yet, as a fearless Samurai, I swear to give him shelter and protect him, unless he gets political asylum. We, the Japanese people, cannot let him die before our eyes.'

A brief pause followed while Rash Behari stood silently and observed the reactions of the bakery workers. Then, a chorus reverberated in the room, 'Very well, Master. We give you our word. We shall risk everything, including our lives, to protect him. We, the Japanese, the honest workers of Nakamuraya Bakery and the faithful people of Aizō Sōma, take oath that we will even sacrifice our lives to protect him.'

Tears appeared in Rash Behari's eyes, and he bowed low in the Japanese way to show his respect. He didn't have words to say. Perhaps he didn't understand much of the conversation that was happening in the local dialect. However, he sensed the sentiment. He was speechless with emotion. In his heart, he made a resolution at that time, 'From today, I shall embrace the Japanese as my own family. I can never forget the love, bravery and compassion that they have shown. From today, I shall dedicate myself to become a true Japanese. Deep in my heart, I shall remain a devoted son of India and fight for her freedom. Added to that resolution, I shall dedicate myself to the service of the Japanese people and do whatever I am able to do for them. I shall never forget this moment in my life!'

Aizō Sōma's house was adjacent to the Nakamuraya Bakery he owned. The shop was in the forefront and the household was behind it. Every day, many customers visited the bakery and Aizō Sōma and Kokkō Sōma were busy with running the bakery. The extended family of the Nakamuraya Bakery comprised many people. Other than the Sōma family, it included all the staff who worked in the business and the household. Strangely, not one person ever thought of betraying him to the authorities. As Rash Behari remained holed up either in the attic or in the basement, the couple often visited him for his daily needs. It was a strangely monotonous life, but Rash Behari chose to bear it patiently.

Hiding within the safety of the Nakamuraya bakery and the residence of the Sōma family, Rash Behari started a new life. Inside the dingy cellar, Rash Behari dedicated himself to learning the Japanese language, and the country's culture and politics. As he remained hidden within the folds of the Sōma family, a bond of affection grew between him and the people who had given him refuge.

Over time, Rash Behari became like a son to the Sōma family while Aizō and Kokkō Sōma became his loving parents. Kokkō Sōma was moderately comfortable with the English language. However, she avoided face-to-face interactions, fearing someone would see her talking to Rash Behari and report it to the authorities. She preferred to communicate with him in English through hand-written messages. But this too was extremely dangerous. What if the notes were intercepted… messages in English in a Japanese household? Yet compassion grew in her motherly heart for the young man hiding in her cellar.[1]

Meanwhile, the British Embassy in Tokyo grew frustrated by Rash Behari's disappearance from the city. They were sure he had not travelled out of the city. He could not have just vanished in thin air. In their frustration, they blamed the Japanese Foreign Affairs Ministry for Rash Behari's disappearance. It was a bitter blame-game and the political relations between the two imperial powers deteriorated. In their effort to appease the British, many eminent persons in Tokyo were questioned and accused of hiding Rash Behari. However, this yielded very little information about Rash Bihari's whereabouts.

Within the damp and cold chamber of the attic, Rash Behari kept himself concealed with utmost determination. It was not just a challenge of patience, but also a challenge of psychological stability. With limited resources and heavily curtailed human

---

1 Historical facts taken from: *Two Great Indian Revolutionaries-Rash Behari Bose & Jyotindra Nath Mukherjee* by Uma Mukherjee.
Rash Behari Basu: His Struggle For India's Independence by Radhanath Rath. The statements of his mother-in-law were noted in this book.

interaction, he tried to focus himself on visions of brighter days. Learning Japanese language kept him occupied and soon Rash Behari was able to cross the communication barrier with his hosts. With his novice accent but very amicable as a person, Rash Behari befriended the people who attended to his daily needs. In those long monotonous hours, he even learned from them about Japanese cuisine and culture.

It was 1916. The war in Europe was still raging and colonial India was very much a part of it. His fugitive status had put a halter on Rash Behari's active participation in the subcontinent's political struggle. The month was that of April and spring was in the air. Cherry-blossoms were ready to bloom, and an atmosphere of positivity was everywhere.

After hiding for four long months, like a gust of fresh air came some glad tidings. Aizō Sōma and Mitsuru Tōyama came to see Rash Behari in his hideout. A visibly happy Aizō Sōma said to him, 'At last the Extradition Warrant has been withdrawn. The impending threat of your deportation is now gone.'

Rash Behari breathed a sigh of relief. He felt he had won in this strange battle of nerves. He hugged his host as tears rolled down from his eyes.

Tōyama was a wise man. He sat quietly for some time and then said, 'The danger is not completely over. Even though the Extradition Warrant has been nullified, the British spies are still active. My experience tells me, they will now become hyperactive, anticipating that you will come out of hiding. They will have just one mission… to seek out Rash Behari Bose and kill him.'

Tōyama looked at the others present and after a pause, continued, 'It has come to my knowledge that the British spies have got a hint of Rash Behari's presence here, at the Nakamuraya Bakery. They know that you are here, in the house of the Sōma family. You must be moved from here, as soon as possible.'

Kokkō Sōma was listening to the conversation keenly. She commented, 'Mr Bose is still unfamiliar with the streets of Tokyo. Even though he is moderately conversant in the local language, but he is still a stranger here. How can we ensure his safety after he leaves here and starts living at a new location?'

Tōyama said, 'For that, someone has to be with him, whenever he ventures out. One of us needs to accompany him. Else, there is the danger of his being discovered anytime. Moreover, his location needs to be frequently changed, so as to avoid being discovered by the moles.' However, the Sōma household was no longer safe for Rash Behari, if Mitsuru Tōyama's informers were correct.

After long hours of discussion, it was finally decided that Rash Behari would relocate to a new hideout. The Sōma family and Tōyama's men would accompany him like shadows, whenever he needed to venture out. His urgent letters and secret correspondences to India would be handled by them as well. An agreement was reached between them and Rash Behari left, accompanied by Mitsuru Tōyama and Aizō Sōma. He said his goodbye to the Sōma family and thanked everyone in the household for all the love and security they had showered upon him.

Thus, despite the eyewash of the Extradition Warrant being withdrawn, Rash Behari spent several more months as a fugitive, hiding from the clutches of the Japanese authorities and the radar of the British Intelligence. It was just his hosts' Samurai spirits that kept him alive and well.

CHERRY BLOSSOMS

THEN, A WONDERFUL proposal changed the course of Rash Behari's life, perhaps forever.

One day, Mitsuru Tōyama came to visit the Sōma family and said to Aizō Sōma and Kokkō Sōma, 'Bose is still not safe. Attempts are being made by the British agents to capture him secretly and assassinate him. Moreover, it is impossible for you and my men to be his protector throughout the day and night. In this scenario, he needs a companion who will be like his shield. Thus, I have a proposal… a proposal that can change everything and perhaps bring him political asylum in Japan. Marry your eldest daughter, Toshiko Sōma, to Bose. With a familial connection with Japan, he will soon become naturalised in the country. Moreover, Toshiko will be with him always and thus be his protector.'[1]

The proposal was surprising and Aizō and Kokkō Sōma remained speechless for a while.

---

1 Historical facts taken from: *Rash Behari Basu: His Struggle For India's Independence* by Radhanath Rath. Pages 34-36. The statements of his mother-in-law were noted in these pages.

Then, Kokkō said, 'Please give us a month to ponder. Mr Bose has indeed become like our son, but we had not thought about such a proposal even in our wildest dreams. Let me speak with my daughter. She is still very young. I must seek her consent, before I can give my opinion'. In the world of politics and patriotism, unusual courage and Samurai convictions now entered cupid with his arrows.

In a few days, Kokkō Sōma sat with her young and docile daughter and told her about the Indian fugitive they were hiding, Rash Behari Bose. Then, she said, 'My dear, this is an extraordinary moment that I had never even imagined.'

'It is your life and you must take your own decision. You are, and will always be, my loving child. However, today, you must delve deep inside the chambers of your heart and ask yourself... do you really want to be Bose's protector? Will you sacrifice all happiness to shield a man who lives like a fugitive for the freedom of his motherland? It is too big a mission for you... but there is no one else who can do it. Will you take this risk for the sake of four hundred million people of India? Will you be able to love Bose and become his partner in life? It is a mammoth question, my dear. I, your mother, ask you for your own brave decision.'[2]

Toshiko Sōma was a beautiful young woman, even more beautiful in her heart. She was shy and timid yet courageous. She asked her mother for a month's time to ponder over the proposal.

---

2 Historical facts taken from: *Rash Behari Basu: His Struggle For India's Independence* by Radhanath Rath. Pages 35-38.
The statements of his mother-in-law were noted in these pages.

As time flew, the month-long thinking period came to an end. Then, Toshiko came to her mother, looked into her eyes and said fearlessly, 'Mother, let me go… Let me be the shield for Rash Behari Bose. Yes, I will be able to love him and become his partner in life. I shall protect him with my love at every cost. Even though this marriage might not bring enormous joy and hope into our lives immediately, I am confident that together with Bose, I shall be able to create a beautiful and happy family.' The moment was blissfully ethereal and Toshiko Sōma hugged her mother. When Tōyama received the news, he was equally elated. It was his Samurai plan and he saw success. He arrived at Rash Behari's hideout to seek his consent for the proposal. And this is how Mother India got a real Japanese wife for her brave son.

Rash Behari was even more surprised. Secretly he had always admired Toshiko as a beautiful young woman but the thought of marriage, that too to a Japanese woman, had never crossed his mind. He pondered awhile and then said, 'Marriage is something that I have never contemplated. From the age of fifteen, I have devoted myself to the struggle for freedom of my motherland. This has been a dangerous life. Yet, at this juncture of my life, when it is the will of my guardians here in Japan, including you and the Sōma family; when it is by the free will of the beautiful Miss Toshiko… I humbly bow to all your wishes and accept the proposal.'[3]

---

3 Historical facts taken from: *Rash Behari Basu: His Struggle For India's Independence* by Radhanath Rath. Pages 35-38.
The statements of his mother-in-law were noted in these pages.

Rash Behari with Toshiko Sōma

In 1918, even as the war in Europe ended, Rash Behari got married to Toshiko Sōma, the daughter of Aizō Sōma and Kokkō Sōma. It was the conjugation of two cultures that merged into a wonderful blend and showed the entire world that love is beyond every artificial barrier. Along with the sense of belonging, this was a marriage that brought unconditional and unselfish love into Rash Behari's life that cultural barriers and social constructs could not restrict.

In the next five years, Rash Behari and Toshiko Sōma built a beautiful family. The couple had two children and an abundance of love. Yet, they were people who lived in the shadow of fear and could not enjoy the freedom of a normal life. British spies were still on the lookout for Rash Behari, who, despite his long absence, continued to be an inspiration to all Indians who believed only armed struggle could bring freedom to India.

Along with Rash Behari, Toshiko had to move from one location to another, to avoid the eyes of Japanese and British intelligence. The couple had to change their residences as many as seventeen times. Despite being a young woman, the constant tension of changing homes made Toshiko fearful and filled her heart with turmoil. However, not even for a moment did she leave Rash Behari's side.

In Japan, Rash Behari Bose started a career as a journalist and a writer, beginning an overt life after being under cover for all his years of existence as an adult in India. He established himself as an educationist and also participated in various socio-cultural and political activities. Having arrived as a fugitive amidst an alien civilisation, Rash Behari gradually established himself as a much-respected man in Japanese society. He was a protégé of Samurai warlords, Japan's military elite, and finally, he was granted Japanese citizenship in 1923. After five years of marriage, the sun was finally rising for him.

Toshiko Sōma (Right) with Kokkō Sōma in Indian Saree

Toshiko had embraced Indian culture, just like he had embraced Japanese culture and the couple created a harmony that came from their hearts. The naturally elated Rash Behari rushed to Toshiko and said, 'My dear, with your unconditional love and support, I was able to gain respect and affection in Japan. Now, after years of perseverance, we have been awarded the best gift from my adopted country. I am now a Japanese citizen. Protected by this shield, I am now naturalised in a territory that is beyond the control of the British. God has indeed finally showered his blessings upon us.'

Toshiko smiled, held his hands softly, and said, 'Yes, now we can have our own small home, where only love will foster....'

Though his life moved on in an even tenure, Rash Behari remained glued to the political progress in his beloved India. The British had failed to extradite him from Japan and had almost given up their hunt for him, With citizenship and a beautiful and loving family, Rash Behari was now again ready to revive his India connections.

He was a dormant watcher but Rash Behari had re-established his contacts with his companions in India including with Shrish Ghosh, Amarendra Chatterjee and Moti Lal Roy who were now out of British jails. Moreover, he remained in touch with other Indian political personalities like Tarak Nath Das, Ram Chand and Narendra Bhattacharya in America.

Indian Independence League

Though in slow motion at times, the life of a revolutionary is never meant to be flat. Ripples of uncertainty and volatility are constants in that journey. In the year 1924, Rash Behari's wife, Toshiko passed away suddenly. Bliss had blessed him only for six years. An ocean of pain and emptiness filled his life, but Rash Behari focused on looking after his children.

Even at the Nakamuraya Bakery, Rash Behari did something radical. It was no less than a revolution in the culinary history of Japan that redefined the Nakamuraya Bakery. Rash Behari involved himself in developing new products the bakery offered and introduced as an experiment an Indian-style curry. British 'curries' were known in Japan. The innovative recipe Rash Behari developed gradually became popular among the locals and then its fame spread among the gourmand population of Tokyo. The curry was called the Indian Curry of Nakamuraya. It was more expensive than other dishes at the restaurant but its popularity was phenomenal. Soon, Rash Bihari Bose too became known as the Bose of Nakamuraya in Japan's social circles.

However, within him, a storm was brewing. With the colossal emptiness surrounding his lonely soul, Rash Behari again began to dream his dream of a free India. 'I was fighter, I am a fighter, and I shall be so in future too. My mission will be to strive for the dream that I have dreamt ever since I was a child', he told himself. Soon, his life became that of a hermit's, with his sight fixed on one supreme achievement. A free India.

Rash Behari never remarried. His parenting, however, was somewhat remote, considering that his attention was on his motherland. Once, Toshiko's mother Kokkō Sōma told Rash Behari, 'Dear son, we are here to take care of the children. However, without a companion how will you spend your entire life? You are now an honorable citizen of Japan. I urge you to get married again and settle down in life....'

Rash Behari only laughed and replied, 'Mother, my life's purpose has never been marriage. Yet, Toshiko's love was like a tsunami that swept me away. I was a mere fugitive and she sacrificed everything to protect me and love me.... Yes, for me, who was a stranger to her. That love is divine and incomparable.'

As Kokkō Sōma stood speechless, Rash Behari continued,

Rash Behari in Japan

'It is impossible to find the love that Toshiko harbored for me. I can't even think of another marriage. I have my loving family here and that is more than enough. The love of Toshiko is with me even today and will be so forever. Mother, my life is dedicated to my motherland. It is not mine; it is devoted to my countrymen so that, one day, they can see the dawn of Freedom.'[4]

In Japan, Rash Behari had established himself as a gentleman of repute, whose social and cultural standings were of the highest order. Yet, in his heart, he was the son of Mother India, for whose freedom he could sacrifice everything. His helplessness made him restless as he heard of fellow revolutionaries sacrificing their lives, victims of British wrath. His companions in Japan as well as in India knew that Rash Behari was pining to do something drastic to shake up the colonial rulers.

At an important meeting of India supporters in Japan, Rash Behari said, 'The fire of freedom must remain ignited. Across the countries of Asia, the brotherhood of Indians must join

---

4 Taken from the accounts of his mother-in-law Kokkō Sōma, as mentioned in the following book on page 37 - 38.
Rash Behari Basu: His Struggle For India's Independence by Radhanath Rath | Sabitri Prasanna Chatterjee.

their hands to carry forward this struggle. I am a mortal; my body can perish. However, the flame of freedom must never get extinguished. The almighty has given me everything. At this juncture of life, I am now left with a final task. Yes, I must do something so that an anti-colonial wildfire sweeps across the globe which the British Raj will not be able to put out.'

Just like his Nakamuraya curry, in his mind Rash Behari started to brew yet another masterplan to free India from British rule, even though he remained far away from his beloved country and countrymen.

'A league of legionnaire needs to be formed who will struggle together like an army! It must be a league that will not only strive to fight for the freedom of India, but also create the sentiment to throw off the colonial Raj. Yes, it must be a... League Of Extraordinary Children Of India. That must be my mission. I don't know where this effort will lead us to. However, in Japan, I must sow the seed of empathy for this league among Japanese politicians and the army.'

In his mind's eye, Rash Behari saw Toshiko's loving face glow as he said to himself, 'It will be called the... Indian Independence League'. By 1924, Rash Behari was ready with his new plan and he used his social standing to promote the Indian League in Japan. As his voice continued to echo the slogan, 'Asia for Asians', Rash Behari devoted all his energy to put the Indian Independence League on a firm footing.[5]

---

5 Rash Behari Bose organised a conference for Asian youths at Sankaido in Tokyo (27 October 1937) where he officially raised this slogan.
The Historical facts are referred from: *Two Great Indian Revolutionaries-Rash Behari Bose & Jyotindra Nath Mukherjee* by Uma Mukherjee, page numbers 150 to 158.
Cross referenced by Uma Mukherjee from *The Political Philosophies Since 1905, Vol II, Part II, Lahore 1942.* pages 356-358.

In his secret correspondence to his friends in India, Rash Behari wrote, 'This is a revolution to expel British imperialism from Asia! Looking at the political emancipation of India as a stepping-stone, a Greater Asian Liberation from bondage will be the larger vision. My sole purpose now is to generate an Indo-Japanese political understanding, cooperation, and goodwill. We need more friends across the world. With strong allies, we can create a huge impetus to liberate our country'. Thus, the 1920s saw the formation of the Indian Independence Leagues in Japan and across Southeast Asian countries. They were political organisations and included numerous Indian nationalists. The primary motto of these organisations was to create a buzz against colonial rule that would lead to the ouster of the British Raj in India.

Over the years, the growing community of Indian expatriates abroad gradually came under the protection of Japan. Moreover, across various Southeast Asian countries, Indian emigrant communities steadily garnered local support to voice their concerns and protest against the British Raj. Even though the local and disparate clusters of the Indian Independence League did not have any lasting impact, their memberships continued to grow. Many of these separate groups, however, established connections with each other with the intention of creating a unified global body.

THE ALLIES vs THE AXIS

Flags of the Axis Powers in Tokyo

THE DECADES ROLLED on as Rash Behari waited with hope in his heart. It was by the end of the 1930s that Rash Behari finally found advantage India as yet another global war loomed. By 1937, Japan was at war with China. Imperial Japan began to dream of dominating the Asia-Pacific region. At the same time, in 1939, the invasion of Poland by Germany created unrest in Europe. It was clear that Germany was spoiling for a fight again. Within the next two years, Germany forged a series of alliances with Italy and Japan and that created the Axis power bloc for the world.

The Soviet Union at the time had a peace pact with Germany. The United States had not joined the war and watched from a distance. The relationship between China's patron Britain and Japan was at its lowest point and the Japanese economy began to shrink.

At the opposite end were the 'Allied powers', including Britain, France and China which joined the alliance in 1941. By June 1941, Soviet Union too joined the Allies when Hitler attacked its western frontier.

In the beginning of the 1940s, the Japanese Intelligence found a new source of information about British plans in the pro-independence Indian organisations. Outstanding officers of the Japanese army, like Iwaichi Fujiwara, successfully established secret intelligence depots with them in connection with Malay, a region coveted by both, the British and Japanese. Creating an environment of mutual coexistence and sustenance, the Japanese government gradually started to provide financial support to these organisations in South Asia, including Rash Behari's, in return for vital information about the movements and tactics of the Allied troops.

Major Iwaichi Fujiwara

Major Fujiwara was an extraordinary officer of the Imperial General Headquarters (IGHQ). With Japanese aspirations soaring, he established a special Japanese operations unit by the name, F Kikan. The unit was established in September 1941 and was stationed in Bangkok at the end of that month. This intelligence unit was headed by Major Fujiwara himself. The primary task of the unit was to support the Indian independence movement, as well as the aspirations of the overseas Chinese and the Malayan Sultans, respectively, with the target of increasing friendship and cooperation with Japan. It was a forward-looking political and military strategy.

Rash Behari Bose was now an important figure in Japan and his political views mattered. His relentless pursuit of India's independence was not unknown to the Japanese, and Fujiwara found a mutually beneficial purpose in Rash Behari's opinions. Much before the 'Malayan Campaign' and even during the year of the campaign's active state, Rash Behari directed all his efforts to generate Japanese interest in the Indian independence movement. This was what Major Fujiwara wanted to cash in on.

At a secret meeting with Rash Behari, Fujiwara said, 'Japan is highly empathetic towards your sentiments and the sentiments of your countrymen. We respect the desire that you harbour for the freedom of India. I assure you and your fellow countrymen that we shall assist you with support and funds in your endeavours.'

Rash Behari, himself a shrewd man, understood Fujiwara's concerns and replied with a smile, 'I am honoured by your support and kindness. The people of India and the emigrant Indians communities will always remain faithful friends of Japan. I assure you my full cooperation with the IGHQ and we shall remain loyal friends forever.' In the ongoing turmoil, the Bose of Nakamuraya saw a golden opportunity to use the Japanese army under Fijiwara's able command to achieve his own end, a free Indian army.

Before him was the question, if not now, when?

An aging Rash Behari could see the massive unrest unfurling across the globe. One stormy night, Rash Behari sat in front of his biggest guide and supporter, Mitsuru Tōyama, and said, 'This second World War is a devastating episode in the history of human existence. Yet, as a true son of my country, I feel a sentiment that I can only call selfish….'

The old and frail Tōyama looked at his protégé and smiled. Rash Behari continued, 'Under the pressure of the Axis powers, Britain is now most fragile in her colonies. The time is ripe to free Asia from His Majesty's Government and usher in independence for all Asian countries. I can again visualise a free India. I too am getting on in years and my limbs have become feeble, but my mind has grown sharper. Indians can garner support from Japan, Italy and Germany and get military assistance that will help us attain freedom.'[1]

1 The historical facts are mentioned in the book: *Rash Behari Basu: His Struggle For India's Independence* by Radhanath Rath.

Then, Rash Behari sighed, 'Alas, many of my countrymen are taking the path of self-destruction. The anti-Japan propaganda of many important political figures in India is extremely inimical to India's national interest. At this moment, India needs more powerful allies. By criticising Japan, they are hampering the prospect of a Pan-Asia support.'

Mahatma Gandhi's call for Swaraj, self-rule in India had become a distinct possibility.

Following the war by Japan on China, Rash Behari had written a letter to Rabindranath Tagore, saying, 'Indian merchants, students and residents here in Japan request you to prevent the Congress's and Pundit Nehru's anti-Japanese activities for the sake of Indian interest and Indo-Japanese ties.'

The bard's reply came as a bolt of thunder, reminding Rash Behari '... Japan has not taken long to betray the rising hope of and repudiate all that seemed significant in her wonderful progress....'[2]

Rash Behari, therefore, chose to carry forward his own vision of building a pan-Asian brotherhood. He went ahead and founded the Asia Lodge in Tokyo for Asian students in Japan.

The Indian National Army

It was Japan's Malayan Campaign that unfolded another chapter in history and Japan-India relations. The Malayan Campaign was a series of bitter battles fought between the Japanese and

---

2 *Two Great Indian Revolutionaries-Rash Behari Bose & Jyotindra Nath Mukherjee* by Uma Mukherjee, page number 150.
Cross-referenced by Uma Mukherjee from *Amrita Bazar Patrika*, 11 October 1937. It is not known in which language the correspondence took place.

the British forces in the Malayan peninsula in 1941 and created a permeant fracture in their diplomatic relationship. The gruesome war lasted for about a year and left thousands dead and many more taken as Prisoners of War by the Japanese.

In these tropical battlefields, the British Army comprised the British Indian Army, Indian soldiers in thousands. Many of those men were fighting a war that they didn't have any reason to fight. Unlike the Japanese soldiers who were their opponents, the cause for the Indians was alien, so was the landscape and yet the Indians were sent to die in foreign lands for a colonial master. These Indian soldiers were brave but without any inspiration and most of these men were taken prisoners by the Japanese Army during the Malayan Campaign.

At the height of the World War II, more than two million Indian troops were fighting Axis forces around the world under the British banner. The confrontation between the Allied and Axis forces in the South Asian countries led to a huge number of POWs among the combating Indian soldiers. The men were captured in different battlefields but destiny created a connect, woven by the master planner Rash Behari Bose.

Rash Behari's dream was at last becoming a reality. Not because of his clarion call to British Indian soldiers to rise in rebellion. It was because Britain was being defeated on the Asian fronts and Japan had taken thousands of Indian soldiers prisoners. It was Rash Behari, the Indian Japanese, who told them what to do with these prisoners. It was he who threw a lifeline to the captured Indian soldiers.

Rash Behari had spent more than twenty-five years in Japan, espousing India's freedom. The fruit of perseverance finally fell on his lap. The Japanese Imperial General Headquarters finally met Rash Behari Bose to seek his help in consolidating the efforts of the independent and disparate Indian movements against the British Raj. Thus, it was Rash Behari who had the opportunity to propose an Indian National Army that would include all the captured soldiers.

Rash Behari had been highly critical of the members of the Indian Congress Party when they spoke against Japan as a strong Axis Power. He openly condemned Pundit Nehru for advocating a pro-British Indian Foreign Policy wherein Nehru was actively condemning Japan.

Rash Behari saw the salvation of his motherland in the rapidly precipitating international crisis and changing geopolitics of the world. Taking a strategic overview of all different streams of India's freedom movements, Rash Behari decided to go along with the Congress viewpoint and adopted Mahatma Gandhi, the prophet of non-violence, as his walking stick for his militant endeavour.

In a meeting with General Tojo, the Prime Minister of Japan at the end of December 1941, Rash Behari declared, 'As long as British imperialism in India continues, Japan cannot expect a final victory in the war. Over the years, I have tried to create the stage for an Indo-Japan partnership. Now is the time to utilise the power of that relationship.'

General Tojo

With unwavering confidence in his voice, he said, 'On 8 December, we, the Indian community in Tokyo, met at the Rainbow Grill to contemplate upon a course of action. My compatriots have formed a committee and have asked me to lead the movement. I gladly abide by their decision and aspire to take this mission forward. Then, on 26 December, for the first time in the history of Indians in Japan, fifty representatives from four cities met at the Railway Hotel in Tokyo to decide the modes of this action. Our representatives have been sent across the East Asian countries to establish a uniform resolution and gain unanimous support for our cause. The future is bright... The Sun shall rise in the Land of the Rising Sun and will bring in the Dawn of Freedom to India! I echo my resolve, Asia for Asians. Together, we can achieve this victory.'

The power in his words held the gathering spellbound. General Tojo openly declared in front of the Imperial Diet, 'Our government is prepared to help Indians in their efforts to free their country from the bondage of the British Raj.'

Before the meeting with Rash Behari, General Tojo had told the Imperial Japanese Diet, 'It is a golden opportunity for India, with several thousand years of historic and splendid cultural traditions, to rid itself of the ruthless British rule and to participate in the construction of the Greater East Asia Co-Prosperity Sphere. Japan expects that India will regain her proper status as "India for the Indians" and Japan will not stint herself in extending assistance to the patriotic efforts of the Indians. Should India fail to awaken to her mission, forgetting her history and tradition, and continue as before to be beguiled by British manipulation, I fear that an opportunity for the renaissance of the Indian people will be lost forever.'[3]

In March 1942, General Tojo again reiterated his support for the Indian Struggle spearheaded by Rash Behari and openly said, 'For the Indian people Japan, of course, entertains not the least thought of antagonising them. I desire, however, to reiterate clearly that the determination of Japan to crush thoroughly the American and British influences will undergo no change whatever…, It is my firm belief that now is the time to establish "India for Indians", which has for many years been the aspiration of four hundred million Indian people.'

General Tojo asked the delegation of Indians, 'Will India rise as "India for the Indians" to have the honour of cooperating in the establishment of the Greater East Asia Co-Prosperity Sphere? Or, will India permanently stoop under the Anglo-American shackles to leave her name in posterity as a slave nation? India is now face to face with the time when she should dismiss her past, read the new situation correctly and make her final decision'. The success of the meeting was phenomenal and Rash Behari was ever more confident.

Rash Behari sent a detailed account of his meeting with General Tojo to his prime collaborators in India, Prafulla Sen of Anushilan Samiti and Sirdar Pritam Singh. In open support for Japan, Rash Behari organised three important conferences. In March 1942, Rash Behari Bose organised a conference of local leaders of the Indian Independence Leagues in Tokyo.

---

3 Historical facts referred from: *Two Great Indian Revolutionaries-Rash Behari Bose & Jyotindra Nath Mukherjee* by Uma Mukherjee, page numbers 150-160.
Cross-referenced by Uma Mukherjee from: Presidential Address by Rash Behari Bose at the Bangkok Conference.

However, there was no consensus with Rash Behari's point of view at this gathering. Later, the leagues again convened in Singapore and then in Bangkok in June 1942. The Bangkok Conference turned out to be historic in the backdrop of the raging world war, letting Rash Behari's dream of an army of free Indians flower.

The 1942 Bangkok Conference was truly significant in many ways. Attended by important Indian and Asian members, it established many important things. Foremost, a formal constitution of the Indian Independence League was framed. In the formal structure, it comprised a Council for Action and a Committee of Representatives. Below the committee was to be the territorial and local branches. Rash Behari was honoured with the role of the President.

In an emotional address to the congregation on 15 June, Rash Behari said, 'It is a great honour that you have bestowed upon me and I am not unaware of the great responsibility that you have conferred upon my shoulders. With full respect, I accept this responsibility and promise to take this mission forward, despite all the difficulties that may come in our path. During and since 1857, hundreds and thousands of Mother India's brave children have sacrificed their lives for our motherland. With their own blood, they have nourished the seed of *Swaraj* and it is their supreme sacrifice that has brought us together at this juncture wherein we can dream to form this association to take forward their dreams. The world knows only a little about the long list of those valiant children of Mother India. Let us today pay homage to all those men and women, as we embark upon a great journey. Let us also pay tribute to all the leaders and legionnaire of Indian men and women who have taken up that struggle through their untiring efforts to free our country from colonial bondage.'

Mahatma Gandhi

Rash Behari's words echoed the words of Mahatma Gandhi, while he spoke to compatriots across East Asia, to garner unanimous support for free India, 'Remember the words of Mahatma Gandhi when he said that freedom is not a gift which will come down from the sky but you have to fight for it. Let us prepare ourselves. Let us set aside our selfish motives and join this race for the freedom of our nation.'

Adding further, Rash Behari said, 'Let us pay our tribute to the greatest living Indian, Mahatma Gandhi, who has with his magic wand woken the Indian masses from their centuries long slumber and has created in them self-confidence. We can have no doubt that when the new and true history of India will be written, Mahatma Gandhi's name will have to be mentioned as the saviour of India!'[4]

He spoke with confidence and command, 'The mission of the Indian Independence League is no different from that of the Congress's. Perhaps our methods are different, but our

4 Historical reference from: *Rash Behari Basu - His Struggle For India's Independence* by Radhanath Rath | Sabitri Prasanna Chatterjee. Pages 69-70.

goals are one. Today, we express our heartfelt support for the efforts of the Indian National Congress and their leaders and we sincerely hope that they will support us. We must remember that whatever be our approach, we are all Children of Mother India. Our mission and our vision remain the same… Freedom of our Motherland.'

'As an integral part of the Indian Independence League and under the complete control of the Council of Action, the "Indian National Army is being invested with the powers and status of a free National Army" of an independent India', he continued.[5]

Rash Behari spoke of the struggles that he and his companions had faced throughout his early days, before he took the painful decision to abandon his country and live in a foreign land, just to bring freedom to his nation. The heart wrenching tale of his journey towards freedom and the extreme hurdles placed before him by the British melted the hearts of everyone present in that conference.

Talking of the first World War, he said, 'During the war of 1914 to 1918, the British were partially successful in receiving India's cooperation by telling lies and making false promises. They promised us freedom after that war, the same as they are doing now, in the present war. Alas, the British did not mean to keep their promises then. When our countrymen questioned their intentions, the response from the British were bullets. Needless to mention the tragedy at the Jallianwala Bagh in

---

5 *Rash Behari Basu - His Struggle For India's Independence* by Radhanath Rath | Sabitri Prasanna Chatterjee. Page Nos 60-65 and 70-74.
The texts are from Rash Behari Bose's Presidential address on 15 June 1942.

1919 that is still fresh in my memory like a festering wound. Yet, every tragedy has a lesson and the Jallianwala Bagh tragedy too had its own lesson for our country. The result was the Non-Cooperation and Civil Disobedience Movements that the Indian National Congress has steered ever since.'

He paused a bit and then continued, 'With the commencement of the second World War, the British have once again begun the jugglery of words to seek India's cooperation. However, I am glad that our nationalist leaders have refused to be misled. I am elated by the manner in which the great Mahatma Gandhi has led the nation in dealing with these treacherous dialogues.'

Then with a serene smile, he said, 'With this Great East Asia War, being an Indian, I heartily believe that every Indian patriot, whatever be his political attitude towards Japan and wherever he might be residing, he or she is indeed honestly delighted to see how Japan has waged war against the Anglo-Saxon races and will one day soon impart a crushing blow to the British imperialist bases and end colonialism in Asia.'

'We, the Indian fraternity, have a very amicable relationship with Japan and we have their complete support and confidence. Moves on the world's political chessboard over the last one decade has inevitably shown that a global conflict was inescapable. I am elated that amid this raging crisis lies the salvation of India.'

'I don't want to test your patience with more speeches. It is now time for us to act. Yes, we have engaged in dialogues for a long time and now is the time to act. I must reiterate the words of Pundit Jawaharlal Nehru… *Success often comes to those who dare and act; it seldom goes to cowards.* Remember, our enemies have always been successful in keeping us divided. I can only hope that we shall not repeat that folly. Let us stand together shoulder-to-shoulder and march ahead hand-in-hand to our moment of glory and success.'

He added, 'As I stand here, my heart goes out to the unfortunate aeroplane accident last March, that claimed the lives of four of our valuable comrades including Sirdar Pritam Singh, Satyanand Puri, Captain Akram and Mr Nilkanth Ayer. Under the auspicious leadership of Sirdar Pritam Singh and Captain Mohan Singh, we had planned to establish the commands of the Indian National Army. Alas, the accident snatched away our precious companions.'

'We have the full support of Japan and their Army, especially Major Fujiwara. However, Major Fujiwara being a Japanese Officer, will not be perfectly suitable for the role of a supreme leader for an Indian armed force. Thus, we bestow upon Captain Mohan Singh, the role of the Supreme Commander of the Indian National Army.'

Captain Mohan Singh

He concluded with a solemn resolution, 'Let us remember we have one indivisible nation, India. – One enemy, England, – One Goal, Complete Independence or *Purna Swaraj*.'[6]

The Bangkok Conference documented a thirty-four-point resolution that was duly forwarded to the Japanese government. The League Committee expected the Japanese government to respond to each point. Rash Behari's message to the Japanese government was very clear. The Indian National Army or INA must be given the status of an allied army and be treated equally.

'The equal respect and honour will empower our brave soldiers to fight this decisive war. All Indian POWs must be released and handed over to the INA. These men are not mere soldiers of the enemy. They are sons of India. They were fighting a war that was not meant to be theirs. These men didn't deserve to fight and die in a foreign land for a foreign cause and be buried far away in foreign graves. They deserve to be free. Economic difficulties have forced them to fight the war on behalf of the British Raj. They don't deserve to be taken as POWs and be tortured. This is sheer injustice. With the freedom Japan gives them, these men will rise like shining knights and fight for their motherland like fearless lions.'[7]

'Finally, with our humble demands of financial assistance from the Japanese government, we expect that the help will allow us to carry out our efforts towards India's independence. An Army not only needs soldiers, but also needs ammunitions,

6 Complete self rule.

7 *Rash Behari Basu - His Struggle For India's Independence* by Radhanath Rath | Sabitri Prasanna Chatterjee. Page Nos 69-75.

ration and money to wage an assault during the battle', he added. From that moment his entire focus became the INA and the Indian Independence League.

Sitting alone in his room, one night, the 56-year old Rash Behari whispered to himself, 'Time is running out. I must act soon. An inner voice tells me that I don't have much time on earth left. My courage is sky-high, but my body is failing. When my subconscious mind takes me into the oblivion of sleep, the face of my beloved Toshiko appears in front of me. With a serene smile upon her countenance, she summons me... *Come my dear, I am waiting for you with all my love! Finish your supreme duty and come to me so that together we can rest in peace.* Her voice is clear in my mind and I know that I must act fast. Time is indeed running away....'

Treachery was, however, never far from Rash Behari. This time it was Mohan Singh, his dream army's supreme commander and his most trusted lieutenant, who opened a personal communication channel with the Japanese and for personal gains, promised that the INA could be used as a personal army under his command and taken away from the supervision of the India League's Council of Action. When he learnt of this treachery, despite his age and ailing health, Rash Behari pounced on Mohan Singh like an angry lion and with the help of the Japanese government, dismissed him from his position. The swift retribution proved Rash Behari as an able administrator.

Nevertheless, a murmur of concern began to reverberate across the ranks of the INA and the Indian Independence League, 'Who will lead us ahead?'

The voices echoed... 'The INA needs a commander. Yes, it

needs a commander who will be the face of the youth. It needs a man on whom every soldier of the INA will be able to repose his faith. It needs a leader on whose command, every soldier will be ready to sacrifice his life for the sake of mother India.'[8]

The aging Rash Behari knew he could not be that leader. His ailing body could not lead young soldiers through deep jungles towards an India in shackles that awaited such an army of liberation. Rash Behari was the strategist with a great world vision. It was not 1912 and he was not an Anushilan Party field action cadre. Old Man Time had taken its toll.

Sitting in his study-room in the Nakamuraya house in the Shinjuku prefecture of Tokyo, Rash Behari pondered, 'The INA needs to be commanded with an iron fist, like any professional army. This is the time when we cannot afford to make any more mistakes. My task… my final task, has taken on a golden shape… I cannot let it get dismantled. Perhaps it is the will of Destiny that I again make a supreme sacrifice.' Tears appeared in his eyes.

'My mortal being is fading with every passing minute. I know, I may not be able to lend that iron fist to this endeavour until we win this battle. The INA needs a new leader. The vital question that needs to be addressed immediately is who will lead the INA? It must be a man whom everyone looks up to. It must be a man whose valiance is like a fierce tiger and who will be revered by the entire world. I must seek out that man who will lead forward this war.'

---

8 Historical fact from: *Two Great Indian Revolutionaries-Rash Behari Bose & Jyotindra Nath Mukherjee* by Uma Mukherjee.
Two Great Indians In Japan, pages 55-65.

'I MUST… I MUST!', Rash Behari told himself.

As the world slept, in the darkness of the night, Rash Behari sat awake thinking. From the mist of questions and the probables, appeared a face. It was the face of another heroic son of India, who, just like Rash Behari, believed in the ideology that the little Rasu had himself upheld throughout his bold and adventurous life. As he sat with gleaming eyes, quietly and composed, Rash Behari said aloud, 'Yes, he is the man… Subhas Chandra Bose.'

PEACE BIDS

RASH BEHARI BOSE had always led a radical life. Rash Behari did not believe non-violence could be a weapon in India's battle for freedom. Neither did he believe that the freedom of India would come through any individual effort. He was fully aware that the future of India depended upon her will and power to utilise the new emerging world forces in her favour.

From a penniless fugitive in a foreign land, he had now become an honourable and respected citizen of Japan with the helm of the Indian Independence League and the INA in his hands. Along his long journey through the decades of isolation in a faraway country, Rash Behari had continued to participate in India's political struggle through his trusted friends like Shrish Ghosh. However, considering the diplomatic atmosphere between Britain, Japan and India and his own failing health, one thing became clear to Rash Behari. Even though he was the mastermind behind the mammoth design, he understood that to lead the mission of armed struggle forward, a leader with a magnetic personality was required who would be able to lead the INA into ground action. He had never met Subhas, but having chosen him as leader, Rash Behari now began an exercise of wooing the Congress Party's sympathy. He had changed tactics and this time, he was sure, his grand dream would not fail.

Thus, the year 1943 was a significant year for Rash Behari's endeavours for India's freedom struggle. In the whirlwind of events, he wrote some urgent letters to the stalwarts of the Indian National Congress and sought their consent in recognising the Freedom for India movement as an integral part of the Great East Asia War. It was his intention to join the efforts of the leaders within India with the efforts made globally to create immeasurable pressure upon the British Rule. In the eyes of the world, he wanted to depict a portrait of a united India whose children fought together for her dignity, across the globe.

In his letter to Mahatma Gandhi, he praised the adoption of 'Satyagraha' as the rallying point for Indians of all classes, creeds and sects because it was a principle that appealed to the people of every religion and community. It made everyone revisit the foundation of their faiths and each of these foundations were the pillars of the term 'Satyagraha' where everyone would be able to protest as one national community.

He concluded his letter with the words:

> *In conclusion, I must say that the principle of Satyagraha is the essence of all great religions and antidote to sectarianism, dogmatism and demagogy. India's mission lies in turning this principle into a living force. Yet she cannot accomplish this until she achieves complete freedom from British Rule. I have therefore decided on this occasion to contribute my quota to the cause of making India for Indians, and to cooperate with Japan whose objective in the present war of Greater East Asia is to make Asia for Asians. I shall*

be greatly pleased to receive your blessings in my present undertaking.[1]

In his letter to Pundit Jawaharlal Nehru, he urged:

Dear Pundit Nehru,

Pundit Jawaharlal Nehru

personally and on behalf of the Indians in East Asia, I think it is fortunate for the Congress and for India, to have chosen you as the leader at this critical juncture. Mahatma Gandhi too, I believe, has shown another instance of his depth of vision, by declaring you as his successor, even during his lifetime. My faith in you is based upon sound reasoning. You were the first Congress President due to whose influence the Congress did away with Dominion Status as its ultimate goal and substituted it with Complete Independence. By claiming that, the defense, foreign policy and finance of India must have nothing to do with British control, you made it clear as to what constitutes the substance of Independence. I strongly support your statement that

1 The historical statement contained in a letter to Mahatma Gandhi dated 13.03.1942 (from Tokyo) mentioned in the book: *Rash Behari Basu: His Struggle For India's Independence* by Radhanath Rath. Page 165.

Independence cannot be accepted with conditions as a gift, but must be won as a prize for itself. I feel confident that you will guide India safely through the impending crisis. And yet, times being as critical as they are, a slight mistake is liable to ruin the destiny of our nation. In the first place, I wish to warn you that the star of England is setting. In other words, whether India actively comes to her support or not, England is not going to win this war. Conversely speaking, whatever might befall England for losing this war, would befall India also if she fights on her side. The only way to escape from its cajolery is to firmly reject any offer that England makes through Sir Stafford Cripps or any other representative. Rather, start a Civil Disobedience immediately, which is the only weapon left to you under the prevailing circumstances. I must mention that during your last Civil Disobedience, we were not in a position to offer you, our help. However, today we are fully capable to contribute with our full might to the success of the movement started by you. On behalf of the Indians in East Asia, my only prayer to you at this moment is that you realise that the doom of the British Empire is a historic necessity, and the rise of free India as a member of the Asiatic comity of nations, is the wish of Providence itself.[2]

In his letter to Muhammad Ali Jinnah, he advocated,

Years ago when the Indian National Congress, and the national movement sponsored by it, was still in its

---

2 The historical statement contained in a letter to Nehru dated 18.03.1942 (from Tokyo) is mentioned in the book: *Rash Behari Basu: His Struggle For India's Independence* by Radhanath Rath. Page 171.

Muhammad Ali Jinnah

infancy, you were among the few leaders whose fiery nationalism was a subject of admiration among the Indian people within the country and abroad. I, on behalf of every Indian in East Asia, acknowledge this and thank you for the leadership. At present, as the President of the Muslim League, you are looked up to, at home and aboard, as the leader of the vast masses of Indian Muslims. Alas, I am reluctant to consider you as the sole leader of only a section, however big and important it may be. In my eyes, you are the same old Jinnah of years ago, who thought, spoke and moved as one of the leaders of the entire Indian Nation. Today, the whole East Asia stands together to throw off the century old yoke of Anglo-Saxon control. Amid the reverberating sounds of Asia for Asians, India is called upon to be India for Indians. But India can never be India for Indians unless her sons, Hindus and Muslims, begin to identify service to the nation with service to their respective Gods. For, if truth be regarded as the essence of religion, then there is no reason why the followers of Hinduism and Islam should fall out on religious matters. A great mission awaits you Janaab Jinnah, in this connection. On behalf of the Indians living in East Asia, I assure you that we are all awaiting your emergence once more as a National Leader.[3]

To both Jawaharlal Nehru and Muhammad Ali Jinnah, he wrote earnestly,

> *In the hands of you both lie, in a large measure, the destiny of India of today and tomorrow. As heads of the Congress and the Muslim League respectively, you have fought heroically against the oppression of British imperialism in India and led the nation against insurmountable obstacles on the path of complete independence. Today, thanks to the mighty efforts of the great children of India, alive or dead, we are fortunate enough to have a glimpse of the first streak of the dawn of independence over Indian skies… The solution of the Indian problem is in the Indian hands and not in Britain's. The freedom that shall crown India can be fashioned only by the suffering and sacrifices of the millions of the sons and daughters of India, and not by the decree of the Anglo-Saxon tyrants. Not in England, but on Indian sacred soil, is that battle for freedom to be fought and won. The plan to invite you to London is an obvious British mechanism to draw you away from the scene of action, where the last decisive battle is impending. Let not British cajolery succeed in robbing you of your leadership at this vital moment in Indian history. At this critical period, the sufferings of millions of India's children wait and watch*

3 The historical statement contained in a letter dated 10.03.1942 (from Tokyo) is mentioned in the book: *Rash Behari Basu: His Struggle For India's Independence* by Radhanath Rath. Page 169.

> *for a sign from you to march ahead to their freedom. If you but join hands and bid the nation reach out its hands for its own freedom, which is its birthright, as rightly stated by the great Tilak, India will be free that very moment. Then why waste further time on negotiations with the British intruders and their accomplices in Washington and elsewhere? The Time Spirit is calling out to you both and looking at your faces for a sign. May that sign be not long delayed.*

As he corresponded with the leaders in India for a unanimous cooperation by dissolving all differences, the resolution of the Bangkok Conference received the approval of the authorities of the Imperial Government of Japan. The positive reply from the Japanese government came as a breather and finally the plans for an armed revolution started to take shape with the INA at its centre. However, this involved massive coordination and it made an already indisposed Rash Behari more ill. He continued to dream, however, of the day when his dream would come and hold his hand – of the day Subhas would come and hold his hands.

Subhas Bose was a young and dynamic leader. During all the years of watching India from a distance, just one man had passed Rash Behari's metrics of leadership. Subhas Bose came across as one person who had progressively risen from being a faithful son of his motherland to a staunch political activist who first demanded *Purna Swaraj*, or complete independence from the British Raj.

Destiny had never arranged a physical meeting between Rash Behari and Subhas Chandra, but the two had conversed over many written correspondences. In those hand written

Subhas Chandra Bose

letters, Rash Behari Bose smelt the fragrance of the strong urge within Subhas to lead his countrymen into the light of freedom. Another common ideological position that connected Rash Behari with Subhas was their uniform view that a dormant protest would never bring independence to India and only a revolutionary military retaliation was capable of doing so.

In various meetings of the Indian Independence League for augmenting the INA, many senior members of the league had expressed their views in agreement with the fact that a magnetic leader like Subhas Chandra Bose must lead the way forward. Contemplating the global political and war situation, the interested POW leaders also opined that they would be willing to join the INA only if it was led by Subhas Chandra Bose.

In the interest of India, the prisoners and his brainchildren, the creator of the Indian Independence League and the INA shed his ego, and with open arms Rash Behari welcomed Subhas Chandra Bose and invited him to take up the reins of these organisations and lead his beloved India into the daylight of freedom.

Sitting with his closest associates in Japan, Rash Behari told them about Subhas. 'Despite being a member of the Congress party, Subhas Chandra Bose has always been a revolutionary in his fundamental political faith. Many a times he has adopted a path that has been in tangent to the path followed by the Congress, and he has time and again refused to ally himself with the moderate policy of the Congress party. He is a true revolutionary at heart, who has dared to confront his mighty opponent without any fear.'

With a smile upon his face, Rash Behari added, 'I have been a disobedient boy throughout my life. Yet, the almighty has not made me the only one to be so. Subhas Chandra is another man who has been born to be disobedient of authorities and power structures, a boy who is destined to take a radical path for the sake of his beloved motherland. Even though we have never met each other or spoken with one another, I feel a strong connect with his soul. Through the years, I have been a keen observer and admirer of his work. Elected as the president of the Indian National Congress in 1938, his influence has grown by leaps and bounds.'[4]

'In the zealous youth of India, he has infused a new spirit and has given the national movement a radical turn. It was through his influences that a resolution was passed by the Congress to disassociate itself from any imperialist war undertaken by Britain against Japan, Germany and Italy. At a time when eminent members of the Congress, like Jawaharlal Nehru, were carrying on a bitter anti-Japan propaganda, Subhas Chandra stood for a more sober and realistic line of action and policy

4 Historical fact from: *Two Great Indian Revolutionaries-Rash Behari Bose & Jyotindra Nath Mukherjee* by Uma Mukherjee, page numbers 155 to 158. As many of the references are works in Bengali, the scenes here have been created by the author using his creative liberty to explain the essence of the sentiments of the great leader at that point in time.

for India. Personally, I hold him in high regard for his courage and bravery.'

Rash Behari paused a while and continued, 'Many Congress veterans tried to oust him and secretly carried out propaganda against him. Even Mahatma Gandhi got convinced and wrote to him personally to not contest the next presidential elections. However, bravery and courage always wins. Subhas Chandra contested and won the elections again and proved his popularity to the world.'

'He is a man for whom the dream of freedom for his nation is far greater than any personal gains. Hence, to keep the internal turmoil in the party under control, he renounced his role and went ahead alone and founded the Forward Bloc as a separate political entity. However, the shrewd British Raj got him arrested and sent him to prison.'

'Subhas is an untamed lion who cannot be kept caged. He took great risks to escape from India in April 1941 and headed towards Germany. He understood that India could not attain liberty from slavery if he remained a prisoner in the country. Friends, in this man, I can see a reflection of my own journey, and perhaps a much greater one for him. He commands the love and the hearts of millions in India and across the world. He is called Netaji. In him, I see my dream come true.'

With a determined countenance, Rash Behari said, 'With the help of VD Savarkar, I have already expressed my wish to Subhas Chandra. During a private meeting at Bombay, Savarkar has urged Subhas Chandra to join hands with us, in Japan, to carry forward his mission. Fortunately, Subhas has heard the voices of India's revolutionaries to unite with the efforts of Germany, Italy and Japan to carry out a modern warfare by the

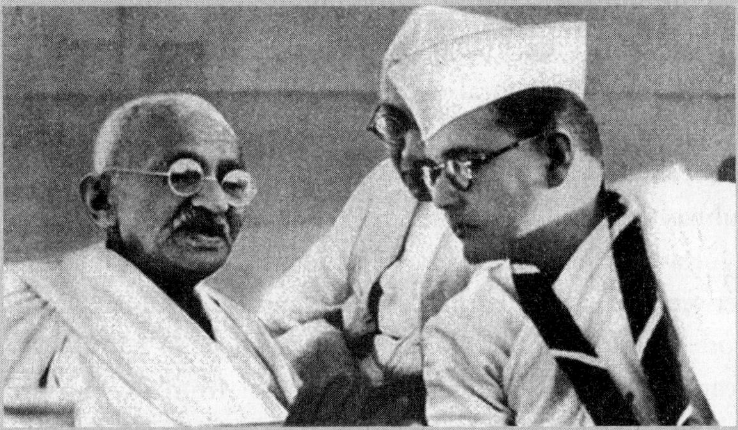

Gandhi and Subhas

Indian youth and oust the cunning British from the country for good.'[5]

Rash Behari smiled and added, 'My message to Subhas is very clear ... NOW OR NEVER, NOR FOR EVER.' With a clear vision of the future, at the Bangkok Conference, Rash Behari

5 In 1940 (22 June) Subhas had met with and spoken to VD Savarkar in Bombay. It seems that by 1940, Rash Behari had begun to take into account the surrender of Indian soldiers of the British army and planning the INA and looking at leaders for his pet project. Subhas may have been in his radar as early as the beginning of 1940s. By April 1943, Rash Behari was already ready with all the arrangements for armed struggle and boasted of a military training center in Kuala Lumpur. The official invitation to Subhas was sent thereafter.
Two Great Indian Revolutionaries-Rash Behari Bose & Jyotindra Nath Mukherjee by Uma Mukherjee, page numbers 150 and 158.
Cross referenced by Uma Mukherjee from *The Two Great Indians in Japan*, pages 59-65.
Desh Sahitya issue 1372, for Sudhakanta Roy Choudhury's article/ Letter of Savarkar to Khitish Chandra, Joint Secretrary, Rash Behari Smarak Samity, dated 2 June 1954.

had already framed a resolution that said, 'This Conference requests Shri Subhas Chandra Bose to be kind enough to come to East Asia, and appeals to the Imperial Government of Japan to use its good offices to obtain the necessary permission and conveniences from the Government of Germany to enable Shri Subhas Chandra Bose to reach East Asia safely.'

Rash Behari knew very well that without an arrangement between Japan and Germany, the safe passage of Subhas Chandra Bose to Tokyo would be impossible. Indians in East Asia had heard Subhas Chandra's radio broadcast from Berlin during the Bangkok Conference, wherein he had confidently told his audience he would soon be in Asia.

THE LAST BATTLE

IT WAS A historic moment for India, when Subhas Chandra Bose arrived in Japan in March 1943, following a turbulent submarine ride across seas under British warship surveillance. When they finally met, an elated Rash Behari embraced him like a son. Greeting Subhas Chandra, the frail and aging Mitsuru Tōyama said with enthusiasm, 'You both have the same surname. I believe that you both have, by now, one soul. I pray to the almighty that you both may together fight for the freedom of India.'

That night, within the confines of his house, Rash Behari sat in front of Subhas Chandra and spoke his mind. 'In your valorous face, I see the glow of a stellar leader. Yes, a leader who will lead our motherland into the daylight of freedom. The hazardous journey of the last one year has left me frail from exhaustion. My health is broken, and I know that I don't have many more days on earth left. Yet, the true struggle for freedom has just begun to take a beautiful shape. How can I abandon this task at this critical juncture?'[1]

---

1 Historical reference from: *Rash Behari Basu: His Struggle For India's Independence* by Radhanath Rath | Sabitri Prasanna Chatterjee. Pages 47-49.

He looked at Subhas Chandra, who was looking at him with full attention, and said, 'We have never met before. However, I feel a strong connect with your heart. It is not just my will, but the will of every person associated with the Indian Independence League and the Indian National Army, that from this moment, you take up their reins and lead us to victory.'

With tears rolling down their cheeks, the two men sat in front of each other like a teacher and a disciple, as a few minutes of silence prevailed. The dark night remained witness to that wonderful moment. Subhas Chandra broke the silence and said in a emotional voice, 'I am awestruck by your magnanimity. You are about to make the supreme sacrifice and entrust what you cherish most to someone else yet your face is unperturbed. My heart melts with regard for you and I cannot express my emotions in words.'

'You strived for the freedom of India from such a tender age. Your valiant deeds are legends in our country, yet destiny always sent hurdles in your path. Like a fugitive you came to Japan and created a world of your own and set up these massively successful organisations, the INA and the Indian Independence League. Yet, today, at this historic juncture, you are putting aside all personal pride and prejudice and handing over all the powers to me. This is something that I can only call, fantastic heroism of an ultimate degree. You are truly the Father of the Indian Independence Movement in East Asia.'[2]

---

2 The conversations, presumably taking place in Bengali, have been visualised under creative license for reader facility, supported by evidence of the meeting provided in Radhanath Rath and Sabitri Prasanna Chatterjee's book, Pages 47-49.

Rash Behari held his hands, smiled and added, 'Dear Subhas, the sacrifices that you mention now is nothing when compared to the supreme sacrifices of the sons and daughters of India who have given their lives for her independence. The faces of all my companions are still fresh in my mind. I can never forget their smiles. Shot, hanged, their gruesome deaths pierce me like swords every day. This little sacrifice is nothing in comparison to those deeds.'

Rash Behari stood up, looked at the ceiling, as if searching for a glimpse of the almighty, and said, 'Netaji Subhas Chandra Bose… from this moment, you are the messiah of the people of India, within the country and across entire East Asia. I, Rash Behari, choose to remain your constant supporter and advisor as long as I live. In the history of India and for the entire world, I voluntarily choose to remain as the OTHER BOSE.' Patriotism bound these two brave sons of India as one handed over the baton of revolution to the other with tears in their eyes and hope in their hearts.

As the dark clouds of war hung low over Asia, Rash Behari Bose addressed INA leaders and India League members gathered at the Cathey Building in Singapore. Rash Behari stood in front of the crowd and said in a brave voice, 'Friends and Comrades in Arms. In your presence today, I resign my office and appoint Deshsevak Subhas Chandra Bose as president of the Indian Independence League. I have full faith in the almighty that India's best is represented in him.' It was 4 July 1943.

Perhaps a turmoil raged in his aging heart, where a tinge of pain mingled with untamed happiness. Rash Behari continued his discourse, 'You know, In my own humble way, I have dedicated my life to the cause of our sacred motherland. That

Subhas Chandra Bose with the Indian National Army

is my life's mission and will remain so forever. As long as there is breath in my body, I shall be the soldier that I have always been – the soldier in the battle for Mother India's freedom. And of course, I shall not spare myself in giving Subhas Chandra all that I can give him – wholehearted cooperation, assistance and advice in the battle that is now ahead of us.'

Addressing the soldiers of the INA gathered at the Padang on 5 July, Subhas Bose took control of the INA. 'Comrades', he said, 'You have voluntarily accepted a mission that is the noblest that the human mind can conceive of. For the fulfilment of such a mission, no sacrifice is too great – not even the sacrifice of one's life. You are today the custodians of India's national honour and the embodiment of India's hopes and aspirations. So, conduct yourselves in a manner that your countrymen may bless you and posterity may be proud of you.'[3]

Rash Behari had already designed a flag of Azad Hind and he handed this over to Subhas Bose at the ceremonial event. As Rash Behari Bose sat back, the charismatic Subhas announced the name AZAD HIND FAUJ for the Indian National Army.

Flag of Azad Hind Fauj

The wheel of destiny were turning fast as the months moved on under the glorious wings of the heroic Subhas Chandra's leadership, while the astute and courageous Rash Behari stood behind him and provided all the support he could from the core of his hearts.

---

3 Reference from the following says 5 July 1943: *Rash Behari Basu: His Struggle For India's Independence* by Radhanath Rath | Sabitri Prasanna Chatterjee, Pages 511-512 and 514. However, it is 6 July as per reference: https://www.nas.gov.sg/archivesonline/online_exhibit/indian_national_army/revival.htm

Subhas Chandra Bose with the Indian National Army

Subhas Bose's famous call on 12 October 1943, rang in every Indian soldier's heart…

'In the name of God, in the name of bygone generations who have welded the Indian people into one nation, and in the name of the dead heroes who have bequeathed to us a tradition of heroism and self-sacrifice, we call upon the Indian people to rally around our banner and strike for India's freedom. We call upon them to launch the final struggle against the British and their allies in India and to prosecute that struggle with valour and perseverance and full faith in final victory until the enemy is expelled from Indian soil and the Indian people are once again a Free Nation.'

By the end of 1943, the balance of power favoured Japan and her allies. Britain and her allies were losing in the Asian fronts.

Subhas Bose held the helms of the INA from July 1943 to August 1946. The most significant contribution of the Indian National Army under his command were in the various Asian fronts of the Japanese U-Go offensive into India in 1944. Having overrun Indo-china, Andamans and Myanmar (then Burma), the Japanese made a bid to enter the Indian subcontinent through the north east – at the Imphal-Kohima front. The Japanese were supported by the INA units who were supposed to entre first and take these posts from the British and their Indian soldiers. The battle took place in three stages from 4 April to 22 June 1944 around the town of Kohima, now the capital of Nagaland.

The Japanese attempted to capture Kohima ridge, a geographical feature which dominated the road by which the besieged British and Indian troops of the IV Corps at Imphal were supplied. However, from mid April to May, the British with Indian reinforcements counter-attacked to drive the Japanese from the positions they had captured and chased them back. The INA troops involved in this battle too were killed and defeated.

This defeat dealt a big blow to Rash Behari's and Subhas's soaring hopes. Nevertheless, the war in East Asia was a see-saw battle between the two imperial giants. While Japan was fighting alone, the Americans had brought air support to the British. It still seemed, the war could end either way but for Japan, December 1944 was a bleak month of uncertainties.

Middle Of January 1945

Across a wintry junction of Tokyo city, inside the closed chamber of the old hospital building, the first rays of a new morning poured in, bathing the bedstead of a frail old man. Yes, it was the Bose of Nakamuraya, Rash Behari Bose, who looked at the rising sun that brought a smile upon his face. 'I have always been a disobedient boy. Yet, I am happy that my battle is being efficiently led forward valiantly by another son of my Mother India whom I can proudly pronounce as the true leader for my countrymen.'

Around the middle of December 1944, Rash Behari's son Masahide, who was in the Japanese Army, had returned from the battlefront and met his father after two and a half years.[4] That was an emotional moment, a moment of union connecting the souls of a father and his son who had been apart for years, yet their hearts had remained united in a soft bond forever. Rash Behari's daughter, Tetsu Higuchi, was always at his bedside, when he became terminally ill.[5]

Rash Behari looked at the hospital window and sighed. 'So much is happening outside. So much will unfold soon. Perhaps, I shall never see the day when my beloved country, my Mother India, will open her eyes to embrace the dawn of freedom. Yet, I am happy… generations to come will live a life of freedom for which I have had the good fortune to strive for. In the bright light outside, I can see the face of Toshiko and I can hear her soft voice. As destiny takes me away from this

---

4 Historical facts from: https://www.thestatesman.com/opinion/unsung-warrio-rii-1502765179.html

5 Rash Behari Bose was suffering from Tuberculosis after the enormous strain he undertook to fulfil the dream of Freedom for Mother India. It ultimately led to his death. Historical facts from: *Karmabir Rash Behari* by Bejon Behari Bose (1959). *Rash Behari Basu: His Struggle For India's Independence* by Radhanath Rath | Sabitri Prasanna Chatterjee.

Rash Behari Bose

mortal body, I shall be happily reunited with my beloved and rest with her in the eternal kingdom. Almighty God, take me into the oblivion of eternal sleep, wherein I can perpetually dream my Undying Dream.'

As a cold wind blew, the Other Bose told himself softly, 'I pray to the almighty… my Last Wish is to be reborn as a little infant in my beloved… AZAD HIND. '

The old and frail warrior sighed as he told himself, 'Now it is time for me to go home.'

Shortly afterwards, Rash Behari Bose was taken home from the hospital. He passed away on 21 January 1945 in his home. Before his death, the Japanese Government honoured him with the Order of the Rising Sun (2nd grade).

Rash Behari did not see the bombing of Hiroshima and Nagasaki on 6 and 7 August 1946, nor witness Japan's defeat in the World War. Subhas Chandra Bose reportedly died on 18 August 1945 from third-degree burns sustained after an overloaded bomber in which he was being transported by the Japanese crashed in Taihoku (now Taipei), Japanese Taiwan. He was allegedly fleeing from being captured alive by a victorious Britain. Subhas Bose was declared officially dead in August 1946.

BIBLIOGRAPHY

Two Great Indian Revolutionaries-Rash Behari Bose & Jyotindra Nath Mukherjee, by Uma Mukherjee.

Rash Behari Basu: His Struggle For India's Independence by Radhanath Rath | Sabitri Prasanna Chatterjee.

Rash Behari Bose - The Father Of The Indian National Army by Elizabeth Eston.

Revolutionary Organization: A Study Of The Ghadar Movement by Harish K Puri.

Chandernagore: From Bondage To Freedom, 1900-1955 by Sailendra Nath Sen.

Online Reference Sources: National Digital Library Of India (https://ndl.iitkgp.ac.in)

Source: West Bengal Public Library Network

https://frontline.thehindu.com/the-nation/bose-in-singapore/article9968319.ece

https://knowledgeofindia.com/list-of-freedom-fighters-of-india/

www.chandernagorecollege.org

www.fridu.edu.in/pages/2/history

https://www.quora.com/What-was-the-Gadar-Partys-role-in-the-Indian-freedom-movement

https://www.shaheedbhagatsingh.org/martyrs.html

https://www.wikiwand.com/en/Indian_independence_movement

https://boseofjapan.wordpress.com/rash-behari-bose-the-father-of-the-indian-national-army-kindle-edition/volume-2/

https://www.thehindu.com/opinion/op-ed/bose-of-nakamuraya/article22661567.ece

www.architecturaldigest.in

www.nas.gov.sg/archivesonline/online_exhibit/indian_national_army/provi.htm

www.economictimes.indiatimes.com/news/politics-and-nation/was-ina-an-army-of-freedom-fighters-or-deserters/articleshow/57185286.cms

www.edition.cnn.com/2020/05/09/asia/japan-indian-freedom-fighter-hnk-intl/index.html

Photo Credits

Wikipedia, Wikimedia and Creative Commons sources

ACKNOWLEDGEMENT

Firstly, I must acknowledge the efforts of eminent researchers and historians whose works had been the source of my own study while exploring the various incidents encapsulated within this book. With a blend of both official and non-official records from these sources, I hope I have been able to uphold the true spirit of this book that entails the life and journey of one of the bravest sons of Mother India, Shri Rash Behari Bose. I humbly acknowledge all the books and resources that I have diligently studied and referred to while creating the backdrop of this book and also used the chronological references to various significant incidents mentioned in the book. The bibliography of this book respectfully acknowledges my sincere gratitude towards these references and their authors.

My heartfelt thanks to my entire family for being my constant support system. Especially, I must mention the name of Brinda Roy, my beloved wife, who has been a wonderful partner for me in love, life and work. Without her presence and inspiration, I am always incomplete.

Special thanks to the team at The Book Bakers, one of the leading literary agencies in the country today, for believing in my work. I thank you for not only working as an agent for this book, but also as a constant support for my literary journey. Suhail Mathur, you are one person who has always vested your faith in this manuscript and all my works. With your fantastic insight, you have always encouraged me to explore various literary ideas. I feel fortunate for being associated with you and your team.

My sincere thanks to Papri Sen Sri Raman, my editor from Vitasta Publishing Pvt Ltd, for her undeterred dedication in refining this manuscript to its best form.

At last, I would like to thank my dynamic publisher Renu Kaul Verma from Vitasta Publishing Pvt Ltd for her personal commitment and expert touch in shaping out this story into a fine book.

A Samurai Dream of Azad Hind - Rash Behari Bose is a book for readers of all ages that provides a glimpse into the life of a valiant man whose unsung sacrifice for his beloved motherland is one of the finest examples of patriotism. I sincerely hope that everybody will get an exhilarating reading experience from this book.